THE UN SECURITY COUNCIL
AND HUMAN RIGHTS

Also by Sydney D. Bailey

ASPECTS OF AMERICAN GOVERNMENT (*editor*)
BRITISH PARLIAMENTARY DEMOCRACY
THE BRITISH PARTY SYSTEM (*editor*)
CEYLON
FOUR ARAB–ISRAELI WARS AND THE PEACE PROCESS
THE FUTURE OF THE HOUSE OF LORDS (*editor*)
THE GENERAL ASSEMBLY OF THE UNITED NATIONS
HOW WARS END (2 vols)
HUMAN RIGHTS AND RESPONSIBILITIES IN BRITAIN AND IRELAND (*editor*)
THE KOREAN ARMISTICE
THE MAKING OF RESOLUTION 242
NAISSANCE DE NOUVELLES DÉMOCRATIES
PARLIAMENTARY GOVERNMENT IN BRITAIN (*editor*)
PARLIAMENTARY GOVERNMENT IN THE COMMONWEALTH (*editor*)
PARLIAMENTARY GOVERNMENT IN SOUTHERN ASIA
PEACE IS A PROCESS
PROBLEMS OF PARLIAMENTARY GOVERNMENT IN COLONIES (*editor*)
THE PROCEDURE OF THE UN SECURITY COUNCIL
PROHIBITIONS AND RESTRAINTS IN WAR
THE SECRETARIAT OF THE UNITED NATIONS
THE UNITED NATIONS: A Concise Political Guide (3rd Edn)
VOTING IN THE UN SECURITY COUNCIL
WAR AND CONSCIENCE IN THE NUCLEAR AGE

The UN Security Council and Human Rights

Sydney D. Bailey

palgrave
macmillan

This book is printed on paper suitable for recycling and made from fully managed and sustained forest sources. Logging, pulping, and manufacturing processes are expected to conform to the environmental regulations of the country of origin.

First published in Great Britain 1994 by
THE MACMILLAN PRESS LTD
Houndmills, Basingstoke, Hampshire RG21 2XS
and London
Companies and representatives
throughout the world

A catalogue record for this book is available
from the British Library.

ISBN 10: 0-333-56489-8 hardback
ISBN 13: 978-0-333-56489-9 hardback
ISBN 10: 0-333-62982-5 paperback
ISBN 13: 978-0-333-62982-6 paperback

Printed and bound in Great Britain by
CPI Antony Rowe, Chippenham and Eastbourne

First published in the United States of America 1994 by
Scholarly and Reference Division,
ST. MARTIN'S PRESS, INC.,
175 Fifth Avenue,
New York, N.Y. 10010

ISBN 0–312–12324–8

Library of Congress Cataloging-in-Publication Data
Bailey, Sydney Dawson.
The UN Security Council and human rights / Sydney D. Bailey.
p. cm.
Includes bibliographical references and index.
ISBN 0–312–12324–8
1. United Nations. Security Council. 2. Human rights.
I. Title: The United Nations Security Council and human rights.
JX1977.A593B345 1994
341.23'23—dc20 94–19511
CIP

11 10 9 8 7 6 5 4
04 03 02 01 00 99 98 97

Contents

List of Tables and Figures

List of Abbreviations

ANC African National Congress (South Africa)
ASEAN Association of South East Asian Nations
CSCE Conference on Security and Cooperation in Europe
ECOMOG Military Observer Group of West African States
ECOWAS Economic Community of West African States
FMLN Frente Farabundo Martí para la Liberación Nacional
FRETILIN Revolutionary Front for the Independence of East Timor
GA UN General Assembly
GAOR General Assembly Official Records
GOC Good Offices Committee in Indonesia
ICJ International Court of Justice
ICRC International Committee of the Red Cross
IHL International Humanitarian Law
MICIVIH International Civilian Mission in Haiti
MINURSO Mission for the Referendum in Western Sahara
MPLA Popular Movement for the Liberation of Angola
OAS Organization of American States
OAU Organization of African Unity
ONUCA Observer Group in Central America
ONUSAL Observer Mission in El Salvador
ONUVEH Observer Group for the Verification of the Elections in Haiti
PFLP Popular Front for the Liberation of Palestine
POLISARIO Frente Popular para la Liberación de Saguia el-Hambra y Río de Oro
POW Prisoner of war
SC Security Council
SCOR Security Council Official Records
SWAPO South West Africa People's Organization
UDI Unilateral Declaration of Independence
UNAMIC UN Advance Mission in Cambodia
UNAVEM UN Angola Verification Mission
UNCIP UN Commission for India and Pakistan
UNDP UN Development Programme
UNFICYP UN Peacekeeping Force in Cyprus
UNITA National Union for the Total Independence of Angola

UNMIH UN Mission in Haiti
UNPMS UN Police Monitors in Haiti
UNRWA UN Relief and Works Agency for Palestine Refugees in the Near East
UNTAC UN Transitional Authority in Cambodia
UNTAG UN Transition Assistance Group in Namibia
UNTSO UN Truce Supervision Organization in the Middle East

Introduction

In a study on war-termination published in 1982, it was noted that more than half the wars in the Third World since 1945 had been caused by the perception that human rights were being denied.[1] That being the case, one would expect that the Security Council, being concerned with the prevention of armed conflict, would have developed procedures for dealing with human rights issues, either by the establishment of a permanent subsidiary organ under Article 29 of the Charter, or by close collaboration with the Commission on Human Rights under Articles 65 and 68. Yet for more than four decades, the Security Council did its best to avoid taking up human rights issues, and it has not yet developed consistent procedures for dealing with such matters.

The Council, like the other five principal organs, has to keep within the Charter. It has no power to intervene in matters which are 'essentially within the domestic jurisdiction of any state' unless enforcement measures under Chapter VII of the Charter are being applied, and enforcement measures depend on a prior determination that peace is being threatened or breached, or that an act of aggression has occurred (Article 2.7).

In reaching decisions on intervention, the Council has to bear in mind not only the constraint of Article 2.7, but also the provisions under Articles 55 and 56 of the Charter and, in particular, the obligation of UN Members to cooperate for the achievement of universal respect for and observance of human rights and fundamental freedoms.

In the early days, UN Members and UN organs laid great stress on the non-intervention requirement of Article 2.7, but increasingly since 1989, the Security Council has taken the view that the agreement of the parties, or a determination under Chapter VII of the Charter, whether or not enforcement measures are applied, or grave breaches of international humanitarian law have occurred, may sometimes override the non-intervention provisions of Article 2.7. The International Committee of the Red Cross has expressed the view (which I share) that violations of human rights can be of such a magnitude that their continuation would represent a threat to peace within the meaning of Article 39 of the UN Charter.[2]

Two important international trends were visible for all to see while this book was being written, not only in foreign offices and defence ministries but also in the homes of those with television sets. On the one hand was the tragic deterioration of the world situation, with new wars breaking out with alarming regularity, mainly in the Third World. On the other hand was the feeble response of the outside world, mainly in the form of words. It was while atrocities were taking place in Rwanda, for example, that the UN organized a major international conference on human rights and appointed an international high commissioner for human rights. Both these steps had their uses, but they needed to be reinforced by more vigorous action.

In fact, the Security Council did its best to avoid becoming embroiled in such matters. We therefore have a picture of the world situation steadily deteriorating while the Security Council was manifestly failing to keep pace with external events. The United Nations seemed unable to act effectively, other than to utter pious words.

The purpose of this book is to provide factual information about the Security Council's handling of human rights issues. Any reader who consults the notes on pages 143–64 will notice that, in the various cases, I have to the greatest extent possible drawn only on UN documentation. All the members of the Security Council had access to national sources of information; but the one source that was common to them all was UN documentation: speeches in the Council, reports from the UN Secretariat and subsidiary organs, documents from UN Members circulated to Council members. Scholars and practitioners have written articles and books about the early cases, drawing on national archives and using vital information that was not available to all the members of the Council when decisions were taken. If, to take a hypothetical case, Britain and the United States should have reached a secret agreement by which the United States would take the lead on Middle Eastern issues and Britain would take the lead on Southern African matters, the two States would exchange information from open or covert sources, some of which might not be available to other members of the Security Council. But reports, documents and speeches that have been issued by the UN for general distribution are public property, available to all members of the Council on equal terms. It is on these documents that I have relied for describing the various cases.

Documents of the Security Council and cited with S/ followed by a number were issued in mimeographed form on a provisional basis.

Table 1 Arrears in contributions, permanent members of the Security Council, 1993 (in $ millions)

	Regular budget	*Peacekeeping*	*Total*
China	0	7	7
France	0	54	54
Russian Federation/USSR	49	467	516
United Kingdom	0	0	0
United States	286	131	416

Official records are issued in printed form and are cited as Security Council Official Records (SCOR).

One aspect of the problem of dealing with human rights issues that I have not dealt with is how the Security Council's decisions are to be financed, since this is a matter which the Charter assigns to the General Assembly (Article 17). This is by no means a trivial issue, since Members seem much more willing to authorize expenditures than to contribute their assessed share. A recent report of the Secretary-General showed arrears on the regular budget of $542 million, and $1033 million of arrears for peacekeeping on 31 October 1993.[3] Four of the permanent members of the Security Council were in arrears, as shown in Table 1. After 50 years the UN finds itself overburdened and underfunded especially by the powers who should be paying the most.

One other issue related to human rights I have not dealt with. Article 1.3 of the Charter distinguishes between 'international co-operation in solving international problems of a humanitarian character' and cooperation in promoting and encouraging 'respect for human rights and for fundamental freedoms for all'. One of the main humanitarian problems confronting the Security Council as this book went to press was providing protection, sometimes armed, for the movement of medical supplies and food for civilians in war zones. This subject deserves a book on its own.

I have included a chapter on violations (or alleged violations) of international humanitarian law, since human rights instruments are an essential source for such law.

The author of a book on contemporary affairs has great difficulty in keeping up with events. I have tried to confine the book to its subject matter – the UN Security Council's role regarding human rights but not concerning other social and humanitarian matters – and to relevant developments up to 31 December 1993. The result has been that some cases stop abruptly and incomplete. This is so regarding the following: Angola, Cambodia, East Timor, El Salvador, former Yugoslavia, Haiti, Iraq, Kuwait, Liberia, Mozambique, and Western Sahara. There is no way of avoiding this difficulty, but the author can at least warn the reader of its existence.

SDB
January 1994

1 Self-Determination in Africa

Respect for 'the principle of equal rights and self-determination of peoples' is one of the purposes of the United Nations (Articles 1.2 and 55). It seems that the word 'principle' was chosen by the founders deliberately, since it was realized that self-determination might in practice have to be balanced against other equally valid principles such as non-intervention in the domestic affairs of States or the territorial integrity of States. In 1960, the UN General Assembly declared that self-determination was not only a principle but 'the right' of all peoples, and the two UN Covenants on human rights, approved by the General Assembly in 1966, affirmed 'the right' of self-determination.[1]

It was the intention of the founders of the United Nations that the Security Council and the General Assembly should not deal simultaneously with the same issue. There was therefore included in the Charter a provision that the General Assembly shall not make recommendations regarding a matter while the Security Council is exercising the functions assigned to it in the Charter regarding that matter (Article 12.1). The wording of the Charter in this, as in some other respects, is not completely clear: does the inclusion of an item in the list of matters of which the Security Council is seized necessarily mean that the Council 'is exercising . . . the functions assigned to it' in the Charter? Is the General Assembly precluded only from making recommendations but not from taking other actions? Is it plausible to maintain that the two organs may deal simultaneously with the same question so long as they are dealing with different aspects of that question?

These are interesting questions for international lawyers, but the fact is, as the UN Legal Counsel put it in 1964, that 'the General Assembly, beginning in 1960, adopted several resolutions clearly containing recommendations in cases of which the Security Council was then seized and could reasonably be regarded as exercising its functions in regard to that question'.[2] In all the cases dealt with in this chapter, aspects of the matter were considered by both the Security Council and the General Assembly, and often by other UN organs as well.

ANGOLA, MOZAMBIQUE, AND GUINEA-BISSAU

The question of Angola came to the attention of the Security Council in 1961, when Liberia asked the Council to take immediate action 'to prevent the further deterioration and abuse of human rights and privileges in Angola'. When the Council met, Liberia and two other non-aligned members proposed that the Council should appoint a sub-committee to consider what might be done to secure due respect for human rights and fundamental freedoms, but this received only 5 out of 11 votes (the three non-aligned co-sponsors, the Soviet Union and the USA) and was therefore not adopted.[3]

Later in 1961, a group of mainly non-aligned countries alleged that the suppression of human rights in Angola constituted a serious threat to international peace and security. A draft resolution included a preambular reference to the effect that the continuance of the situation was 'an actual and potential cause of international friction and threat to international peace and security', but 'threat to' was amended to 'is likely to endanger the maintenance of'. The amendment was approved. In its operative paragraphs, the resolution called on Portugal to desist from repressive measures, and expressed the hope that a peaceful solution would be found. This was approved by 9 votes with 2 abstentions.[4] In 1963, the wider question of Portugal's overseas territories was brought to the Council's attention on the ground that Portugal 's refusal to comply with UN resolutions constituted a definite breach of peace and security in Africa. An attempt was again made to include in a preambular paragraph of a draft resolution a determination that the situation threatened international peace and security, but this reference was deleted before the vote was taken. An operative paragraph found that the situation was 'seriously disturbing peace and security in Africa'. The proposal was then approved.[5] In 1970, following a complaint that Portugese forces from Guinea (Bissau) had invaded the Republic of Guinea, the Security Council decided by unanimous vote that a special mission should visit the region 'to report on the situation immediately'. The mission considered that an invasion of Guinea by Portugese forces had indeed taken place. 'The operation seems to have been well planned and carried out with professional skill and precision.' On the basis of this report, the Council adopted a comprehensive resolution which included a declaration that 'Portugese colonialism on the African continent [was] a serious threat to the peace and security of independent African States.'[6] By referring to a threat to peace, this was deemed to bring Portugese colonialism in Africa within the scope of Chapter VII of the UN Charter, thus making possible mandatory enforcement action.

There were only a few references in the debates to violations of international standards regarding human rights.[7] Six of the Council's decisions affirmed the goals of self-determination and independence, three asked Portugal to desist from repressive measures, two asked States to refrain from helping Portugal to continue its repressive measures, three called for an amnesty, and two called for free political activity.[8] As Portugal's critics wished each resolution to be stronger than the previous one, the operative verb relating to Portugal changed from 'deprecates' in 1963, to 'deplores' in 1965, to 'condemns' in 1972.[9]

The overthrow of the Salazar–Caetano dictatorship in Portugal in 1974 led to rapid decolonization. Guinea-Bissau was admitted to UN Membership in 1974, Mozambique in 1975, and Angola in 1976.[10]

SOUTHERN RHODESIA (ZIMBABWE)

The Southern Rhodesia case in the Security Council was bedevilled from the start by a certain amount of double-think. From the point of view of a majority of Council members, Southern Rhodesia was a non-self-governing territory administered by the United Kingdom, and Britain was regarded as legally responsible for developments in the territory. From the British point of view, on the other hand, Southern Rhodesia had enjoyed internal self-government since 1923, and for a time before the Unilateral Declaration of Independence (UDI), Britain maintained that internal developments in Southern Rhodesia were essentially matters of domestic jurisdiction and therefore beyond the scope of UN intervention.[11]

The United Kingdom regarded the Unilateral Declaration of Independence in 1965 as illegal and invalid, but the UK had no coercive military presence in the region by which British policy could be imposed.[12] In that case, said Third World countries, the United Kingdom should send an expeditionary force to repress the rebellion: 'in the recent past the United Kingdom used force, scorning right and justice, to repress what it called at the time the rebellion or insubordination of the peoples it had colonized' (Senegal).[13] When the Falklands–Malvinas crisis arose in 1982, Britain found it possible to send an expeditionary force halfway round the world to expel the invaders, thus confirming the view of Third World countries that decisive military action was possible far from metropolitan territory.

The Southern Rhodesian question first came before the Security Council in 1963, after a conference at Victoria Falls had decided to break up the Central African Federation into three separate units. African members of the Council were worried because they considered that Southern Rhodesia was to receive a disproportionate amount of the Federation's military hardware. The nature of the problem changed with the UDI by Ian Smith in 1965. The Security Council condemned this act 'by a racist minority' and called on States not to recognize or assist the illegal regime.[14]

Third World countries would have liked the Council to make an immediate formal determination under Article 39 of the Charter ('threat to the peace, breach of the peace, or act of aggression'), thus making it possible for the Council to take binding decisions, but such a move was resisted by Britain at this stage. US Ambassador Arthur Goldberg then devised a formula which was acceptable only because nobody knew what it meant: 'the situation . . . is extremely grave . . . [and] its continuance in time constitutes a threat to international peace and security'.[15] In the following year, the Council determined that the situation constituted a threat to peace, thus bringing it within the scope of Chapter VII of the Charter, and later in 1966, there were specific references in the Council's resolutions both to Chapter VII of the Charter and to Article 25, by which UN Members agree 'to accept and carry out' decisions of the Security Council.[16]

Between 1963 and 1980, the Council held 128 meetings devoted wholly or mainly to Southern Rhodesia. The aim was variously described as 'to allow the people of Southern Rhodesia to determine their own future', 'freedom and independence', 'self-determination, freedom and independence', 'the free and fair choice of the people', and 'full independence and majority rule'.[17]

The African States were somewhat miffed that the initiative for convening the Council after UDI in 1965 had been taken by Britain.[18] At crucial junctures thereafter, there was competition as to who would be the first to put in a request for a Council meeting, and there was an unseemly row in 1966 when the African president of the Council (Mali) delayed calling a meeting which Britain had requested.[19] On one occasion when it was Britain's turn to preside over the Council, the British ambassador (Lord Caradon) ceded the presidency under Rule 20 of the Council's Rules of Procedure, which allows the president to cede the presidency to the member next in alphabetical order, the procedure that is followed if the question before the Council is one with which the president is 'directly connected'.[20] From time to time, African members of the Council spoke on behalf of the Organization of African Unity or the Group of African States.[21]

As in the case of Portugal's African territories, it is surprising, in retrospect, that there were not more references in the debates and resolutions on Southern Rhodesia to international human rights standards. On one occasion, Zambia cited the Universal Declaration of Human Rights,[22] and on another occasion, the Council received a statement of consensus from the Commission on Human Rights concerning 'the illegal killing of three African political prisoners and freedom fighters', leading the Council to condemn 'the recent inhuman executions' as a flagrant affront to the conscience of mankind.[23]

Because the Security Council always took the line that the United Kingdom was legally responsible for the administration of Southern Rhodesia, its appeals were addressed to Britain rather than to the Smith regime. In 1965, shortly before the UDI, the Council endorsed a request of the General Assembly, asking the United Kingdom 'to obtain' the release of political prisoners, detainees, and restrictees, the repeal of repressive and discriminatory legislation, the removal of restrictions on political activity, and the establishment of full democratic freedom and equality of political rights. Later in 1965, after UDI, Britain was asked to act vigorously in quelling 'this rebellion of the racist minority' and to eliminate the authority of the usurpers. In 1968, the call to Britain to 'bring to an end the rebellion' was repeated, and Britain was also asked to ensure that no settlement was reached which failed to take account of the views of the Southern Rhodesian people; and the measures whose termination Britain had been asked 'to obtain' in 1965 were condemned. The measures were again condemned in 1970, and Britain was asked 'to rescind or withdraw' existing agreements for the presence of trade or consular representatives in Southern Rhodesia. In 1979, Britain was asked 'to take all necessary measures' to prevent illegal executions and to ensure the departure of all external military forces, 'regular or mercenary'.[24] The request about military forces was repeated in 1980 after the Lancaster House agreement, and Britain was also asked to ensure the release of political prisoners and freedom fighters, the release of any South African political prisoners in Southern Rhodesia and 'their safe passage to any country of their choice', the rescinding of emergency legislation, equality of treatment for all parties, and also 'to ensure that eligible Zimbabwe nationals will freely participate in the forthcoming electoral process'.[25]

As for the application of non-military sanctions, the Security Council first called on States to apply oil sanctions, later ordered selective economic and diplomatic sanctions, and then comprehensive sanctions.[26] In 1976, Mozambique informed the Council that it had suffered special economic problems as a result of imposing sanctions against Southern Rhodesia and was therefore consulting the Council in accordance with Article 50 of the Charter. The Council commended Mozambique and appealed to States and UN agencies to provide assistance.[27] After the conclusion of the Lancaster House agreement, mandatory sanctions were terminated, and UN Members were asked to respect 'the free and fair choice of the people of Zimbabwe'. Zimbabwe had achieved genuine independence and was admitted to UN Membership in 1980.[28]

NAMIBIA

Namibia (or South West Africa, as it was called in Security Council documents until June 1968) was the only territory formerly under League of Nations mandate that was not brought within the UN trusteeship system. The matter was placed before the General Assembly in 1946 and before the Security Council in 1968. In 1966, the General Assembly decided to terminate the League of Nations mandate over the territory and, the following year, the Assembly established a Council for Namibia with the ostensible purpose of administering the territory until independence would be achieved. In 1969, the Security Council recognized the General Assembly decision to terminate the mandate; and the following year, the Council declared that the continued presence of the South African authorities in Namibia was illegal. In 1971, the Security Council agreed with, and the General Assembly welcomed, an advisory opinion of the International Court of Justice that South Africa's presence in Namibia was illegal. South Africa, as the former Mandatory power, had pledged itself to respect human rights and fundamental freedoms for all. To introduce restrictions based on national or ethnic origin constituted a denial of fundamental human rights and was a flagrant violation of the UN Charter. In 1978, the Security Council asked the Secretary-General to appoint a Special Representative to ensure early independence for Namibia through free elections under UN supervision and control.[29]

In 1977, the Western members of the Security Council, the so-called Contact Group (Canada, France, the German Federal Republic, Britain, and the United States), had initiated their own search for a solution which would accord with the Council's decisions. This involved intensive consultations with South Africa, the South West Africa People's Organization (SWAPO), and the neighbouring front-line States. In 1978, the Contact Group issued a paper elaborating the proceedings for an impartial electoral process. This contained many of the elements that were to find a place in the Security Council's later plan for Namibian independence, but the proviso that primary responsibility for maintaining law and order during the transition to independence would rest with 'the existing police forces' was not in full conformity with the Security Council's 1976 decision that the election should be under UN supervision 'and control'. Be that as it may, the 1978 plan of the Contact Group was accepted with qualifications by South Africa and SWAPO, and was approved by the Security Council (Czechoslovakia and the Soviet Union abstaining). The Council reiterated at regular intervals the principle of free elections under UN auspices.[30]

Following a decision of the Security Council of 27 July 1978, the Secretary-General appointed Martti Ahtisaari as his Special Representative. Ahtisaari visited Namibia in August 1978 and put forward a plan elaborating the proposals of the Contact Group. South Africa and SWAPO were to observe a ceasefire and their forces would be confined to bases; political prisoners and detainees would be released; discriminatory legislation would be repealed; and refugees and political exiles would be allowed to return. An Administrator-General would be appointed by South Africa to work with the UN Special Representative and to maintain law and order during the transitional period. A UN Transition Assistance Group (UNTAG) would be established with both military and civilian elements, acting with complete impartiality in monitoring the cessation of hostilities and ensuring free and fair elections. This plan was approved by the Security Council in resolution 435.[31] This became the benchmark for the Security Council's role regarding the decolonization of Namibia, though it was to take more than a decade before the Ahtisaari plan could be implemented.

External events were to have a major bearing on the Namibian issue. First came the *coup* against the Salazar–Caetano regime in Portugal in 1974; the consequent decolonization of Angola in 1975; the outbreak of civil was between the Angolan Government formed by the MPLA (Popular Movement for the Liberation of Angola) and

Jonas Savimbi's guerrilla movement UNITA (National Union for the Total Independence of Angola); the breach between UNITA and SWAPO; and the intervention of Cuban forces to assist the Angolan Government, and South African forces to assist UNITA. The consequence of these events was to make inevitable a linkage between the Namibian and Angolan problems. Another major event was the gradual ending of the Cold War after 1985 and increasing Soviet efforts to contribute to the solution of regional issues.

The installation of the Reagan Administration in 1981 and the appointment of Chester Crocker as US Assistant Secretary of State for African Affairs led to a shift of emphasis in US policy, from confrontation with South Africa towards what was called 'constructive engagement'. Gradually the Contact Group lost its solidarity, and its last collective act was the issuance in 1982 of a set of principles for the election of a constituent assembly, which principles (it was claimed) had been accepted by 'all the parties to the negotiation'.[32] By 1988, the United States was conducting talks involving South Africa, Angola and Cuba, and a new tripartite agreement was reached on the principles for a peaceful settlement. SWAPO accepted these principles and a *de facto* ceasefire then took effect. Agreements on the phased withdrawal of South African forces from Namibia, and Cuban forces from Angola, were concluded by the end of 1988. It was subsequently agreed that implementation of Security Council resolution 435 would begin on 1 April 1989.[33] An election for a constituent assembly was held in 1989, Namibia became independent and was admitted to UN Membership in 1990.[34]

At no time did the Security Council make a formal determination under Chapter VII of the Charter which would have enabled the Council to take binding decisions, but one resolution included a preambular reference to Article 25 and the obligation of UN Members to comply with decisions of the Council, and two resolutions warned that coercive measures under Chapter VII of the UN Charter might be initiated.[35] The Council's aim was that the Namibian people should achieve self-determination, national independence, and their territorial integrity.[36] The Council censured, condemned and strongly condemned South Africa.[37] States were invited, requested, called upon, or urged to take specified forms of persuasion and pressure.[38]

South Africa had abstained when the Universal Declaration of Human Rights was put to the vote in 1948, but South Africa was later asked to respect its provisions in Namibia.[39] On particular human rights issues, South Africa was asked to discontinue illegal trials, release political prisoners, abolish discriminatory and repressive laws and practices, and allow the return of exiled Namibians.[40]

SOUTH AFRICA

The treatment of persons of Indian origin in South Africa came before the General Assembly in 1946, and the wider question of apartheid in 1952. In 1960, following the Sharpeville massacre, 29 Afro-Asian States asked the Security Council to consider the situation in South Africa as a matter that was likely to endanger international peace and security. South Africa, supported by Britain and France, maintained that the issues raised were within South Africa's domestic jurisdiction and therefore outside the Council's purview. Italy thought there was a contradiction in the Charter between the provisions regarding human rights and the ban on intervening in domestic affairs. The United States, agreeing that there was tension between various provisions in the Charter, thought it desirable that the Council should at least consider the matter. The sponsors of the item argued that a State that was violating vital provisions of the Charter could not hide behind the ban on intervening in domestic affairs. At the end of the debate, the Council adopted a skilfully drafted resolution, recognizing that the situation in South Africa had led to friction and 'might' endanger international peace and security, and asking UN Secretary-General Hammarskjöld 'to make such arrangements as would adequately help in upholding the purposes and principles of the Charter'. This was a typical formulation in the Hammarskjöld era.[41]

Hammarskjöld corresponded with the South African Government in 1960 and visited South Africa in 1961, and he reported to the Security Council that no mutually acceptable arrangement had been found. In his view, the lack of agreement was 'not conclusive', and he intended to continue the consultations 'at an appropriate time'.[42]

In 1962, the General Assembly asked the Security Council 'to take appropriate measures, including sanctions, to secure compliance with the resolutions of the General Assembly',[43] and at the 1965 session and subsequently, the General Assembly addressed similar but increasingly forceful requests to the Council.

The Afro-Asian members of the Council pressed for many years for a formal determination by the Council under Chapter VII of the Charter so as to make the Council's decisions mandatory, but this was resisted by the main Western members.[44] The Council had decided in 1960 that the situation, if continued, 'might' endanger international peace and security.[45] In 1963, the Council received two reports from a committee on apartheid established by the General Assembly the previous year, together with a request from 32 African States, that the Council should consider the systematic refusal of South Africa to comply with UN resolutions. The Council held seven meetings on the matter. Tunisia, not a member of the Council, said that the situation in South Africa fell within the scope of Articles 55 and 56 of the Charter (international cooperation regarding human rights and related matters), and the Soviet Union maintained that racial discrimination was a violation of the Universal Declaration of Human Rights (which neither South Africa nor the Soviet Union had supported when it was put to the vote in 1948). The Philippines made the same points. In 1963, a resolution declaring that the situation was seriously disturbing international peace and security and calling for a ban on the export of arms to South Africa was adopted, Britain and France abstaining; and this decision was reiterated on four subsequent occasions. None of these resolutions contained a formal determination under Chapter VII of the UN Charter that the situation in South Africa threatened world peace, so these decisions were referred to in a subsequent resolution as 'a voluntary arms embargo' against South Africa.[46]

During this time, paramilitary elements of South African and Namibian liberation movements began to base themselves in neighbouring States, and from time to time South African forces launched armed incursions against these groups. Raids by South African forces against Zambia and Angola during this period were condemned or strongly condemned by the Security Council.[47]

Whether a particular situation represents a threat to world peace is, in part, a subjective matter. If enough people allege often enough that world peace is threatened, the situation tends to take on a threatening appearance. The policy of apartheid was widely regarded as offensive to human conscience and a violation of UN norms regarding human rights, but initially it was difficult to argue that it threatened world peace, as that term is used in Article 39 of the UN Charter. Once South African forces began crossing national borders, however, it became plausible to maintain that peace was threatened and that the Security Council had an obligation to consider coercive measures under Articles 41 or 42 of the Charter. It thus came about that in 1977, the Security Council determined that the acquisition of arms by South Africa constituted a threat to peace and security and decided that States should 'cease forthwith any provision to South Africa of arms and related *matériel* of all types'. Later in the year, the Council established a committee of the whole to verify that the embargo was being effective, and these decisions were reaffirmed from time to time. All the decisions were approved unanimously or adopted by consensus. UN Members were later encouraged to apply more extensive sanctions, but these were recommendations and not binding decisions.[48] A proposal for mandatory and widespread sanctions against South Africa was vetoed by Britain and the United States in 1987.[49]

The mandatory arms embargo did not stop incursions by South African forces against neighbouring States, not only against Angola and Zambia as previously, but also against Lesotho and Botswana. These cross-border attacks were strongly condemned by the Security Council.[50]

The basis of the Council's concern had always been that human rights were being systematically violated in South Africa. One of the first resolutions of the Council declared that racial discrimination in South Africa was contrary to the principles of the UN Charter. A group of experts appointed by the Secretary-General, in accordance with a resolution of the Security Council, recommended in 1964 that South Africa should incorporate into its constitution a bill of rights based on the Universal Declaration of Human Rights. The experts also appealed for an immediate amnesty for opponents of apartheid. The communiqué issued after the 'periodic' meeting of the Security Council in 1970 stated that Council members had affirmed that the peoples of Southern Africa were entitled to self-determination and 'fundamental human rights in freedom and dignity'. Apartheid was described by the Council as 'a crime against the conscience and dignity of mankind' and incompatible with the Universal Declaration of Human Rights, and the Council affirmed 'the legitimacy of the struggle of the oppressed people of South Africa . . . as set forth in . . . the Universal Declaration of Human Rights'. The preamble to a resolution of the Council in 1984 reaffirmed the Universal Declaration of Human Rights. In 1986, a preambular paragraph of a resolution of the Council affirmed that a solution to the South African problem should be based on the UN Charter and the Universal Declaration of Human Rights, and this was repeated the following year in a statement by the President of the Council on behalf of its members.[51]

The Council called on South Africa to take specific measures for assuring human rights, to allow the return of political exiles,[52] to release all political prisoners (including Nelson Mandela by name on four occasions),[53] to stop excessive violence and the killing of African people,[54] and not to carry out death sentences.[55] The policy of creating bantustans or 'homelands' was rejected, a referendum held in 1983 was declared to have 'no validity whatsoever', and the Council solemnly declared its aim to be 'the establishment of a non-racial democratic society based on majority rule, through the full and free exercise of universal adult suffrage'.[56]

It is difficult to judge what effect the decisions of the Security Council had on white opinion in South Africa. There were other external pressures against South Africa, particularly those orchestrated at Commonwealth conferences, and there were internal influences from the black community, from white liberals, and from commercial and industrial circles. In 1989, the hardline State President, P. W. Botha, suffered a stroke, and his successor, F. W. de Klerk, initiated cautious but irreversible moves for political and constitutional reform. In 1990, Nelson Mandela was released from prison and immediately assumed the *de facto* leadership of the African National Congress. The Security Council did not meet to consider South African issues between 23 November 1988 and 15 July 1992.

In December 1991, a Convention for a Democratic South Africa (CODESA) was convened. This brought together the South African Government, the African National Congress, the Inkatha movement, and other significant South African parties. The negotiations soon ran into difficulties, however, and following a tragic incident in Boipatong in June 1992, the Security Council held two long meetings and then adopted a resolution which included a request to the UN Secretary-General to appoint a Special Representative 'to recommend ... measures which would assist in bringing an effective end to the violence and in creating conditions for negotiations leading towards ... a democratic, non-racial and united South Africa'.[57]

The Secretary-General appointed Cyrus Vance as his Special Representative, and Vance recommended the release of political prisoners as a means of 'creating trust and burying the unhappy past'. The atmosphere in South Africa took a sudden turn for the worse with an incident at Bisho in Ciskei, during which 28 demonstrators were killed and nearly 200 were wounded. Nearly 50 UN observers were operating, together with 17 from the Commonwealth, 14 from the European Community, and 11 from the Organization for African Unity. Their task was to observe marches and other forms of mass action, and to maintain contact at all levels with Government agencies, political parties and other non-governmental organizations. Some 13 000 Namibians had returned home from abroad, and a further 5000 had applied to return. Much of Vance's report dealt with measures to reduce violence. UN observers had made informal contact with the Goldstone Commission, which was investigating the prevention of violence and public intimidation. The assassination of Chris Hani, a leading member of the ANC, was described by the Security Council as 'a deplorable and troubling event'.[58] At a meeting of the Government of South Africa and the ANC in February 1993, it was agreed that elections for a constituent assembly should be held within a year. In September, Mandela addressed the UN Special Committee against Apartheid and asked that all economic sanctions against South Africa should be lifted, and the General Assembly passed a resolution to that effect. On 15 October, it became known that Mandela and de Klerk had been jointly awarded the Nobel Peace Prize.[59]

There were critics of the constitutional negotiations from both African and white extremists, but the widespread yearning for peace from moderate white and African opinion meant that the process was virtually unstoppable.

THE ROLE OF THE SECURITY COUNCIL

Decolonization in Africa, while slower than the colonized peoples would have wished, proceeded relatively smoothly after the mid-1950s. The main difficulties were in territories with substantial communities of white settlers. Until the *coup* in 1974, Portugal refused to fulfil its obligation, under Article 73e of the Charter, to transmit to the UN information on the dependent territories which it administered, nor did it cooperate with UN bodies concerned with colonial questions. After 1974, decolonization of Portugal's overseas territories proceeded expeditiously. Southern Rhodesia was in an unusual position, having enjoyed internal self-government since 1923. The UK never transmitted information about the territory under Article 73e, and there was much Third World criticism of Britain for failing to take forceful measures after the illegal declaration of independence. Namibia was, in effect, a colony adjoining the mother country. In 1946, South Africa told the General Assembly that a majority of the inhabitants desired incorporation with South Africa, but the

Assembly always took the line that the territory should be brought within the international trusteeship system. South Africa had in 1910 attained what was then called dominion status, but it was a country run by a white minority numbering only 20 per cent of the population.

Afro-Asian Members of the UN believed that these areas would not be able to exercise self-determination unless pressure were exerted by outside powers, and especially by the West. The Charter envisages various forms of external pressure: expressions of opinion by UN organs, non-military sanctions (Article 41), military sanctions if non-military sanctions prove inadequate (Article 42), suspension of UN Membership in the case of a State against which preventive or enforcement action has been taken (Article 5), expulsion from the UN if a State has persistently violated the principles of the Charter (Article 6). It was never on the cards that Western powers would take military action to secure self-determination in any of the cases dealt with in this chapter, so Afro-Asian efforts were directed towards increasingly vehement condemnations of the offending State and the imposition of non-military sanctions. The West resisted these efforts, partly for reasons of economic self-interest, partly for reasons of military security during the Cold War period, and, in some cases, because of the belief that external pressures might have the effect of consolidating support for intransigent white minorities.

The resolutions of the Security Council condemning repressive measures had a long-term rather than an immediate effect, for they demonstrated that abuses of human rights did not go unnoticed by the outside world, and there was always the possibility that individuals responsible for crimes against humanity might one day be called to account. Moreover, as the catalogue of abuses lengthened, so the pressure for external coercion increased.

Mandatory sanctions against the Smith regime in Southern Rhodesia and the arms ban against South Africa were widely violated, often with the knowledge of the governments concerned. But the fact that mandatory sanctions were in place, comprehensively in the case of Southern Rhodesia and partially in the case of South Africa, and that the screw might be progressively tightened, undoubtedly had its effect in the region: it caused the white elites to wonder how long they could hold out as international pariahs, and it encouraged the black majorities to realize that they were not forgotten.

When the history of this period comes to be written, I doubt whether Western governments will find much cause for satisfaction. The speeches of their representatives in the Security Council, the efforts to water down Third World resolutions, the failure to enforce rigorously the mandatory decisions on sanctions, these did not give the impression that the West attached primary importance to the elimination of racial discrimination and oppression. On the other hand, some of the more vociferous critics of the West represented countries with deplorable records on human rights. However the blame is distributed, the UN Security Council played an essential role in helping the peoples concerned in their struggle to achieve self-determination.

2 Ascertaining the Will of the People

Between the two world wars, a number of plebiscites on the status of territory took place under international auspices: Schleswig (1920), Allenstein and Marienwerder (1920), the Klagenfurt Basin (1920), Upper Silesia (1921), Sopron (1921), and the Saar (1935). Only the last of these was under the direct sponsorship of the League of Nations.[1]

The Atlantic Charter (14 August 1941) stated that one of the hopes for a better future for the world would be respect for the right of all people to choose the form of government under which they would live, but the UN Charter contains no express provision assigning a role to the United Nations in facilitating, organizing, or supervising elections. There are, however, some general affirmations in the UN Charter which have a bearing on the matter: the principle of equal rights and self-determination of peoples (Article 1.2); the goal of self-government or independence for trust territories (Article 76b); the development of 'a full measure of self-government' for other dependent territories (Article 73); and the promotion of respect for human rights and fundamental freedoms for all (Articles 1.3, 55c, and 76c). It was not envisaged at San Francisco that the Security Council would have a role regarding the application of these affirmations, except possibly regarding those trust territories designated as strategic areas.

In 1948, in the Universal Declaration of Human Rights, the General Assembly proclaimed that everyone has the right to participate in government, directly or through freely-chosen representatives, and that the will of the people should be expressed in 'periodic and genuine elections' by universal and equal suffrage, and by secret vote or 'equivalent free voting procedures' (Article 21). In the International Covenant on Civil and Political Rights, adopted by the General Assembly in 1966, the principle of free elections was again affirmed, but the reference to 'equivalent free voting procedures' was eliminated, and the proviso was added that elections should guarantee 'the free expression of the will of the electors' (Article 25).

In the event, the Security Council has perforce been involved in various procedures for ascertaining the will of the people, initially in a rather haphazard manner but since 1989 in accordance with principles that have been developed and refined in the light of experience. On three occasions, the Council has declared elections not held under UN auspices to be invalid. What is still not always clear is how responsibilities for electoral processes should be allocated to the Security Council and other UN agencies, especially the General Assembly, the Human Rights Commission, the Secretary-General and staff, and the UN Development Programme. The International Court of Justice has played an indirect role in a number of cases (e.g. Namibia, Western Sahara, Libya, hostages in Iran, Pakistan and Bangladesh, Bosnia-Herzegovina and Serbia-Montenegro).

In the following pages, I describe those cases where the Security Council had a part in ascertaining the will of the people. I have included a brief section on Nicaragua, though the Security Council's responsibilities related in the main to other aspects of the situation.

INDONESIA

After the uprising of the Indonesian Republicans against Dutch colonial rule, a Good Offices Committee (GOC) was established in Indonesia by the Security Council. According to agreements concluded between the parties on board the USS *Renville*, a plebiscite under the observation of the GOC was to be held within six to twelve months to determine whether 'the population of the various territories of Java, Madura and Sumatra' wished to form part of the Republic of Indonesia or of another State. Madura had been occupied by Netherlands forces after a ceasefire had supposedly entered into force, and the Netherlands authorities had on 23 January 1948 organized a plebiscite in which over 90 per cent of the voters had agreed that relations between Madura and the Indonesian Republicans should be severed. The Republicans complained to the Security Council that the Dutch policy of encouraging separation was contrary to the *Renville* agreements. As a consequence of this complaint, the Council asked the GOC to report on political developments in Madura and Western Java. In the case of Madura, the GOC was not able to do more than report to the Council that the plebiscite had 'conformed largely to traditional practice'.[2]

The situation in Western Java was more complicated. The Dutch authorities had sponsored a movement for local autonomy, and the Republicans had assumed that separatist activities would cease after the *Renville* agreements had been concluded in 1948, pending a plebiscite within six to twelve months. The Dutch had convened two regional conferences of their own appointees in Western Java in 1947 and, after the *Renville* agreements, they announced that a third conference would be held the following month, consisting of 47 Dutch appointees and 53 persons chosen in indirect elections. To the surprise of the Dutch, the conference asserted considerable independence and voted that the status of Western Java should be decided by a plebiscite as agreed in the *Renville* accords. As in the case of the plebiscite in Madura, the GOC was not able to observe the proceedings of the conference at first hand, so it did its best to provide the Security Council with a factual account of what had happened and a statement to the effect that the status of Western Java was 'only provisional', pending a plebiscite or some other method for ascertaining the will of the people.[3] In the event, the *Renville* agreements became redundant after the second Dutch 'police action' in December 1948.

The second 'police action' took place while the Security Council was in the process of moving from Paris (where the General Assembly had been in session) to Lake Success in New York (where the Council normally met, until the UN headquarters building in Manhattan had been completed). There was a widespread sense of outrage at the Dutch action, and the Security Council called for an immediate ceasefire and the release of Indonesian political prisoners.[4] The Council then embarked on a lengthy debate, in the course of which the Dutch delegate fought a rearguard action by claiming that the Indonesian question was within the domestic jurisdiction of the Netherlands and thus beyond the competence of the Security Council. The debate culminated in a comprehensive resolution setting out the terms for a settlement of the conflict. The resolution reaffirmed the *Renville* principle of free and democratic elections to be observed by an appropriate UN agency, to be held before 1 October 1949.[5]

This resolution was soon overtaken by other events, however, for the parties agreed to meet at a Round Table Conference in the Hague. On the initiative of Canada, the Security Council issued a directive to its Commission for Indonesia which, by stressing other elements in its previous resolution, implied that it was no longer essential to proceed with elections.[6]

At the Round Table Conference, agreement was reached on internal self-determination, that is to say, the right of populations to determine the status of their respective territories within the Indonesian federal structure.[7]

KASHMIR

When the Indian sub-continent was partitioned and achieved independence in 1947, it was agreed that the 565 Princely States were free to link up with either India or Pakistan. This led to special difficulties in those States, like Jammu and Kashmir, in which the ruler was of a different community from the majority of his subjects. The Hindu Maharajah of Kashmir, having dithered for some time, finally decided to accede to India, but Lord Mountbatten (Governor-General of India) said that once law and order had been restored, the question of accession should be settled by reference to the people. This was followed by an acrimonious exchange of letters between the Prime Ministers of India and Pakistan. The proposal for a plebiscite to settle the status of Kashmir was taken up by Pakistan at a meeting at Lahore on 1 November 1947 between Mohammad Ali Jinnah and Lord Mountbatten, Pakistan suggesting that a plebiscite should be under the joint control and supervision of India and Pakistan. Nehru suggested in a broadcast the following day that, once peace and order had been restored, a referendum should be held under UN or other international auspices.[8]

On 1 January 1948, India complained to the Security Council that Muslim fighters from Pakistan had invaded Kashmir, had established a regime which called itself Azad Kashmir, and that this was likely to endanger international peace and security. Pakistan, in reply, said that India's occupation of Kashmir was unlawful, and Pakistan denied that it was supporting the invaders.[9]

In April 1948, the Security Council adopted a comprehensive resolution which *inter alia* provided that the future of Kashmir should be decided by a fair and impartial plebiscite conducted by a Plebiscite Administrator nominated by the UN Secretary-General. In the meantime, the government of Indian-held Kashmir would constitute an interim administration, but 'major political groups' should share 'equitably and fully' in the conduct of the administration. A UN Commission for India and Pakistan (UNCIP) was created, and UNCIP subsequently proposed that areas from which Pakistan forces withdrew should be administered 'by the local authorities under the surveillance of the Commission'. In 1949, UN Secretary-General Trygve Lie appointed Admiral Chester W. Nimitz as Plebiscite Administrator.[10]

Both Pakistan and India expressed disquiet about the April resolution, which Pakistan said was one-sided, because the proposed plebiscite would favour India so long as Indian-held Kashmir was under the control of Sheikh Abdullah. Pakistan wanted to be assured that there would be impartial administration in Kashmir before the question of accession was submitted to the people. India was even more strongly opposed to the resolution. India held that there could be no serious consideration of a plebiscite until effective steps had been taken to end the fighting and secure the withdrawal of Muslim intruders. In any case, the Indian view was that the holding of a plebiscite must not be allowed to encroach on the ordinary sovereign powers of the State of Jammu and Kashmir. Sheikh Abdullah, the Kashmiri nationalist leader, who at this stage was cooperating with India, said he was as anxious as anyone to ensure a free vote, but how could the neutrality of the administration of Kashmir be guaranteed? While it might be desirable to have a neutral administrator in Kashmir, said Abdullah, where would the Security Council find a neutral individual? 'Frankly speaking, even if the Security Council were to request Almighty God to administer the State of Jammu and Kashmir during this interim period, I do not feel that He could act impartially. After all, one must have sympathy either for this side or for that side.'[11]

When the UN Commission for India and Pakistan reached the subcontinent, it elaborated a phased plan for a cessation of hostilities, with a commitment that the future status of Kashmir should be determined 'in accordance with the will of the people'. India accepted the plan with the reservation that Pakistan should play no part in the organization and conduct of a plebiscite. Pakistan stressed that it would be affected by the result of a plebiscite at least as much as would India, and therefore the two Governments should be placed in a position of absolute equality and advantage. UNCIP found the attitudes of the parties so divergent that it 'wished to leave open the possibility . . . of alternative solutions mutually agreeable to both parties'.[12]

UNCIP proceeded to work out detailed arrangements for a plebiscite, to be held when the truce arrangements had been carried out. When the truce had taken effect and UNCIP had been satisfied that peaceful conditions had been restored, UNCIP and the Plebiscite Administrator would determine, in consultation with India, the final disposal of Indian and Kashmiri armed forces and, 'in consultation with the local authorities', the final disposal of armed forces in Azad Kashmir. The Plebiscite Administrator would report the result of the plebiscite to UNCIP, which would certify to the Security Council whether the plebiscite had been free and impartial.[13]

When UNCIP returned to the subcontinent in 1949, it found that

India no longer agreed that the future of Azad Kashmir forces should be settled by the Plebiscite Administrator in consultation with local authorities: India was now insisting that there could be no question of withdrawing Indian forces from Kashmir until arrangements had been made for disbanding and disarming Azad Kashmiri forces. UNCIP suggested that this and other matters in dispute should be dealt with at a bilateral meeting at ministerial level, but Pakistan rejected any reference in the proposed agenda to the disbanding and disarming of Azad forces. UNCIP then suggested that outstanding issues be referred to arbitration, but this was unacceptable to India.[14]

In submitting its third report in 1949, UNCIP commented that the holding of a plebiscite still depended on the demilitarization of Kashmir, but that the plan of demilitarization contained in UNCIP's own resolutions was no longer adequate. What was needed was a comprehensive plan for dealing with the disposal of all armed forces in the State.[15]

It was now clear that India regretted its original commitment to a plebiscite. Indian diplomats did their best to postpone Security Council debates on the issue or gave reasons why a plebiscite was impossible or unnecessary: Pakistan must first 'vacate' its aggression; a plebiscite could not be held until demilitarization of Azad Kashmir had been achieved; a plebiscite was unnecessary because a constituent assembly in Indian-held Kashmir had already decided to join the Indian Union. Only the Soviet Union, which had abstained on the April resolution, now opposed the idea of a UN-sponsored plebiscite.

In 1950, the Security Council appointed Sir Owen Dixon of Australia as UN Representative for India and Pakistan, taking over the function of UNCIP. Demilitarization was to be achieved within five months.[16] Dixon duly reported on the 'strange' situation he found in Kashmir. India and Pakistan had agreed on a general plebiscite, but neither had taken the necessary preliminary steps other than to agree on a ceasefire. Dixon had conceived it to be his duty to bring about conditions for an overall plebiscite, but his proposals for demilitarization had been rejected by the parties. He therefore proposed an alternative plan whereby the south-eastern part of Kashmir would go to India, the north and west to Pakistan, with a plebiscite limited to the Vale of Kashmir; but this idea was rejected by both sides. Pakistan claimed the Vale because its inhabitants were mainly Muslim, India by right of occupation. Dixon suggested that the interest of the people, the justice as well as the permanence of the settlement, and the imperative necessity of avoiding another refugee problem, pointed to the wisdom of abandoning the idea of an overall plebiscite and adopting partition. He could not recommend further steps by the Security Council: 'It is perhaps best that the initiative should now pass back to the parties.'[17]

The Security Council did not take Dixon's advice, however, and in 1951, the Council reaffirmed that 'the final disposition' of the State should be settled 'in accordance with the will of the people expressed through the democratic method of a free and impartial plebiscite under the auspices of the United Nations'. Frank P. Graham was appointed the new UN representative for India and Pakistan.[18] Although Graham had no better luck than his predecessor, the Security Council never abandoned the idea that the status of Kashmir should be settled by reference to the will of the people.[19] There was a general feeling that, as this was a dispute between two members of the Commonwealth, Britain should take the lead in coming forward with suggestions for peacemaking, and Britain never gave up the idea that the matter should be resolved by an act of self-determination under UN auspices.[20]

THE CONGO (ZAIRE)

In the Indonesian case, a subsidiary organ of the Security Council had been asked 'to report' on plebiscites in Madura and Western Java. In Kashmir, the plebiscite called for by the Security Council was never held. In the case of the Congo (now Zaire), what was then a quite novel role fell to the United Nations.

The Congo in 1961 was wracked by disorder and disunity. On 21 February, in a resolution authorizing the use of force if necessary and as a last resort in order to prevent civil war, the Security Council also urged that the Parliament of the Congo be convened. The UN was asked to take the 'necessary protective measures in that connexion'. Five months later, the General Assembly reaffirmed the decision of the Security Council, urging also the release of all members of parliament and other political leaders then held by the Belgians, and asking that 'safe conduct and security' be extended to the members of parliament.[21] The parliament of the Congo was due to convene at the University of Lovanium near Léopoldville. The United Nations was able to conclude safe-conduct agreements with the provincial authorities in Orientale (Léopoldville) and Kivu (Stanleyville): an agreement was also concluded with Katanga (Elizabethville), but this was later repudiated by the provincial assembly.[22]

The task assigned to the UN agency in the Congo was unprecedented. It involved not only assuring freedom of passage and absolute safety for members of parliament travelling to and from the University of Lovanium, but also ensuring that the whole area was completely demilitarized and that unauthorized persons were not able to gain access. Of 137 members of parliament, only eight from Katanga and nine others did not participate in the sessions. A coalition government of national unity and reconciliation was formed, with the conciliatory Cyrille Adoula as Prime Minister. Only Katanga under Moïse Tshombe refused to accept the new arrangements.[23] Although there was much inflammatory language in UN circles over the UN operation in the Congo as a whole, criticism of this particular exercise was surprisingly muted.[24]

DOMINICAN REPUBLIC

The United Nations played only a marginal role in the crisis in the Dominican Republic in 1965. The main external impact was from the United States, in part under the banner of the Organization of American States (OAS).

The crisis began in 1963 with a *coup* against the leftist President Juan Bosch. Donald Reid Cabral was named head of the junta. On 24 April 1965, the supporters of Bosch staged an uprising against the junta, and within a few days, the capital (Santa Domingo) was engulfed in civil war. On 28 April, US Marines were landed, ostensibly to protect or evacuate US nationals but in reality to prevent a Communist takeover. The Council of the OAS met the following day and called for a ceasefire.

On 1 May, the Soviet Union called for an urgent meeting of the Security Council to consider 'the question of the armed interference by the United States in the internal affairs of the Dominican Republic'. Before the Council could take a decision, the OAS had decided to create an Inter-American Peace Force which by the middle of July was composed of 12 400 personnel from the United States and 1700 from six Latin American countries. On 14 May, the UN Security Council unanimously called for a ceasefire and asked Secretary-General U Thant to send a representative to the Dominican Republic in order to report to the Council on the situation. U Thant appointed José Antonio Mayobre as his representative and Major-General Indar Jit Rikhye as his military adviser. On 19 May, the Council asked that Mayobre's efforts be devoted to securing an immediate suspension of hostilities so that Red Cross agencies could search for the dead and care for the wounded. The same day, the OAS issued a report in the course of which it stated that the presence of the United Nations 'compromised and interfered with' the work entrusted to a Special Committee of the OAS. On 22 May, the Security Council (the United States abstaining) urged that the suspension of hostilities should be transformed into a permanent ceasefire. On 16 July, Mayobre included in his report to the Security Council a section on alleged violations of human rights, and, on 26 July, the President of the Security Council stated that members of the Council condemned gross violations of human rights and called for strict observance of the ceasefire.[25]

In December, U Thant informed the Council that national elections would be held on 1 June 1966. Although the UN had no role in supervising the elections, the OAS deployed 32 observers and reported that the election had been conducted in an honest and impartial manner. Mayobre reported to the Security Council on the elections, repeating the assessment of the OAS observers that the election had been satisfactorily conducted. Joaquin Balaguer was elected President with 58 per cent of the votes, Juan Bosch securing 39 per cent.[26]

One aspect of resort to international humanitarian law is considered in Chapter 3, p. 65.

SOUTHERN RHODESIA (ZIMBABWE)

In 1969 the President of the Security Council made a statement of consensus to the effect that a referendum to be held in Southern Rhodesia was illegal and that the constitution was invalid[27] and, ten years later, that the forthcoming elections were condemned and the results declared to be 'null and void'. In 1980, after the agreement at Lancaster House, the Council called on the British Government to 'create conditions . . . which will ensure free and fair elections':[28] these were successfully held a few weeks later under international supervision.

BAHRAIN

Bahrain comprises a group of islands in the Persian Gulf. The Bahrainis themselves are Muslims, and there is a significant expatriate population. During the nineteenth century, Britain concluded a series of treaties with the Amir by which Britain assumed responsibility for defence and foreign relations. Sovereignty over Bahrain was, however, claimed by Iran. In 1968, Britain announced that it was abandoning its East-of-Suez military policy. The following year, there was some talk of Bahrain joining Qatar and the Trucial States in a new Arab federation. In 1970, however, the Shah of Iran stated that Iran was withdrawing its claim to Bahrain, and that the people of Bahrain should be allowed to decide their own future.

Following this announcement, the United Kingdom and Iran agreed that the matter should be resolved by reference to the will of the people, and Secretary-General U Thant was asked to designate a Personal Representative to visit Bahrain and consult the people about their wishes regarding the future status of the islands. The published documentation stated that U Thant's report would be transmitted to the Security Council 'for its consideration *and endorsement*' (my italics), and he stated in his memoirs that this was the first time that parties to a dispute had given a prior pledge to accept without reservation the findings or conclusions of his Personal Representative 'provided that the conclusions were endorsed by the Security Council'.[29] U Thant designated Vittorio Winspeare Guicciardi, a senior UN official, to undertake the mission of consultation.[30]

The Soviet Union protested that U Thant's action in agreeing to the request of Iran and Britain without the express authority of the Security Council was 'illegal', but he insisted that his actions in this and similar cases were consistent with the UN Charter and in no way impinged on the authority of the Security Council.[31]

At that time, Bahrain did not have an elected legislature, but in six areas there were partially-elected municipal councils. Winspeare consulted members of these councils and their subsidiary committees, as well as religious leaders, representatives of welfare organizations, professional groups and clubs of various kinds. Only a few women were consulted, but the few that were interviewed were 'well informed and very articulate'. Virtually all of those consulted wanted Bahrain to become a fully independent sovereign State. Winspeare was confident that the method of consultation had been appropriate and adequate, and that the overwhelming majority of those consulted wished that Bahrain should become fully independent and sovereign, free to decide for itself its relations with other States.[32]

Iran and Britain asked for a meeting of the Security Council, and this was held promptly. After a harmonious debate, the Council unanimously endorsed U Thant's report, and this decision was also confirmed by the two chambers of the Iranian parliament. In 1971, Bahrain was admitted to UN Membership.[33]

PACIFIC ISLANDS

The UN Charter states that among the territories that might be placed under the trusteeship system were territories formerly under League of Nations mandate (Article 77.1), and that any territory placed under UN trusteeship might be declared 'a strategic area or areas', in which case, the UN's supervisory functions were to be exercised by the Security Council, with the assistance of the Trusteeship Council (Articles 82 and 83). In 1947, the United States concluded an agreement whereby the Pacific Islands previously under League of Nations mandate to Japan would be placed under the UN trusteeship system, the United States to be the administering authority and the territory to be designated a strategic area. This was approved by the Security Council. In 1949, the Security Council delegated most of its supervisory functions to the Trusteeship Council, but retained the right to amend or terminate the trusteeship agreement.[34] The annual reports of the Trusteeship Council on the Pacific Islands are issued as supplements to the official records of the Security Council, but there was no public debate in the Security Council on the administration of the Pacific Islands between 1949 and 1990.

It had been the original intention that the Trusteeship Council should consist of an equal number of States administering Trust Territories and States not administering Trust Territories. All five permanent members of the Security Council were to be members of the Trusteeship Council, of which three (Britain, France and the United States) administered Trust Territories and two (China and the Soviet Union) did not. The balance between colonial and non-colonial powers was to be met by the election of the requisite number of non-colonial members by the General Assembly (Article 86).

When the Charter was drafted, it seems not to have been envisaged that when a Trust Territory achieved 'self-government or independence', this would affect the composition of the Trusteeship Council and that eventually the balance between administering and non-administering members would be impossible to maintain. When a Trust Territory achieved self-government or independence, the administering authority, if not a permanent member of the Security Council, would cease to be a member of the Trusteeship Council and, in order to maintain the balance, one of the elected members would have to be displaced. If, however, a permanent member of the Security Council that had formerly administered one or more Trust Territories ceased to be an administering authority (as was the case for France in 1960 and Britain in 1962), it would move to the non-colonial side of the Trusteeship Council, thus displacing *two* elected members. The result of this process was that by 1975, the Trusteeship Council consisted only of the five permanent members of the Security Council: the United States (administering the Pacific Islands) and the other four permanent members of the Security Council (Britain, China, France and the Soviet Union); there were now no members elected by the General Assembly.[35] After the People's Republic of China was seated at the UN in 1971, China did not participate in the work of the Trusteeship Council until 1989.

The Pacific Islands placed under trusteeship fell into three geographical groups: the Mariana Islands (now known as the Northern Mariana Islands), the Marshall Islands, and the Caroline Islands. In accordance with its standard policy, the Trusteeship Council regularly sent visiting missions to examine conditions in the islands but, beginning in the mid-1970s, the United States as administering authority also invited the Trusteeship Council to send special missions to observe plebiscites or referenda on constitutional changes. The Soviet Union consistently opposed the sending of these observation missions. The missions were small in size, the two largest having six members, together with a few UN officials. Beginning in 1983, the missions included members from Fiji and Papua New Guinea as well as from members of the Trusteeship Council. A Chinese member took part in the mission to Palau in 1990. The aim was that each mission should be in the territory for a few days before polling, on election-day itself, and for the declaration of the result, but this was not always possible: the mission to Palau in December 1986, for example, did not reach the territory until two days before polling, and the second mission to Palau the following year arrived the day before polling.[36]

Often the people of the territory were asked to say 'yes' or 'no' to a reasonably simple question, but occasionally the voters were asked what were, in effect, hypothetical questions: if proposition no. 1 should not be approved, which of the following other options would you prefer? In the 1983 plebiscite in the Marshall Islands, for example, the voters were asked to ballot for or against a compact of free association with the United States together with a final settlement of radiation claims arising from nuclear tests. The voters were also asked whether, if that proposition should be defeated, they had preferences from a number of other options. This led to the following results (in percentages):

blank ballots	70
Relationship with the USA	
no comment	9
Commonwealth status	4
Statehood	less than 1
Status quo	less than 1
Compact of free association without an agreement on compensation for radiation claims	13
Independence	4
Communism	less than 1

In the case of the 1990 plebiscite in Palau, the complicated question read as follows:

> CONDITIONAL UPON THE INTERPRETATIONS SET FORTH IN SECTION 3 OF RPPL NO. 3–10, DO YOU APPROVE FREE ASSOCIATION WITH THE UNITED STATES AS SET FORTH IN THE COMPACT OF FREE ASSOCIATION SIGNED ON JANUARY 10, 1986, INCLUSIVE OF ITS SUBSIDIARY AGREEMENTS, INCLUDING ITS SECTION 324, WHEREBY THE GOVERNMENT OF THE UNITED STATES, IN CARRYING OUT ITS SECURITY AND DEFENSE RESPONSIBILITIES UNDER THE COMPACT OF FREE ASSOCIATION, HAS THE RIGHT TO OPERATE NUCLEAR CAPABLE OR NUCLEAR PROPELLED VESSELS AND AIRCRAFTS WITHIN THE JURISDICTION OF PALAU?[37]

The missions found the campaigns orderly, with the radio reporting fairly on the issues. In some cases (Palau in December 1986, for example), government employees were told to campaign during working hours for the policy favoured by the government. The main complaint from political and community leaders was that there had been insufficient time to prepare for the test of opinion. There was occasional confusion about proper electoral procedures, and there were a few minor irregularities, but never on such a scale as to affect the outcome. There was usually a high turnout, never less than 62 per cent and in two cases as high as 93 per cent (Mariana Islands in 1975, Palau in 1978).

The various parts of the Trust Territory did not opt for the same status. The Northern Mariana Islands chose free association with the United States.[38] The Caroline Islands other than Palau, now known as the Federated States of Micronesia, opted for independence in free association with the United States, and the federation was admitted into UN Membership in 1991.[39] The situation regarding the Marshall Islands was complicated because of claims arising from US military activities in the territory. Marshall Islanders had been displaced from a chain of atolls in the northern part of the territory consequent on US testing of nuclear weapons: Bikini in 1946, Eniwetok in 1947, Rongelap and Utirik in 1954. In addition, the Kwajalein group of atolls was used by the United States as the destination for test missiles launched from Wanderberg Air Force Base in California. It was not until 1983 that compensation terms were agreed. The Marshall Islands then opted for free association with the United States and UN Membership.[40]

The most difficult situation concerned Palau in the Western Carolines, where no fewer than eight UN-observed plebiscites took place in 1978–92. For many years, and particularly since 1973, the Palauans were seeking a separate political status from the rest of the trust territory. The Visiting Mission to observe the referendum in the Caroline and Marshall Islands in 1978 noted that the situation in Palau was 'appreciably different' from that obtaining elsewhere and that campaigning was taking place in 'a climate of tension'. The question of the future status of the Islands was complicated by differences of view about what rights the United States should have regarding nuclear, chemical and biological weapons. By 1986, the United States had agreed 'not to use, test, store, or dispose of' such weapons 'intended for use in warfare' within Palau's jurisdiction, but – as a matter of standard practice – the United States was not willing to disclose whether or not aircraft or naval vessels passing through Palau's air-space or territorial waters are nuclear-powered or carry nuclear weapons. Moreover, the constitution of Palau requires that any change of status for the Islands must be approved by a 75 per cent majority in a plebiscite. The plebiscite in the Islands observed by the UN in 1990 asked the Palauans whether they favoured free association with the United States, with a ban on placing weapons of mass destruction on the Islands, but with freedom for the United States to have aircraft or vessels using nuclear power or carrying nuclear weapons in transit through Palau's territorial waters or air-space. This received a 'Yes' vote slightly over 60 per cent, but well short of the 75 per cent required by the constitution. The final status of Palau thus remains undetermined, but the Security Council has expressed the hope that the Palauan people 'will be able in due course to complete the process of freely exercising their right to self-determination'.[41]

NAMIBIA

I have indicated in the previous Chapter (pp. 6–9) the role played by the Security Council in the exercise of self-determination by the Namibian people. In 1976, the Security Council declared that the people of the territory should achieve independence through 'free elections under the supervision and control of the United Nations', and it reiterated at regular intervals the principle of free elections under UN auspices. The Council condemned the elections held in Namibia in 1978 without UN supervision and declared that the results would be 'null and void'. In 1978, the Council asked the Secretary-General to appoint a Special Representative to ensure early independence for Namibia through free elections under UN supervision and control, and the Secretary-General appointed Martti Ahtisaari to this post.[42]

One of the issues to be resolved before Namibia could have free and fair elections under UN auspices concerned South African questions about the impartiality of the United Nations. In 1973, the General Assembly had recognized SWAPO as 'the authentic representative of the Namibian people' and in 1976 as 'the sole and authentic representative of the Namibian people'. From the South African point of view, this determined in advance the outcome of the process of decolonization. Pérez de Cuéllar assured South Africa in 1983 that the UN would treat all parties equally, and that 'South Africa was expected to do the same'. These assurances were repeated in 1988.[43] It had been part of the Contact Group's plan of 1978 that the primary responsibility for maintaining law and order during the transition to independence would rest with 'the existing police forces' and that an Administrator-General appointed by South Africa would ensure their good conduct to the satisfaction of the UN Special Representative. This arrangement was confirmed by Pérez de Cuéllar in 1988.[44]

On 23 January 1989, Pérez de Cuéllar reported to the Security Council that, while it had not been possible to reconcile all opposing viewpoints, much progress had been achieved and that the independence of Namibia was 'at last in sight'. The election for a constituent assembly was to be held the following November, the voting to be by proportional representation. The Special Representative of the Secretary-General, with the assistance of the civilian and military personnel of the UN Transition Assistance Group (UNTAG), was to certify whether all stages of the electoral process had been free and fair.[45]

Not all was plain sailing, however. During the night of 31 March/1 April, some well-armed SWAPO fighters, estimated by South Africa to number between 1800 and 1900, crossed from Angola into Namibia. South African security forces were supposed to be demobilized or confined to base, and UNTAG's military forces were not yet deployed. After difficult discussions involving the South African Foreign Minister and the Administrator-General of Namibia, on one side, and Ahtisaari and the Commander of the military component of UNTAG (Lt-Gen. Dewan Prem Chand) on the other side, it was agreed that two battalions of the counter-insurgency unit known as Koevoet (Crowbar) should be reactivated to support the South-West Africa Police. Neither the SWAPO incursions nor the reactivation of the Namibian battalions were in strict accord with the agreements which the parties had concluded, but at least the crisis was defused: most of the SWAPO fighters returned to Angola. The Secretary-General reported orally on these developments in informal consultations with the Security Council on 3 April.[46]

This incident was partly responsible for another crisis. It had been agreed that all Namibian security forces should be disbanded, but Ahtisaari learned that, although the Koevoet unit had been disbanded, most of its members had been absorbed into the South-West Africa Police. The Secretary-General reported to the Security Council that many of the ex-Koevoet members, although now ostensibly part of the police, continued to operate as they had done before Koevoet was disbanded. This included the use of armoured personnel-carriers mounted with heavy machine-guns. 'UNTAG received many complaints of intimidation and other unacceptable conduct by ex-Koevoet personnel.' It was not until 30 October, only a few days before the election, that all ex-Koevoet personnel were disbanded under the supervision of UNTAG.[47]

Other elements of the South African and Namibian security forces were withdrawn, confined to base, or disbanded. Some South African military personnel remained in Namibia to perform civilian functions, such as the operation of airfields. A number of members of bushmen battalions, who had become 'completely alienated from their traditional way of life', were placed in camps under the supervision of UNTAG.[48]

Some 42 000 Namibian refugees returned to Namibia with the help of the UN High Commissioner for Refugees, and other UN agencies helped with their reintegration into Namibian life. All were amnestied under the terms of a Proclamation by the Administrator-General, dated 6 June 1989. A small number of political prisoners in Namibia were released. A UN mission visited Angola and Zambia to investigate allegations that SWAPO was detaining over a thousand Namibian dissidents: the mission concluded that, at the time of their visit (September 1989), there were no detainees in any of the alleged detention centres.[49]

The draft electoral legislation issued by the Administrator-General on 21 July was 'highly problematic from the point of view of the United Nations', and prolonged and difficult negotiations were necessary in order to secure amendments satisfactory to Ahtisaari. All restrictive and discriminatory legislation which might abridge or inhibit the holding of free and fair elections was repealed. Over 700 000 voters were placed on the electoral rolls, and ten political parties were formally recognized. A code of conduct for political parties was prepared by Ahtisaari and accepted by all the political parties contesting the election (see pp. 33–4).[50]

There were some difficulties over the role of the media, and especially the partisan stance of the South-West Africa Broadcasting Corporation (SWABC). A fortnight before the election, the governing body of SWABC was suspended, but Ahtisaari reported that 'arduous negotiations [had] left the problem of editorial impartiality unresolved'.[51]

Ahtisaari was assisted by UNTAG, which consisted of 4500 military personnel, 300 military monitors and observers, 1500 police officers, 885 electoral supervisors, plus civilian administrative staff. Fifty countries contributed personnel, supplies or services. The task of UNTAG was to observe the electoral process, sort out difficulties, and report the results; but it had no enforcement powers.[52]

There were 215 fixed and 143 mobile polling stations, monitored by the UN's electoral supervisors and civilian police. Just over 97 per cent of the registered voters cast their ballots for the 72 seats in the constituent assembly. SWAPO won 41 seats, the multi-ethnic Democratic Turnhalle Alliance, 21: SWAPO's strongest support was

Fig. 2.1 Code of Conduct for political parties (S/20883, 12 September 1989)

An essential part of free and fair elections is freedom of political campaigning. Everyone has the right to put forward their political principles and ideas, without threat or fear, to every other person, without exception. But freedom of political campaigning also carries responsibilities, including the duty to accept every other person's freedom to campaign.

The Namibian political parties whose names are subscribed to this document, meeting together in Windhoek under the chairmanship of the Special Representative of the Secretary-General of the United Nations on 12 September 1989, have agreed as follows:

(1) Intimidation, in any form, is unacceptable, and will be expressly forbidden by the parties in directives to their members and supporters.

(2) Party leaders will instruct their members and supporters that no weapon of any kind, including any traditional weapon, may be brought to any political rally, meeting, march or other demonstration.

(3) Parties will notify UNTAG–CIVPOL as well as SWAPOL in advance of their planned meetings and other rallies.

(4) All practical steps will be taken by parties to avoid holding rallies, meetings, marches or demonstrations close to one another at the same time. Party leaders undertake to co-operate in applying this principle in good faith and in a reasonable spirit should any coincidence of time or venue arise.

(5) Speakers at political rallies will at all times avoid using language which threatens or incites violence in any form against any other person or group of persons. Parties will not issue pamphlets, newsletters or posters, whether officially or anonymously, which contain inflammatory language or material.

(6) All parties will consistently emphasize, both to their supporters and also to voters in general, that there will be a secret ballot, and that consequently no one will know how any individual may have voted.

(7) Party members and supporters will not disrupt other parties' rallies, meetings, marches or demonstrations.

(8) Party members and supporters will not seek to obstruct other persons from attending the political rallies of other parties.

(9) Party members and supporters will not plagiarize symbols of other parties, or steal, disfigure or destroy political or campaign materials of other parties.

(10) Party leaders will use their good offices to seek to ensure reasonable freedom of access by all political parties to all potential voters, whether they be at farms, on State-owned properties, in villages, or at secondary reception centres. They will also seek to ensure that such potential voters wishing to participate in related political activities have freedom to do so. This may, where necessary, take place outside working hours.

(11) Parties will establish effective lines of communication to one another at headquarters, regional and district levels, and will appoint liaison personnel who will be constantly on call to deal with any problems that may arise.

(12) Parties will meet on a fortnightly basis under the chairmanship of UNTAG regional directors or centre heads to discuss all matters of concern relating to the election campaign. A standing committee of party leaders at headquarters will meet on a fortnightly basis under the chairmanship of the Special Representative or his Deputy to deal with such matters on a nation-wide basis. An observer from the Office of the Administrator-General will be invited to attend the meeting of the standing committee. Emergency meetings will be convened as and when necessary.

(13) All allegations of intimidation and other unlawful conduct in the election campaign will be brought to the attention of the nearest UNTAG–CIVPOL and SWAPOL stations or patrols.

(14) Party leaders will issue directives to their members and supporters to observe this Code of Conduct, and take all other necessary steps to ensure compliance.

(15) It is stated in the settlement proposal that: 'The elections will be under the supervision and control of the United Nations in that, as a condition to the conduct of the electoral process, the elections themselves and the certification of their results, the United Nations Special Representative will have to satisfy himself at each stage as to the fairness and appropriateness of all measures affecting the political process at all levels of administration before such measures take effect.' Party leaders undertake to honour the outcome of free and fair elections so certified by the Special Representative of the Secretary-General of the United Nations.

(16) The Special Representative and party leaders undertake to publicize this Code of Conduct throughout Namibia by all means at their disposal.

The Namibian political parties whose names are subscribed below accept and endorse this Code of Conduct as binding upon them. They agree that alleged violations will be brought to and considered by the standing committee referred to in paragraph 12 above.

in Ovamboland, where it polled more than 90 per cent of the votes. Ahtisaari certified that the electoral process had gone smoothly and, at every stage, had been free and fair. The following February the constituent assembly adopted a constitution for Namibia which accorded with the 1982 principles of the Contact Group.[53] As indicated in Chapter 1 (p. 8), the Namibian people opted for independence and UN Membership.

NICARAGUA

Although the Security Council was seized with the situation in Nicaragua and had received two reports from the Secretary-General on the proposal of five Central American presidents that the United Nations and the Organization of American States should verify that the electoral process in Nicaragua would be free and fair,[54] the Secretary-General circulated only to the General Assembly three requests from Nicaragua when they were received in 1989. The Secretary-General explained that the UN had observed elections in various dependent territories but had not previously done so in an independent State. 'Indeed, on a number of occasions over the years, we have declined invitations from Member-States to that effect.' There were, however, special factors in the Nicaraguan case, particularly that it was part of a wider peace process of the Central American presidents, and that supervision would not be limited to election-day but spread over a ten-month period.[55]

The Secretary-General was, of course, correct in saying that it had not been the practice for the UN to supervise elections in independent States, but a small mission from the Secretariat led by the Legal Counsel had observed the plebiscite held in Panama in 1977 and had reported that it took place in a sober atmosphere and in accordance with normal democratic standards.[56]

On 27 July 1989, the Security Council adopted a comprehensive resolution on efforts towards peace in Central America, including preambular references to the proposal of the Central American Presidents for international verification of elections. The first stage of the operation to supervise the elections in Nicaragua began on 25 August 1989, but the General Assembly was not in session, and it was not until 23 October that the General Assembly gave formal support to the Secretary-General's decision to meet the Nicaraguan request. On 27 November, the Security Council decided to establish a UN Observer Group in Central America (ONUCA) to verify the cessation of aid to irregular forces and cross-border military attacks. Thus the Secretary-General, the Security Council, and the General Assembly were all involved, as well as the Organization of American States. In 1990, the UN General Assembly noted the Secretary-General's reports that the electoral process had been orderly, free and fair, but – perhaps surprisingly – the resolution contained no express words of commendation or appreciation regarding the UN's role in observing the election.[57]

HAITI

In June 1990, Secretary-General Pérez de Cuéllar received an approach from Haiti requesting electoral assistance and observation. The Secretary-General suggested certain criteria in the Haitian case, repeated in his annual report the following September, for judging whether the United Nations should take on the task proposed, but he pointed out that these were 'not identical with those [that] have been mounted so far'. He also suggested that electoral verification by the UN should remain 'an exceptional activity'.[58]

Most UN Members were at that stage opposed to the establishment of new UN machinery for providing electoral assistance or verifying elections, but Pérez de Cuéllar considered that a new structure in the UN Secretariat was needed. He therefore designated a senior official as Coordinator for Electoral Matters, assisted by a small staff.[59]

Whichever policymaking organ authorizes electoral verification, it is the Secretary-General who administers the operation. If the electoral process is an element in removing a threat to peace, it would make sense for the operation to be authorized by the Security Council: this would in theory have applied in the Nicaraguan case. There had, however, been a feeling among some UN Members that the Security Council was too dominant a body, and that mood undoubtedly increased as superpower tension diminished. This no doubt is part of the explanation for the Secretary-General's decision to report only to the General Assembly in the Nicaraguan case.[60]

The organization and supervision of the election in Haiti was complex in both origin and operation. Haiti first raised the matter informally with the UN Development Programme, and a number of UN missions were sent to Haiti in 1990 to clarify the Haitian request.

Three documents were then submitted to the Secretary-General, asking for UN assistance regarding the forthcoming election. The first request was from Haiti and was co-sponsored by the Bahamas and Colombia; the second came from the chair for the month of the Latin American and Caribbean Group; the third came from Haiti alone. After receiving the first request, Pérez de Cuéllar consulted members of the Security Council informally. On 25 September, the chair of the Latin American and Caribbean Group asked that the request from Haiti be placed on the agenda of the General Assembly, and the General Assembly agreed to this, three days later. On 5 October, the President of the Security Council informed Pérez de Cuéllar that members of the Council, without prejudice to their positions on the competence of UN organs on requests from UN Members for electoral assistance, hoped that the General Assembly would take urgent action on Haiti's request. On 10 October, the General Assembly decided by consensus to request the Secretary-General, 'in co-operation with regional organizations and Member States', to provide Haiti with 'the broadest possible support'.[61]

Haiti's request raised a number of important constitutional questions. In June 1990, the Secretary-General had consulted members of the Security Council informally about the request, but a number of members of the Council, and especially China and the two Latin American members (Colombia and Cuba), were strongly opposed to the involvement of the Security Council, on the ground that the situation in Haiti did not threaten world peace at that time. It was doubtless because this view was held by some members of the Security Council that the Secretary-General issued the communications from Haiti as documents of the General Assembly. At the beginning of October, however, the Secretary-General reported to the Security Council, this time formally, on developments up to that date, including a further communication from Haiti clarifying its request for UN assistance, including help in drawing up 'electoral security plans' – a notably ambiguous expression. The Security Council responded by expressing the hope that the General Assembly would take urgent action, which it duly did five days later. In the course of the debate preceding the adoption of the Assembly's resolution, Cuba and Mexico stressed that there was no threat to peace in Haiti and that the conduct of elections lay within the domestic domain of States. Cuba added that its delegation had found it necessary 'to foil several manoeuvres over the past few months'. This may have referred to US attempts to have the matter of security assistance during the electoral process dealt with by the Security Council.[62] Be that as it may, three UN organs were involved in addition to the UN Development Programme: the Secretary-General, the Security Council and the General Assembly.

In deciding which policymaking organ should be involved, the Secretary-General no doubt took account of part of the second communication from Haiti: 'The Haitian Government does not wish for, and is not requesting, the dispatch of "Blue Helmets" or of any peace-keeping force to ensure the security of the country.' On the other hand, the third Haitian communication had referred to help regarding electoral security, and the UN staff in Haiti did, in fact, include a small number of security observers.[63]

Haiti had been under the dictatorial control of François Duvalier (Papa Doc) and his son Jean-Claude from 1957 to 1986. This had been followed by a series of *coups d'état* or fraudulent elections until the installation of General Prosper Avril as President in September 1988 and his replacement in March 1990 by a Provisional Government headed by Ertha Pascal-Trouillot. It was President Avril who had first asked for UN help in supervising an election, and President Pascal-Trouillot who renewed the request. In response to these requests and the decision of the General Assembly, Pérez de Cuéllar established the UN Observer Group for the Verification of the Elections in Haiti (ONUVEH).[64]

This was a difficult task for the UN. Most of Haiti is mountainous. There is one major road running north and west of the capital, but secondary roads are very poor and communications networks are undependable. More than three-quarters of the population are illiterate, and 80 per cent of the people live below the poverty level of $150 a year. The country has no democratic tradition, and there were no officials with experience of registering voters or issuing and counting ballot papers. To a large extent, the organization of the election had to be improvised.

The atmosphere in the country in the run-up to the election was calm, even festive. The media were free of governmental pressure or control. There was one grenade-attack at an election meeting at Pétionville, killing seven people and severely injuring more than 50 others, and there was an attempted *coup* by Roger Lafontant between the first and second phases of the election, which was quickly suppressed by the army. All Haitians aged 18 or over were eligible to vote. In most areas, the number of persons registering to vote exceeded the number of persons of voting age, but this was probably due to the unreliability of official statistics and to the fact that the officials responsible for registering electors were paid on the basis of the number of persons registered. To prevent double-voting, each elector had to dip his thumb in indelible ink after voting.

The main candidates were the Rev. Jean-Bertrand Aristide of the National Front for Change and Democracy, an unpredictable and sometimes reckless Roman Catholic priest, and Marc Bazin of the National Alliance for Democracy and Progress; but nine other candidates for the Presidency were approved by the Interim Electoral Council.

In addition to the UN, there were observers from the Organization of American States, the Organization of East Caribbean States, the Carter Center, as well as appointees from a number of governments and representatives of non-governmental organizations. The task of the observers was to monitor the different phases of the campaign and voting, to assess whether political parties were free to organize and mobilize support, to see whether candidates had equal access to the media, to observe whether voters were able to register and vote freely, and to see whether the votes were counted honestly. There was also a separate UN operation to ensure that proper security was observed throughout the process.

The polling took place in two rounds in a calm and peaceful atmosphere. In one area (Cité Soleil) in which Aristide was very popular, ballot papers were late in arriving, and some electors from that area were allowed to vote at other polling stations. There were a few minor violations of the secrecy of the ballot (in Jérémie, far instance, election officials were seen filling out the ballot papers for old and disabled voters), but there was no evidence of organized fraud.

The UN observers estimated that 67 per cent of the registered voters cast their ballots. The Rev. Jean-Bertrand Aristide was elected President, and his party won 13 of the 27 seats in the Senate and 27 of the 83 seats in the Chamber of Deputies. The UN observers concluded that the Haitian people had been 'able to vote in freedom and safety, without pressure of any kind'. Other observers reached similar conclusions.

At this stage, the United Nations might well have congratulated itself on having assisted Haiti in the transition to democracy, but underlying tensions now surfaced. Opposition to Aristide came from the Roman Catholic hierarchy, the armed forces, reactionary elements that had formerly been associated with the Duvaliers, and some ordinary Haitians who had expected that Aristide's government could perform an instant economic miracle. Tension developed between the President and the two Chambers of Parliament.[65] Things came to a head in September 1991, there was yet another *coup*, and President Aristide was forced to leave the country.[66] The Security Council met early in October, and Aristide asked for the help of the Council in protecting the human rights of the Haitian people. Honduras, not a member of the Security Council but speaking for the Group of Latin American and Caribbean States, spoke immediately after Aristide and asked the Council to support the efforts of the Organization of American States, which had already decided to impose a trade embargo and to send a mission to Haiti to help restore and strengthen constitutional democracy and respect for the human rights of all Haitians. The President of the Security Council said that members of the Council wished to see the restoration of the legitimate government in Haiti and supported the efforts of the Organization of American States; but the Council adjourned without taking a formal decision.[67] The General Assembly was not so reticent, and condemned the *coup*, called for the immediate restoration of Aristide's legitimate government and the full observance of human rights, and asked the UN Secretary-General 'to consider providing support' for the efforts of the OAS. In February 1992, agreements were apparently reached for the phased restoration of democracy in Haiti. Aristide would be reinstated as President and would respect the decisions taken and acts ratified by the Haitian parliament. The UN and the OAS would solicit emergency assistance. Once constitutional order had been established, the sanctions authorized by the UN and the OAS would be lifted. Measures would be taken to halt all repression and reprisals and to guarantee public liberties, the parties would refrain from ambiguous statements that could be interpreted as incitements to violence, and a general amnesty would be proclaimed except for common criminals. During the absence of President Aristide, acting Prime Minister Marc Bazin would manage the affairs of State.[68]

In 1993, it became apparent that earlier agreements were not being respected and, in June, the Security Council decided to impose an oil embargo pending compliance by the Haitian authorities. On 3 July, a new agreement was reached (the Governors Island Agreement). Dante Caputo, the Special Envoy of the Secretaries-General of the UN and the OAS, would oversee the deployment of an international civilian mission to monitor respect for human rights and the elimination of all forms of violence. An attempt would be made to strengthen the civilian sphere of government and to separate police and army functions. Caputo would have the advice of 'the Friends of the [UN] Secretary-General', comprising the representatives of Canada, France, the United States and Venezuela. Aristide would return to Haiti by 30 October.[69]

The parties continued the dialogue in New York, focusing again on the reform of the police, the armed forces and the justice system, the abolition of all paramilitary forces, and an amnesty for political prisoners (the New York Pact, 16 July 1993). On 26 August, Secretary-General Boutros-Ghali notified the Security Council that sufficient progress had been achieved for the lifting of sanctions. This was done by the Security Council on receipt of the Secretary-General's notification. The Council authorized the dispatch of a United Nations Mission in Haiti (UNMIH), a contingent of UN police monitors (UNPMS), and an international civilian mission (MICIVIH). These developments did not prevent further violence and political chaos, however, with organized gangs threatening and attacking UN personnel. The situation continued to deteriorate, and in October the Security Council decided under Chapters VII and VIII of the Charter to reimpose oil sanctions so long as the Haitian authorities were failing to respect the Council's decisions.[70]

ANGOLA

As part of the Namibian settlement, agreement was reached for the phased withdrawal of South African and Cuban troops from Angola, the Cuban withdrawal to be verified by the UN. The Security Council, in private consultations, agreed unanimously in 1988 to establish machinery to verify the withdrawal of Cuban forces (UNAVEM). By June 1991, 50 000 Cuban troops had left: the Angolan Government then asked that UNAVEM should remain in the country until after the elections in 1992 in order to supervise a ceasefire between Angolan factions, the elections to be supervised by international observers. The Security Council agreed unanimously to extend the mandate of UNAVEM (thereafter known as UNAVEM II).[71]

The following November, Angola asked for UN technical assistance in preparing the elections and for UN observers 'to follow the Angolan electoral procedure'. This was, in effect, two separate requests, and Secretary-General Boutros-Ghali dealt with them in different ways. Technical assistance on electoral matters was assigned to the UN Development Programme and the UN Secretariat's

Department of Technical Cooperation. As for the observation of elections, the Secretary-General reminded the Council of the criteria his predecessor had laid down. On 24 March 1992, after a brief and amicable debate, the Security Council approved the proposals of the Secretary-General.[72]

In June 1992 the Secretary-General reported on the preparations for the election due to take place in September. The ceasefire was being disrupted by antagonisms and misunderstandings; the political and security atmosphere was 'tense and fragile'; the demobilization process was behind schedule, especially on the part of UNITA (Jonas Savimbi's National Union for the Total Independence of Angola); and UN monitoring of the oil-rich Cabinda enclave had been 'paralyzed' by local guerrilla activities. The Security Council met on 7 July and, instead of adopting a resolution, authorized its President to make a statement that had been agreed in private consultations. This statement stressed that Angola was a sovereign and independent country and that the implementation of the Peace Accords was the responsibility of the Angolan parties. These parties had requested UN observation and verification, and the Security Council was concerned that 'constraints' were holding back the peace process. The Council appealed to the Angolan Government and UNITA to overcome the delays and inadequacies described in the Secretary-General's report, so that free and fair elections could take place in September as scheduled.[73]

The election campaign proper began on 29 August, and ten days later, the Secretary-General reported to the Council that both sides were failing to complete 'certain very important tasks'. In some areas, doubts had been raised as to the impartiality of UN personnel. An 'intractable and volatile problem' had arisen concerning the province of Cabinda which was relatively undeveloped but controlled access to offshore oil. The demobilization of military forces had been slow. Some prisoners of war had been released, but each side had 'outstanding claims against the other'. Some 60 000 refugees had returned from Zaire and Zambia, and the UN High Commissioner for Refugees planned to assist the return of a further 270 000. The process of registering the voters had begun, and it had been estimated that 92 per cent of the eligible voters had been registered. It had not been possible to draw up an agreed Code of Electoral Conduct. Some problems remained regarding access to Government-controlled media. In the light of this report, the Security Council called on the Angolan parties for a speedy implementation of the Peace Accords.[74]

The election duly took place at the end of September. UNAVEM II deployed 400 observers of 90 nationalities. Of some 6000 polling stations, about 4000 had been visited. The observers reported that 'the great majority of the . . . voters had cast their ballots in peaceful and orderly conditions'. While there had been some logistical difficulties, there had been no major or systematic fraud. More than 91 per cent of the registered voters had cast their ballots. The Government candidate, José Eduardo dos Santos, secured 49.57 per cent of the votes for the presidency, while Jonas Savimbi of UNITA polled 40.07 per cent. As neither candidate had secured half or more of the votes, a second ballot was needed. This requirement became irrelevant, however, since Savimbi refused to accept the result because of alleged defects in the electoral process. The Security Council noted that 'one of the parties [meaning UNITA] was contesting the validity of the election', so the President of the Council called on 'UNITA and the other parties' to respect the results.[75]

By the end of November, two months after the election, the tactics of the Security Council changed, because the situation on the ground had changed. The Council was no longer urging the parties to accept the result, but instead to cease hostilities and to engage in dialogue. Both parties were being held accountable for the dangers facing UN personnel. The Council condemned both sides for persistent violations of the peace agreement and demanded an immediate ceasefire. The Special Representative of the Secretary-General, Margaret Anstee, reported orally to the Security Council, whereupon the Council demanded that UNITA should 'accept unreservedly the results of the democratic elections', and strongly condemned the attacks against UN personnel and against international humanitarian flights.[76]

In spite of an escalation in the fighting, peace talks were taking place. UNITA was particularly unyielding and was responsible for some major atrocities. It had, for instance, attacked a train, killing more than 200 civilians. But, as Boutros-Ghali repeatedly stressed, the effectiveness of a relief operation depends above all on the cooperation of the combatants, and such cooperation was lacking in Angola. The election held in 1992 had failed by a minuscule margin to form the basis for a peaceful political settlement, mainly because UNITA refused to accept the judgement of international observers that the election had been free and fair. The Security Council took an unusual step by deciding under Chapter VII of the Charter to impose an embargo on the supply of arms and oil to UNITA, a non-State entity.[77]

CAMBODIA

A matter relating to Cambodia (also known as the Khmer Republic or Democratic Kampuchea) first came to the attention of the Security Council in 1958, when Cambodia and Thailand informed the Secretary-General of difficulties that had arisen along their common border. The Secretary-General appointed a Special Representative to help the parties to find a solution to these difficulties. The following year, it was announced that Cambodia and Thailand were re-establishing diplomatic relations. Shortly after this, Cambodia instituted proceedings against Thailand in the International Court of Justice, alleging that Thailand was occupying a portion of Cambodian territory containing the ruins of a sacred temple: in 1962, the Court found in Cambodia's favour. Later in 1962, renewed trouble broke out between Cambodia and Thailand, and the Secretary-General appointed a new Special Representative, who served until the end of 1964. In 1966, another Special Representative was designated, and he continued his duties until 1968. In none of these cases did the Secretary-General obtain the express authority of the Security Council. Secretary-General Hammarskjöld maintained that the procedure he had followed was a 'much more effective and smooth-working technique' than the usual procedure of meetings and debates: moreover, it was not contrary to the UN Charter. This was a case of 'Leave it to Dag.' It was not to the liking of the Soviet Union, however, which insisted that, according to the UN Charter, decisions relating to international peace and security had to be taken by the Security Council.[78]

Another aspect of Cambodia's problems came before the Security Council in 1964 when Cambodia claimed that it was the victim of aggression by South Viet Nam. After eight meetings, the Council decided by unanimous vote to send to the region three of its members (Brazil, the Ivory Coast and Morocco) to consider what measures might prevent a recurrence of the incidents of which Cambodia had complained. The Security Council mission recommended that UN observers be sent to Cambodia and that a person of high international standing be appointed to help the parties resolve their differences, 'particularly the delimitation and marking of the common frontier'. Cambodia protested against 'everything' in the report, which it said was 'strictly unacceptable to Cambodia'. As the Security Council was unable to give Cambodia the help it had requested, Cambodia asked that its complaint should simply be 'placed on file'.[79]

Trouble had been brewing along the border between Cambodia

and Viet Nam for some years, and in December 1978, military forces of Viet Nam invaded Cambodia, expelled the Pol Pot regime (the Khmer Rouge), and installed Heng Samrin as head of a new regime in Phnom Penh. This was, in part, a subsidiary consequence of the Sino-Soviet dispute – the Soviet Union supporting Viet Nam and the new administration in Cambodia, China being critical of Viet Nam and by implication supporting the Khmer Rouge, now mainly in exile. The new government in Cambodia was not generally recognized.

In January 1979, the Khmer Rouge delegation complained to the Security Council of 'savage acts of aggression' by Viet Nam, and the Council held five meetings. China submitted a draft resolution to strongly condemn Viet Nam, but this was not pressed to a vote. Seven non-aligned members of the Council submitted an alternative draft, calling on the parties to respect Charter principles and asking the Secretary-General to report on implementation, but this was vetoed by the Soviet Union.[80]

A month later, on 17 February 1979, China invaded Viet Nam, and the Security Council was again called into session by four of its Western members (but not France). The Soviet Union, joined by Czechoslovakia, proposed that the Council should strongly condemn Chinese aggression against Viet Nam. China proposed that the Council should condemn Viet Nam for aggression against Cambodia. Five ASEAN States, not members of the Security Council, asked that the Council should call on 'all parties' to cease hostilities, withdraw their forces to their own countries, respect the principles of the UN Charter, and welcome the offer of good offices by the Secretary-General. The first two proposals were not put to the vote and the ASEAN text, voted on at the request of Norway, was vetoed by the Soviet Union.[81]

The Cambodian question was taken to the General Assembly in 1979 at the request of the ASEAN States, and the Assembly called for the withdrawal of foreign forces and affirmed UN Charter principles relevant to Cambodia. In 1990, the situation in Cambodia again came to the attention of the Security Council, following receipt of two communications from the Council's five permanent members. The second communication summarized the views of the Five on a comprehensive political settlement in Cambodia, including provisions for elections under UN auspices and measures for the protection of human rights. The Security Council unanimously approved a resolution that had been drafted in private consultations: this endorsed the proposals of the Permanent Five, welcomed the agreement of the

Cambodian parties (the government in Phnom Penh and the three external factions) to proceed with the implementation of these proposals, in particular by the formation of a Supreme National Council reflecting all shades of Cambodian opinion, called upon the two Presidents of the Paris Conference (established in 1981 in accordance with a resolution of the UN General Assembly and consisting of France and Indonesia) to intensify their efforts, and asked the UN Secretary-General to study what role the United Nations might play in achieving a comprehensive political settlement.[82]

During the following year, significant progress towards a settlement was made. The Cambodian parties agreed to a ceasefire and, after a certain amount of wrangling, agreed that Prince Sihanouk should preside over the Supreme National Council. Agreement was reached at two meetings on a comprehensive political settlement, including procedures for electing a constituent assembly and the return of refugees and displaced persons. The Security Council unanimously agreed in private consultations that the Secretary-General should establish a UN Advance Mission in Cambodia (UNAMIC), consisting of civilians, military liaison officers, 'a military mine-awareness unit', and support staff; and, in a subsequent decision, the Secretary-General was asked to appoint a Special Representative for Cambodia and to establish a UN Transitional Authority in Cambodia (UNTAC).[83] More than 300 000 displaced Cambodians were in camps along the border with Thailand, and the Secretary-General expressed deep concern at the way these unhappy people were being exploited.[84]

The main elements of the second Paris Agreement of 1991 regarding the election were as follows. UNTAC was to be responsible for 'the organization and conduct' of a 'free and fair election of a constituent assembly'. Every person of 18 years of age or over who had been born in Cambodia or was the child of a person born in Cambodia would be eligible to register and to vote. Freedom of speech, assembly and movement would be assured. Political parties could be formed by any group of 5000 electors, and these parties and their candidates should be formally registered. UNTAC would establish a code of conduct 'in a manner consistent with respect for human rights and prohibiting coercion or financial inducement'. Fair access to the media would be guaranteed. Voting would be by secret ballot. Facilities would be provided for foreign observers during the campaign and voting. All the signatories to the Paris Agreement committed themselves to respect the results once the elections had been certified as free and fair. This operation, according to the Secretary-General, represented 'a new departure' for the United Nations 'as this was the first time that the Organization was entrusted with the organization and conduct of elections'[85] – a half-truth.

The main organ for managing the UN's responsibilities regarding the election was to be the UN Transitional Authority in Cambodia (UNTAC). Its first task was to organize a major programme of de-mining, and especially the training of indigenous personnel. At an early stage, UNTAC drew up a timetable, culminating in an election to be held in May 1993.[86]

It became apparent during the course of 1992 that the Party of Democratic Kampuchea was not honouring the assurances it had given; in particular it was interfering with UNTAC's freedom of movement. The result was that it was impossible to adhere to the agreed timetable. The Security Council called on all the parties to comply with the agreements they had assumed. The Security Council strongly deplored 'the continuing refusal by one of the parties' to assist UNTAC.[87]

By the end of September, UNTAC was deploying some 170 international staff, 400 volunteers, and about one thousand locally recruited personnel. The Party of Democratic Kampuchea was continuing to cause uncertainty, with the result that UNTAC feared that it might fail to meet the timetable. By the time the Supreme National Council of Cambodia met in Beijing in November, UNTAC disposed of 16 000 troops and 5000 civilians. Some 170 000 refugees had been repatriated. Eleven political parties had registered, and it had been estimated that there would be half a million voters. The Security Council confirmed the timetable but condemned the Party of Democratic Kampuchea, this time by name, for its failure to comply with its obligations. The parties were urged to take part in a dialogue aimed at national reconciliation.[88]

By the beginning of 1993, 4 640 000 voters had been registered, representing about 96 per cent of the electorate in the areas to which UNTAC had access. The Security Council confirmed that the election would take place in late May, in spite of the non-cooperation of the Party of Democratic Kampuchea. The Council demanded that all the parties should cease acts of violence. During the run-up to the election, 13 UNTAC personnel were killed and 52 injured. The Supreme National Council designated Prince Sihanouk as head of state.[89]

On 20 May, some ten days before the election was due to be held, the Security Council expressed satisfaction at the arrangements

Fig. 2.2 UNTAC Election Calendar (S/23613, 19 February 1992)

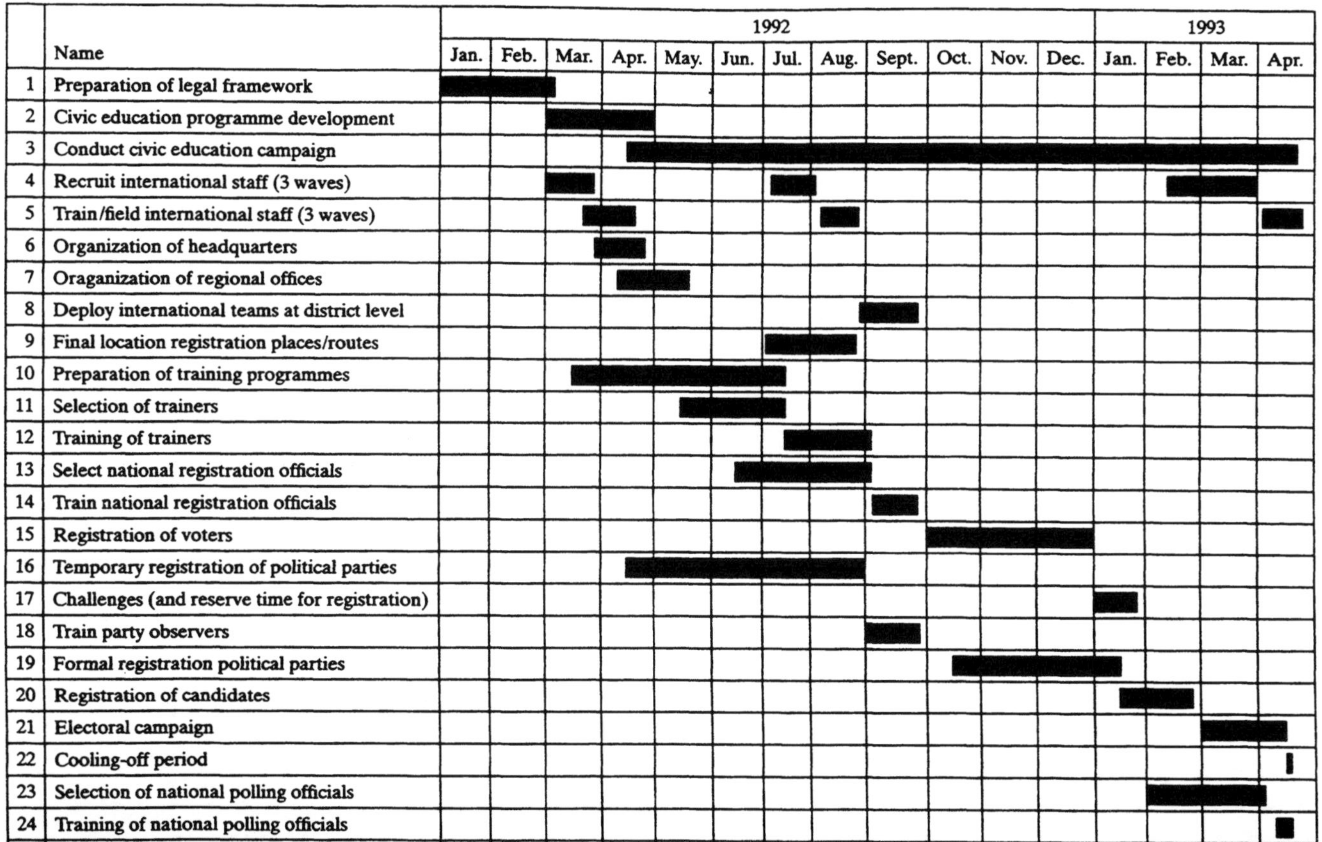

UNTAC had made, demanded that all the parties should adhere to the agreements they had undertaken, and condemned all acts of violence. Some 90 per cent of the eligible voters had registered. UNTAC organized the international observers, including a contingent from the Inter-Parliamentary Union. The observers noted a few scattered incidents of violence but no major disruption. Counting the votes took longer than had been anticipated, but the observers considered that the election had been free and fair. There had been a number of violent outbreaks, and the Security Council demanded that attacks against UNTAC should cease. The Security Council endorsed the results of the election and fully supported the newly-elected constituent assembly. On 24 September 1993, Prince Sihanouk formally promulgated the new Constitution, and the Prince was then elected King of the 'independent, sovereign, peaceful, neutral, and non-aligned' Kingdom of Cambodia. The Security Council expressed its satisfaction at Cambodia's transition to democracy.[90]

WESTERN SAHARA

Like several of the other cases of electoral verification, Western Sahara has been considered by several of the main organs of the UN. The Security Council, the General Assembly, the Secretary-General, and the International Court of Justice have all been involved.

Western Sahara was a Spanish colony until 1974, and a liberation front within the territory, formed in 1973, used the acronym POLISARIO (Frente Popular para la Liberación de Saguia el-Hambra y Río de Oro). In mid-1974, Spain announced its wish to hold a referendum in the territory under UN auspices and supervision. This decision was denounced by Morocco and Mauritania, both of which claimed the territory: Algeria advanced no territorial claim of its own but supported POLISARIO's demand for self-determination. Following a suggestion of Morocco, supported by Mauritania and Algeria, the General Assembly asked the International Court of Justice for an advisory opinion on the status of the territory. The Court's opinion, issued on 16 October 1974, was complex; but in essence the Court advised that there were no legal ties between Western Sahara and Morocco or Mauritania that would impede self-determination through the free and genuine expression of the will of the peoples of the territory.[91]

The following day, King Hassan of Morocco announced the

so-called Green March into Western Sahara of 350 000 unarmed Moroccan civilians, whereupon Spain called on the Security Council to meet urgently to consider a threat to international peace and security. The Council held five meetings, and adopted three resolutions by consensus. The first two called for restraint and moderation, and the avoidance of action that might escalate tension, and asked the Secretary-General to consult the parties about measures to defuse the situation. The third resolution deplored the holding of the Green March, called on Morocco to withdraw from Western Sahara all the participants in the March, and reaffirmed the mandate of the Secretary-General.[92] King Hassan heeded the wishes of the Security Council and called off the March and, on 19 November, Spain, Morocco and Mauritania (but not Algeria) agreed a set of principles for the temporary administration of Western Sahara.[93]

In the penultimate sentence of his fourth report in 1975, the Secretary-General noted that the question of the decolonization of Western Sahara was before the General Assembly and that it seemed appropriate 'that the Assembly should express itself on the subject'. This the General Assembly did not hesitate to do, asking the Secretary-General and the Organization of African Unity to exert every effort to persuade Morocco and POLISARIO to negotiate a ceasefire and agree on procedures for a referendum.[94] In 1988, the Secretary-General was able to inform the Security Council, initially in private consultations and then in open meeting, that these efforts had been successful. A Special Representative of the Secretary-General would be 'the sole and exclusive authority, particularly with regard to all questions pertaining to the referendum'. UN observers would verify the cessation of hostilities, the positions of the parties when the ceasefire would take effect, and the exchange of prisoners. Morocco would withdraw a substantial number of troops from Western Sahara, and the remainder of Moroccan forces and those of POLISARIO would be stationed at sites under UN surveillance. The Security Council, without debate, approved unanimously a draft resolution that had been prepared in private consultations, authorizing the Secretary-General to appoint a Special Representative and asking him to report 'as soon as possible' on the organization and supervision of a referendum by the UN in cooperation with the Organization of African Unity.[95]

Nearly two years were to elapse before the Secretary-General was able to report to the Security Council, and then it was only to elaborate some of the provisions of the 1988 agreement. The Security

Council, again without debate, unanimously adopted a draft resolution that had been prepared in private consultations, approving the Secretary-General's report and welcoming his intention to send a technical mission to the area 'to refine the administrative aspects of [his] plan and to obtain the necessary information for the preparation of a further report'.[96]

Nine months later, the Secretary-General issued a further amplification of his previous proposals, suggesting a timetable for a ceasefire and referendum, and recommending the establishment of a UN Mission for the referendum in Western Sahara (MINURSO).

Reports had been circulating in the media that Morocco had been moving tens of thousands of its citizens into the disputed territory and that some UN officials were acting so as to benefit Morocco in the pending referendum. It was clear that one of the main problems for the UN would be the identification of those eligible to vote. The Security Council, again without debate, unanimously agreed to establish MINURSO, and called on the parties to cooperate in implementing the plans of the Secretary-General. Subsequently, Morocco and POLISARIO accepted the Secretary-General's proposal that a formal ceasefire should take effect from 6 September 1991: UN military observers would be deployed to verify the cessation of hostilities.[97]

A further report from the Secretary-General at the end of 1991 made it clear that many difficulties remained. Morocco and POLISARIO each complained of ceasefire violations by the other. The identification of voters was proving more difficult than had been expected. The UN operation had fallen behind the Secretary-General's timetable, and his Special Representative was planning to resign at the end of 1991. On 31 December 1991, Pérez de Cuéllar's last day in office, the Security Council, again without debate, unanimously adopted a resolution in similar terms to the one it had approved the previous April.[98]

It was now clear that the UN plan for a ceasefire and referendum was seriously at risk, and this was highlighted in a staff report to the Committee on Foreign Relations of the US Senate. This was outspokenly critical of the UN operation and of Morocco's uncooperative attitude. The UN, it was alleged, was failing to respond politically to ceasefire violations. MINURSO was receiving inadequate logistical support, and there were said to be irregularities in MINURSO's financial procedures. MINURSO's officers were living in unnecessarily harsh and sometimes life-threatening conditions.[99]

The first report in 1992 of the new Secretary-General, Boutros

Boutros-Ghali, was frank about the difficulties he was encountering. One of the parties had not responded to his letter clarifying those acts which, according to UN practice, constituted violations of the ceasefire; one of the parties had failed to provide information about the strength and location of its armed forces; one of the parties had refused to cooperate with the process of identifying voters. Nobody was in any doubt that the unnamed party was Morocco, and it was beyond doubt that Morocco had committed 75 of the 77 ceasefire violations. If it should not prove possible to resolve outstanding issues by the end of May 1992, reported the Secretary-General, it would be necessary to consider 'alternative courses of action' and possibly 'a new approach to the whole problem'. A month later, the Secretary-General informed the Security Council that he had appointed a new Special Representative, and the Council reiterated its support for the efforts of Boutros-Ghali and the new Representative.[100]

Morocco then announced that it intended to hold municipal elections in the areas to which it had access, and a plebiscite on constitutional reform. While there had been a reduction in the number of confirmed violations of the ceasefire, more than 90 per cent had come from the Moroccan side. At the beginning of March 1993, the Security Council urged the Secretary-General to intensify his efforts, but one wonders what more he was supposed to do in the face of persistent Moroccan evasion and obstruction.[101]

The new Special Representative of the Secretary-General reported that, after consultations with the parties, it had been decided to solve the question of eligibility of voters by means of an Identification Commission. Boutros-Ghali paid a personal visit to the region and put forward a compromise plan based on two earlier agreements (18 June 1990 and 19 April 1991). This compromise, it was hoped, would produce a 'final list of Saharans qualified to participate in the voting during the referendum on self-determination for the people of Western Sahara'.[102]

There the matter stands. Morocco's reputation has hardly been enhanced. Most of the ceasefire violations originated from the Moroccan side, Morocco had fired on POLISARIO and on UN observers, preventing the latter from entering certain crucial areas. Morocco was also refusing to provide the UN with minimal logistical support and was consistently making it difficult to determine who would have the right to vote. Indeed, Morocco provided an object lesson on how easy it is to agree to UN supervision of electoral matters and then to make it impossible for the UN to do the job.

MOZAMBIQUE

The civil war between the Government of Mozambique and the dissident faction known as RENAMO was ended by an agreement signed in Rome on 7 August 1992, and confirmed by a detailed agreement on 4 October, Protocol III of which provided for assistance and verification of elections by the United Nations and the Organization of African Unity. Shortly thereafter, the Security Council approved a report of the Secretary-General which provided for the appointment of an interim Special Representative and the dispatch to Mozambique of 25 military observers. In December, the Council approved a timetable for an electoral process.[103]

In April 1993, the Secretary-General elaborated the plan for providing technical assistance and the monitoring of the electoral process, and this was endorsed by the Security Council, which also expressed serious concern at delays in implementing the peace agreement. In June, the Secretary-General issued a mildly encouraging report, though RENAMO had refused to attend a meeting to consider a draft electoral law. In August, the Secretary-General reported that RENAMO was now conducting talks with the President of Mozambique, Joaquim Alberto Chissano, and UN experts were in Maputo to assist in electoral preparations. The Security Council welcomed these developments but again expressed concern at the continuing delays in the implementation of major aspects of the peace accords. In October, Secretary-General Boutros-Ghali paid a personal visit to Maputo. Considerable progress was made on electoral matters, and it was hoped that elections would take place no later than October 1994.[104]

LIBERIA

The mayhem in Liberia began with the overthrow of President Samuel Doe in 1990. The Security Council first became seized of the matter in January 1991. The Council met again in May 1992, and a Presidential statement was issued which included the hope that events in Liberia would develop in such a way as to make possible 'free and fair elections'. Later in the year, the Council invoked Chapter VII of the Charter and imposed 'a general and complete embargo on all deliveries of weapons and military equipment' other than those needed for the peacekeeping forces of the Economic Community of West

African States (ECOWAS). The Council also reaffirmed the need for the conditions required for free and fair elections.[105]

A peace agreement was eventually concluded at Cotonou (Benin) on 25 July 1993, and one Article of this provided that elections would conform to UN and internationally accepted codes of conduct. The Security Council then agreed to the dispatch of a technical team and a UN observer mission (UNOMIL). The Interim Government of Liberia had already raised with the Secretary-General the possibility that the forthcoming election should be monitored by international observers, and the UN had sent two experts to advise the Liberian authorities. On 9 September 1993, the Secretary-General submitted to the Security Council his plan for discharging the UN's obligation, commenting that the UN peacekeeping operation in Liberia 'would be the first peacekeeping operation undertaken by the United Nations in cooperation with a peacekeeping mission already set up by another organization', namely, the force known as ECOMOG set up by the Economic Community of West African States.* On 22 September, the Security Council decided that among UNOMIL's tasks would be the monitoring of the embargo on the import of arms; it should also 'observe and verify' the elections for a legislature and president due to be held by February or March 1994. By mid-December 1993, it had become apparent that the timetable for elections could not be adhered to, but the Secretary-General and the Security Council agreed to a new target date: 'possibly . . . by May' 1994.[106]

THE ROLE OF THE SECURITY COUNCIL

Thomas M. Franck has pointed out that self-determination postulates the right of a people organized in an established territory to determine its collective political destiny in a democratic manner, and that this democratic entitlement is being transformed from moral prescription to international legal obligation. This will, moreover, be increasingly promoted and protected by collective international processes.[107] In the year ended 30 September 1992, the UN received 31 requests for electoral assistance, of which five fell within the competence of the Security Council (Angola, Cambodia, El Salvador, Haiti,

* The Secretary-General seems to have forgotten DOMREP, the operation in the Dominican Republic in 1965, though this operation was included in the official review of UN peacekeeping, *The Blue Helmets* 1990, pp. 199–212.

Western Sahara) and five were not proceeded with because of shortage of lead-time.[108] In two cases, the election took place satisfactorily but the result was subsequently undermined. In Haiti, there was a *coup d'état* nine months after the election and President Aristide fled the country. In Angola, the main opposition party (UNITA) was not satisfied with the result and took to arms. The referendum in Western Sahara has not yet taken place because of obstruction by one party. Only in Cambodia did the election proceed satisfactorily with UN supervision, though partially boycotted by one party.

In all cases since Namibia, the verification procedure was spread over months rather than days, as had previously been thought adequate as, for example, in the case of the Pacific Islands. UN observers should be present during the registration of voters, the election campaign, on polling day, during the counting of votes and the announcement of the result, and during the hearing of any appeals. In many cases, the United Nations will have to devise constructive procedures for cooperating with observers from regional organizations, friendly governments, and non-governmental organizations.

The United Nations has been gaining experience and can now be trusted to decide whether an election was free and fair. But the UN can do this only if the parties in the field cooperate to the full. It only needs a few mischief-makers to cast doubt on the result. The presence of international observers has a significant psychological impact at all levels of society and contributes to a smooth electoral process.[109]

Until the Namibian operation in 1989–90, the Security Council had very little experience in the organization or the verification of elections. In the case of Madura and Western Java in 1948, the UN Good Offices Committee (GOC) reported to the Security Council on the basis of information supplied by the occupation authorities or what was available in the public media: this would not now be considered a valid means of UN supervision. The referendums in Kashmir and Western Sahara have not yet taken place. In the cases of the Congo and the Dominican Republic, subsidiary organs of the Security Council had the not very onerous responsibility of enabling the legislature to meet. The task in Bahrain became relatively simple once Iran had renounced its claim to the territory. The role of the Security Council was nominal regarding the US-administered Trust Territories in the Pacific. The Namibian operation, on the other hand, was a major task, in spite of the fact that it did not coincide in all respects with the resolutions of the Security Council. Moreover, the Code of Conduct for political parties during the election campaign in Namibia set a standard which the UN can draw on in future operations. By the time Haiti had requested UN assistance in 1990, the Secretary-General was able to be guided by a set of criteria which had to be satisfied before a UN organ should agree to supervise an election in a UN Member State. Such operations should be authorized only:

1. When such operations are called for primarily in situations with a clear international dimension.
2. The monitoring of an election or referendum should cover the entire electoral process in order to secure conditions of fairness and impartiality.
3. UN operations can be mounted only at clearly defined points in location and strategy, and not in situations of an indeterminate character.
4. Where a UN presence in the electoral process has broad public support for the UN assuming such a role.
5. The approval of a competent UN organ should be obtained.

These criteria were repeated in a report of the Secretary-General in 1991, with the additional proviso that an essential element in the credibility of an election is the maintenance of a peaceful environment in which public order and the political freedom of citizens are guaranteed during the whole electoral process.[110]

If a request for electoral verification is received or seems imminent, the Secretary-General will send a survey mission to the area concerned to discover if more help is needed than simply the monitoring of the electoral process – assistance in training officials, for example, civic education, the provision of computers and communications equipment, the presence of peacekeeping units at different stages, and so on. If armed conflict had been taking place, there need to be clear, unconditional and indefinite ceasefire agreements, including the possible demobilization of forces or their concentration in agreed locations. It may also be necessary to remove mines or other obstacles that might impede movement and communication. Prisoners of war, political prisoners, and other detainees should be released by all parties, and displaced persons and refugees allowed to return to their homes to live in peace with their neighbours.

At an early stage, the Secretary-General will seek authorization for the operation from the Security Council or other policymaking body, to ensure that the necessary personnel and financing will be forthcoming. In appropriate cases, the Secretary-General will need to seek the cooperation of any regional agency, governments willing to provide assistance, and qualified non-governmental agencies. Status of Mission Agreements will be concluded with the local authorities, providing for the privileges and immunities of international personnel, and guaranteeing their full freedom of movement.

A calendar or timetable should be established for all phases of the electoral process. Any discriminatory or restrictive legislation should be repealed. The parties should negotiate a Code of Conduct, and this should prohibit threats of violence, other forms of intimidation, and bribery. Every effort should be made by the local authorities to ensure that the media report fairly, refrain from making unsubstantiated allegations against political opponents, and avoid inflammatory language. All political parties should have equitable access to State-controlled radio and television.

UN observers will be expected to verify the registration of voters, including any procedures for registering qualified voters living abroad; the registration of political parties; the monitoring of the election campaign; observation of voting, either at all polling stations or by spot-checks; agreement on penalties for personation and other fraudulent practices; the counting and tabulation of votes; the announcement of results; and machinery for dealing with complaints, petitions or appeals. Any threats to a free and impartial electoral process or breakdown of law and order should be reported promptly to the Secretary-General, so that peacekeeping units may be dispatched or strengthened or other remedial measures taken.

The head of the UN mission should certify whether the election had been free and fair, and appropriate reports on the operation should be issued as public documents. Local officials should behave in a neutral manner and not campaign for or against their employers, as happened in Palau in December 1986. Care should be taken to avoid a situation in which UN and local personnel are at loggerheads: it is not the job of observers to administer nor of administrators to observe. It is no reflection on the UN to invoke the cooperation of regional agencies, friendly governments, constitutional political parties or experienced non-governmental agencies, for they may have knowledge and resources not available within the UN. Every effort should be made to avoid a situation, as in Nicaragua, in which the General Assembly and the Security Council both claim to be exercising jurisdiction. If those whose job it is to register electors are local officials, they should not be paid on a *pro rata* basis, as happened in Palau in 1986 and Haiti in 1990, because this inevitably encourages fraud.

In many of the cases studied in this book, one of the parties behaved in an obstructive manner: India in the case of Kashmir, UNITA in the case of Angola, the Party of Democratic Kampuchea in the case of Cambodia, Morocco in the case of the Western Sahara, Islamic extremists in the case of the Palestinian territories occupied by Israel, Turkey in the case of Northern Cyprus, Iraq in the cases of the Iraq–Iran and Iraq–Kuwait wars, the Serbians in the case of former Yugoslavia, and the Administering Authority in the case of several actual or former dependent territories. The presence of a UN Force before and during an election may help to deter, but cannot wholly prevent, deliberate obstructionism, especially when the obstructor is the government of a UN Member. Moreover, there is no magic way of knowing when to start and when to terminate a UN peace mission. There are objective considerations which should be borne in mind, but when it comes to the crunch, it is in large part a matter of feeling and instinct.

3 International Humanitarian Law[1]

International humanitarian law (often called simply IHL) is concerned with the protection of war victims. It corresponds in most respect to *jus in bello*, as that term is understood in ethics. It overlaps with the law of human rights, but in no circumstances may its provisions be suspended, as is possible with certain provisions of human rights law in time of war or public emergency threatening the life of the nation. International humanitarian law has been codified in the four Geneva (Red Cross) Conventions of 1949 and the two Additional Protocols of 1977, supplemented in some respects by the Regulations attached to Hague Convention IV of 1907 (which was itself based on Hague Convention II of 1899), the 1954 Convention on the Protection of Cultural Property in time of war, the 1980 Convention on the prohibition or restriction of indiscriminate or excessively injurious weapons, and by other treaties to restrict or prohibit the use of particular weapons. Many of these instruments include a clause drafted by F. F. Martens for the Hague Conference of 1899, by which the parties affirmed that, in cases not included in the Regulations attached to the Conventions, the inhabitants and belligerents remain under the protection of 'the principles of the law of nations, as they result from the usages established among civilized peoples, from the laws of humanity, and the dictates of the public conscience'.[2] The Nürnberg Tribunal declared in 1946 that the rules of land warfare expressed in Hague Convention IV of 1907 had, by 1939, been 'recognized by all civilized nations, and were regarded as being declaratory of the laws and customs of war'. The International Court of Justice, in its 1986 judgement on *Nicaragua v the United States*, expressed the view that the Geneva Conventions are in some respects an expression of international humanitarian law and in other respects a development of them.[3] One important difference between international humanitarian law and human rights is that IHL contains no provisions for derogation, even in time of war or public emergency which threatens the life of the nation. Important aspects of IHL were dealt with in reports of the UN Secretary-General following the international Conference on Human Rights in Tehran in 1968 under the rubric 'Human Rights in Armed Conflict'.[4] The International Committee of the Red Cross

(ICRC) invited the United Nations 'by regular accession, formally [to] undertake to have applied the Geneva Conventions and other provisions of a humanitarian character each time the forces of the United Nations are engaged in operations', but the UN Secretaries-General have hitherto taken the view that improved legal protection of human rights would come from the wider acceptance of humanitarian conventions by States contributing military forces to UN operations rather than from having the United Nations 'undertake obligations whose discharge would involve the exercise of an authority it has not yet been granted'.[5]

The Security Council has been concerned with the application of IHL in a wide variety of circumstances.

JERUSALEM, 1948

In May 1948, the International Committee of the Red Cross (ICRC) was able to arrange for three zones of sanctuary for non-combatants in Jerusalem. One zone was in the centre of Jerusalem and comprised the King David Hotel, the YMCA hostel, the Terra Santa convent, the Shamaria Children's Home, and the surrounding land. Count Bernadotte, the UN mediator, wished to instal UN staff in either the King David Hotel or the YMCA hostel, but the ICRC delegate 'strongly objected' on the ground that the presence of the UN mediator would violate the neutrality of the zone. Bernadotte, who had previous experience of dealing with the ICRC, told the ICRC delegate 'in very definite terms' that he could not accept the decision. Finally, in June, with the agreement of the parties, the ICRC handed over the King David Hotel to the United Nations. When the first ceasefire expired in July, UN staff left the King David Hotel, which was immediately occupied by Israeli forces. The YMCA hostel was subjected to bombardment by the Arabs, as a consequence of which the ICRC arranged for its evacuation and the termination of Red Cross protection as from 22 July. The YMCA was handed over to the US consulate and the Terra Santa property was restored to the Franciscan Order. The second Red Cross zone, on a hill a few miles from the city, comprised Government House, the Arab College, the Jewish Agricultural School and the married quarters at Allenby Barracks. Britain had agreed to hand over Government House to the ICRC for the duration of hostilities, and the Arabs and Jews agreed orally that the surrounding area should be a place of refuge for women, children, old people and wounded. The zone remained in being until 16 August, when Israeli forces attacked and occupied two of the buildings in the zone, whereupon the Arabs placed defensive positions around Government House. Direct meetings between the two sides were arranged with the help of UN observers and the ICRC. On 27 August the UN Truce Supervision Board decided to create a demilitarized zone around the Government House area, and by 4 September all combatants had been withdrawn. The Red Cross zone thus became the nucleus of a demilitarized zone, and on 7 October was transferred to the United Nations. Part of the demilitarized zone surrounding Government House was occupied by Israel during the 1967 war. The third Red Cross zone, comprising the Italian School and the Italian Hospital, was occupied by Israel when the British Mandate expired on 15 May. There were no negotiations between the parties about the creation of the three zones: the ICRC addressed notes to the belligerents, and the substance of the note was accepted by the local Arab authorities on 9 May and by the Jews (by then, the Israelis) on 17 May. The three zones were under the protection of the Red Cross flag. Women and children were admitted to the zones at all times, and temporary asylum was given to refugees while fighting was taking place. Those entering the zones surrendered any arms, and no weapons were introduced. The ICRC was responsible for internal administration and relief.[6]

KOREA, 1950–53

The relationship of the Security Council to the war and armistice in Korea was ill-defined. The third resolution of the Council in 1950, sponsored by Britain and France, asked UN Members to provide military and other assistance to 'a unified command under the United States of America', and the command thus created always called itself the United Nations Command, and reported to the Security Council 88 times during the course of the war. On the other hand, the Security Council had removed the Korean item from the list of matters of which it was seized before the armistice negotiations began in 1951, and the Security Council as such made no input into the armistice negotiating stance of the Unified Command. The 16 countries supplying combat forces to the Unified Command met as needed at the State Department in Washington from February 1951, but the United States insisted that these were briefings and not consultations.

During the armistice negotiations and at the Geneva conference in 1954, the Communists maintained that the UN was not able to perform an impartial role as it was itself a belligerent in the conflict.[7]

The question of how to dispose of prisoners of war was one of the most difficult substantive issues to be resolved during the armistice negotiations in 1951–53. As the war was taking place within the borders of one nation, both sides had an incentive to indoctrinate POWs so that they would elect to stay on the detaining side after the cessation of hostilities. Shortly after the outbreak of the war, a memorandum was prepared in the US State Department which included the recommendation that 'the treatment of POWs . . . shall be directed toward their exploitation, training and use for psychological warfare . . .', and this policy was approved by President Truman. The Communists adopted a similar policy and trained their own combatants to resist indoctrination. General Mark Clark, commander of the forces of the Unified Command, reported to the Security Council that the Communists did not regard their POWs held by the Unified Command as in need of care and protection but as active soldiers determined to fight on.[8]

Geneva Convention III of 1949 on POWs states plainly that POWs shall be 'released *and repatriated*' without delay after the cesstion of active hostilities (Article 118, my italics). There thus arose a contradiction between a basic humanitarian principle (no coercion against protected persons) and the strict letter of an international treaty. Winston Churchill and Anthony Eden (Prime Minister and Foreign Secretary) were against using force to compel a POW to be repatriated against his will, but Eden had not at first understood the legal complications. He minuted in March 1952, 'I did not know that our legal grounds were so poor; but this doesn't make me like the idea of sending these poor devils back to death or worse.' Britain had strong reservations about the proposal of the Unified Command to settle unrepatriated POWs in Taiwan. 'H.M.G. certainly have no interest at all in seeing Chiang Kai-shek's army built up at the expense of additional suffering to British and Commonwealth prisoners.'[9]

China and North Korea were initially unwilling to accept that any of their POWs held by the Unified Command would refuse to be repatriated, and the United States took it for granted (mistakenly, as it turned out) that all POWs from the Unified Command held by the Communist side would opt for repatriation. The obvious solution to the clash of principles and policies was for monitors from an impartial body like the International Committee of the Red Cross to screen POWs on both sides, but North Korea and China were initially unwilling to disclose to the ICRC or the Unified Command how many POWs they held, or to allow the ICRC to visit their POW camps. When the armistice negotiations opened, the Unified Command had given to the ICRC the names of 163 539 POWs held in South Korea, whereas North Korea had given the ICRC the names of only 110 POWs held by them.[10]

This inevitably led to long arguments at Panmunjom about numbers, the figures given by the Unified Command varying slightly from meeting to meeting and those given by the Communist side being manifestly implausible. General Matthew Ridgway estimated that between 3000 and 5000 North Korean POWs and between 11 000 and 11 500 Chinese POWs would resist repatriation. As the Unified Command then held some 132 000 POWs, the Communist delegation to the armistice negotiations was told on 1 April 1952 that 'possibly 116 000' of their POWs would be willing to return home when the war ended. This turned out to be a serious blunder, for when a US screening of POWs actually took place later that month, it was found that only 30 756 would accept voluntary repatriation, though a subsequent rescreening brought the figure up to 39 485. As not all POWs had been screened in April, a further US screening took place in July, and this gave a new figure of 83 071 voluntary repatriates and 86 867 who would refuse repatriation.[11]

In the middle of 1952, China suggested that the negotiators at Panmunjom should stop arguing about principles and discuss actual numbers: China would be satisfied if about 20 000 Chinese POWs agreed to be repatriated. US screening of POWs held by the Unified Command had produced a variety of figures for Chinese POWs willing to be repatriated, the highest being 6388. There was thus no way that the Unified Command could meet China's target figure without using force to compel unwilling POWs to return home, and in fact the number of Chinese voluntary repatriates when the war ended was 6670.[12]

The solution finally adopted was worked out by India, with the assistance of Britain and Canada, during the 1952 session of the General Assembly. All POWs willing to return home would be repatriated after the armistice. Others would be handed over to a Commission consisting of Czechoslovakia and Poland (nominated by the Communist side), Sweden and Switzerland (nominated by the Unified

Command), with India as chairman and provider of a military custodial force. The POWs would then have their rights explained to them and could decide whether or not to go home. The disposition of those refusing repatriation would be decided after ninety days by a political conference. If the political conference should fail to reach agreement within a further thirty days, the remaining POWs would simply change from POW to civilian status.[13]

A number of developments complicated the implementation of the plan of the General Assembly, three before the armistice was finally concluded. First, the Communists stated that they had captured 65 000 persons in the first nine months of the war and that 'large numbers' of these had been re-educated and released at the front. Second, some 37 500 prisoners in the hands of the Unified Command were reclassified as 'civilian internees' and released to their homes. Thirdly, on 18 June 1953, just as the armistice negotiations were at last coming to a successful conclusion, President Syngman Rhee of South Korea released 27 000 POWs without consulting the Unified Command. When the Unified Command negotiators disclaimed prior knowledge of Rhee's action, the Communists wanted to know if the South Korean Government would abide by the terms of an armistice agreement. After a month of havering, the Unified Command was able to give a categorical assurance that South Korea would abide by an agreed armistice.[14]

Following these unilateral acts, there remained just over 105 000 North Korean and Chinese POWs in the hands of the Unified Command, and nearly 14 000 Unified Command POWs in North Korea. Those willing to be repatriated returned home in two phases, as a result of which 78 per cent of the North Korean and Chinese POWs returned to their own side, and 97 per cent of the Unified Command POWs returned to South Korea in accordance with the letter of Article 118 of the Geneva Convention on POWs. The Neutral Nations Repatriation Commission and the Indian custodial force then took custody of the non-repatriates, 22 604 North Korean and Chinese previously detained in South Korea, and 359 Unified Command POWs previously detained in North Korea. The agreement had been that unrepatriated prisoners should receive explanations as to their rights, but the violent opposition of many of the prisoners to receiving explanations, especially those previously held by the Unified Command, reduced the procedure to a farce. During the period set aside for explanations, only around 3200 of the 22 600 North Korean and Chinese prisoners had received explanations, and only 255 of the

359 prisoners previously held by the Communists. Of these, 369 and eight respectively had opted for repatriation, some after receiving explanations and some not. Around 50 prisoners had died, escaped or were missing, but that still left over 22 500 prisoners on 23 December 1953 whose fate was to be decided within 30 days by the political conference.[15]

The final difficulty was that the political conference had not convened by the expiry of the 90-day period in December 1953, and did not do so until the following April. The Neutral Nations Commission and the Indian force had to decide what to do with the remaining prisoners. Having referred the matter to the two military commands and having received contradictory advice, and having tried to reconvene the UN General Assembly but without success, the Neutral Nations Commission and the Indian force released the prisoners into civilian status on the detaining side, except for 12 Chinese, 74 North Koreans, and two South Koreans, who opted to go to a neutral country. These left for Madras on 8 February 1954.[16]

DOMINICAN REPUBLIC, 1965

This chapter is mainly concerned with violations, or alleged violations, of international humanitarian law. This law is designed to benefit the parties to armed conflict equally, and it is a pleasure for the author (and, I hope, also for the reader) to turn to two instances from the civil war in the Dominican Republic in 1965 in which the implementation of IHL was of mutual benefit to the warring factions.

The first was the establishment on 5 May 1965 of a safety zone in Santo Domingo, the country's capital, organized by a committee of the Organization of American States. The belligerents agreed to ratify a ceasefire agreement, to provide protection and safety for all persons within the zone, to allow the evacuation of those who had sought asylum in foreign embassies, and to facilitate the distribution of food and medical supplies.[17]

The second instance was an agreement reached with the assistance of the International Committee of the Red Cross and the World Health Organization for a ceasefire for twenty-four hours (21–22 May) to allow the opposing parties to collect the wounded and transport them to hospitals, to remove the dead to cemeteries, and to resupply the hospitals with medical supplies, food and staff.[18]

ISRAEL AND THE OCCUPIED TERRITORIES SINCE 1967

The application of IHL following the Israeli–Arab war of 1967 and the Israeli invasions of Lebanon in 1978 and 1982 has mainly concerned the Fourth Geneva Convention (civilians under occupation), but the first resolution of the Security Council in 1967 also contained a preambular reference to the Third Geneva Convention relating to POWs, and three resolutions on Lebanon in 1982 also cited the Regulations attached to the Hague Convention of 1907.[19] Israel informed the Security Council in 1967 that it would respect fully the provisions of the POW Convention, but made no mention of the Convention on civilians under occupation: Arab POWs in Israeli hands, said Israel, would be 'treated with humanity and with full regard to their legal and human rights'. The Council's first resolution, adopted unanimously, called for compliance by all parties with the POW Convention and for scrupulous respect for the humanitarian principles of both the POW Convention and the Convention on civilians.[20]

Israel has taken a position on the applicability of the Fourth Geneva Convention on civilians in the Occupied Territories which, in the words of Yoram Dinstein, 'is based on dubious legal grounds'. While Israel has claimed to respect the humanitarian *principles* of the Convention, it has asserted that the Convention is inapplicable on the ground that Israel had never recognized the sovereignty of Jordan over Judea and Samaria (the West Bank) or Egypt's right to administer the Gaza Strip.[21] The International Committee of the Red Cross has consistently taken the view that the Fourth Convention on civilians is applicable in all the territories occupied by Israel, and has so informed Israel on numerous occasions.[22] The UN Security Council, between 1967 and 1992, adopted 40 resolutions or statements of consensus affirming the applicability of the Fourth Convention or deploring Israel's failure to respect its provisions (see Table 3.1 on p. 76). Information on which the Council's decisions were based came from a variety of sources, including:

(1) a report in 1967 by Nils-Göran Gussing on the suffering of POWs and civilians following the 1967 war;
(2) a report, also in 1967, by Ernesto A. Thalmann on the situation in Jerusalem;
(3) a report in 1970 by a Special Working Group of Experts established by the UN Commission on Human Rights;

(4) regular reports from a Special Committee of the General Assembly, established in 1968 to investigate Israeli practices affecting the human rights of the population of the Occupied Territories;
(5) a report issued in 1970 by the International Committee of the Red Cross.

I will take each of these sources in turn.

(1) Gussing's report on the humanitarian needs of civilians and POWs arose from a request of the Security Council immediately after the war of June 1967, endorsed some weeks later by an Emergency Session of the General Assembly.[23] According to Gussing, over 300 000 Palestinians had been newly displaced as a result of the war, of whom 113 000 were already refugees from 1948. The Jordanian authorities estimated that 170 000 Palestinians had applied through the ICRC to go back from Jordan to the West Bank, and that 14 150 had already returned. Syria 'strongly desired' the return of those Arabs displaced by the Golan fighting but 'was not willing to enter into direct negotiations with Israel'. Displaced Palestinians in Egypt wished to return, and Egypt was leaving the arrangements to the United Nations and the ICRC.

Gussing reported that both sides were treating prisoners of war correctly, but Egypt objected that 289 Egyptian civilians from Gaza were being detained by Israel in El Arish. Israel alleged that some 500–600 members of the Jewish community in Egypt had been detained and held incommunicado, but Egypt maintained with some pedantry that the resolution of the Security Council did not apply to the Jewish minority in Egypt, so that this matter was outside Gussing's mandate. As for the Jewish minority in Syria, then thought to number about 4000, Syria said they were treated 'in exactly the same way' as other Syrians: it was true that some Syrian Jews were restricted in their movements because they were suspected of anti-government activities, but so were some Christians and some Muslims. This last point did nothing to make Jewish Israelis happy.

Gussing said that he had received excellent cooperation from the Israeli authorities. He had been accompanied on all official travels by a representative of the Government of Israel, but some conversations would have been franker if he had been able to meet and talk without witnesses. The Arab Governments had complained that Israel had made systematic efforts to expel Palestinians from the Occupied Territories. Gussing found it difficult to determine the line between physical and psychological pressure, but 'certain actions authorized or allowed by local military commanders' had been an important cause of the flight of the Palestinians. The 'extensive looting' in Quneitra had been largely the responsibility of Israel, but it was difficult to from a firm opinion regarding Jordanian complaints of Israeli looting. There had undoubtedly been 'vast destruction' of villages, but some of this had been a direct consequence of military operations, and there had been some deliberate destruction by Israel 'for strategic and security reasons'.

Gussing had visited Bethlehem, Hebron, Nablus (Schechem), and Qalqiliya and had found that the general Arab economy had come to a standstill as a result of the June fighting.

(2) Thalmann's report on Jerusalem arose from a request of the General Assembly on 14 July 1967, but was circulated as a document to the Security Council as well as the General Assembly.[24] Thalmann reported on the legislative measures by which Israel had extended its law, jurisdiction and administration to East Jerusalem and the surrounding area. (Israel did not formally annex East Jerusalem until 1980.) The East Jerusalem municipality had been dissolved and the controls and barriers which had formerly separated the two parts of the city had been abolished. The Israeli authorities stated unequivocally that 'Israel was taking every step to place under its sovereignty those parts of the city which were not controlled by Israel before June 1967.' The process of integration was 'irreversible and not negotiable'. Thalmann commented on the orderly appearance of the Old City. 'Arabs and Jews were mingling.' Walls and buildings in the No Man's Land between the two front lines were being bulldozed, and 'one could see the debris of levelled houses'. A number of shops were closed but most of the hotels had reopened. Municipal services were being restored, and the economic situation was improving. St Anne's Church, near St Stephen's Gate, had been damaged during the fighting, as had the Augusta Victoria Hospital and the YMCA in East Jerusalem. One gate of the El Aqsa mosque had also been damaged. Israel alleged that several synagogues had been destroyed during the Jordanian occupation and that a Jewish cemetery on the Mount of Olives had been desecrated. Arabs complained to Thalmann about the desecration of Islamic Holy Places, the application of Israeli laws, the dissolution of the municipal authorities, the attempt to apply the Israeli educational system to Arab schools, ecconomic dislocation and strangulation, and the incorporation of East Jerusalem

into the Israeli State system without consulting the people. Israel, on the other hand, said that it was determined to maintain freedom of access to the Holy Places of all faiths and to protect them from desecration. Most of the Christian churches were adopting a policy of 'wait and see' about Jerusalem, but the Roman Catholic Church still favoured an international regime, as it had in 1947. The World Council of Churches expressed appreciation for the way the Christian Holy Places were being cared for.

(3) and (4). The question of territories occupied by Israel in 1967 was raised in 1968 in the Commission on Human Rights, which requested the Secretary-General to keep it informed about the application of the Universal Declaration of Human Rights and the Geneva Conventions in territories occupied by Israel, as well as affirming the right of those who had left 'to return . . . without delay'. The Secretary-General's report consisted of a digest of various UN decisions and reports relating to the humanitarian needs of the people following the June war, together with a summary of a reply from Israel on the return to the West Bank of those who had fled.[25] After the Commission had considered this report, it set up a Special Working Group of Experts to investigate allegations that Israel had violated the Fourth Geneva Convention relating to civilians. The Working Group had six members appointed as individuals, the identical membership of an *ad hoc* Group which had previously reported on conditions in Southern Africa. By this time, however, the Security Council had requested the Secretary-General to send a Special Representative 'to the Arab territories under military occupation by Israel' and had asked Israel to receive him and 'to cooperate with him and to facilitate his work'. On 14 October 1968, the Secretary-General reported that Israel was not prepared to cooperate with the proposed mission of the Special Working Group unless its mandate were to include the treatment of both Arabs and Jews in all the States which had taken part in the June war. U Thant therefore reported that he was unable to give effect to the Security Council resolution.[26]

In spite of this rebuff, the General Assembly decided to establish a Special Committee to investigate Israeli practices affecting the human rights of the population of occupied territories, the membership to be determined by the President of the General Assembly. Israel was asked to receive the Committee, cooperate with it and facilitate its work, and the Committee was asked to report 'as soon as possible and whenever the need arises thereafter'. Before the

Special Committee could be appointed, however, the President of the 1968 Assembly session, Emilio Arenales of Guatemala, died following an operation for a brain tumour, and the question arose as to how the Committee should be appointed. Israel has alleged (and there is no reason to doubt the truth of this) that before his death Arenales had approached a large number of UN Members but had been unable to persuade any to join the Special Committee. The situation facing the UN upon the death of Arenales was not covered by the General Assembly's Rules of Procedure, nor were there any exact precedents. Secretary-General U Thant, acting under the article of the Charter which designates him as 'chief administrative officer of the Organization', felt that he had no alternative but to consult UN Members in writing. Unfortunately this led to an inconclusive result, but U Thant noted that 'more than an absolute majority' preferred a procedure which was 'consonant with the spirit' of the Charter and rules of procedure – that is to say, the designation of one of the Vice-Presidents to undertake the appointment. Accordingly, a meeting of all the Vice-Presidents of the previous General Assembly session was held, and they decided to entrust the appointment of the Committee to Dr Luis Alvarado of Peru. On 12 September 1969, four days before the 1969 session of the Assembly was due to convene, it was announced that Ceylon, Somalia and Yugoslavia had agreed to serve on the Committee.[27]

> The only countries willing to become members of the Committee were Somalia, Yugoslavia and Ceylon [Sri Lanka]. All three have no diplomatic relations with Israel . . . Somalia even denies Israel's right to independence and sovereignty.

Israel again asserted that any UN inquiry into human rights in the Middle East should not be confined to Arabs in territory occupied by Israel, but should apply also to the Jewish minorities in Arab States.[28]

The situation at the end of 1969 was thus that there were two UN bodies concerned with human rights in the Occupied Territories, the Working Group established by the Commission on Human Rights and the Special Committee under the terms of a decision of the General Assembly. Not surprisingly, both bodies received full cooperation from Arab governments and the Arab League. Besides holding meetings in New York and Geneva, the two bodies paid separate visits to Amman, Beirut, Cairo and Damascus. Each heard over 100 witnesses, most of them in open meeting. Both bodies consulted representatives of the ICRC and visited refugee camps in Syria and Jordan. Both also asked the Commissioner-General of the UN agency for Arab refugees (UNRWA) to provide information. The Commissioner-General expressed his understanding and sympathy with the needs and purposes of the Working Group, but he doubted whether its requests fell within the terms of the Agency's mandate or were consistent with UNRWA's activities. The Special Committee was critical of UNRWA's refusal to 'make . . . information available, without condition, to investigating bodies'. This, in the view of the Committee, might appear to be a dereliction of a humanitarian duty.

Neither investigating body was able to visit territory occupied by Israel, which considered the activities of the Working Group to be 'a purely propaganda exercise', and informed the Working Group that there was no basis for cooperation. Israel took the same view of the Special Committee: 'The history of this matter has from the beginning been tainted with political bias and procedural irregularity.'

Besides hearing witnesses, the two bodies examined documentation including, in the case of the Working Group, specific Egyptian complaints of violations of the Geneva Conventions. The Working Group stated that it was 'not in a position to verify juridically the allegations which were received' and that the evidence presented to it was 'one-sided' because of Israel's refusal to recognize or cooperate with it. Nevertheless, the Working Group felt able to evaluate the evidence profferred. The Special Committee also felt that, despite the absence of cooperation on the part of Israel, it had established 'a basis upon which a responsible opinion can be given'.

The Working Group was of the opinion that the Fourth Geneva Convention of 1949 was being violated; that persons were being detained without trial; that houses and villages had been destroyed after the ceasefire; and that people had been expelled or transferred from their homes. It recommended that the Fourth Convention be fully implemented; that allegations of torture, looting and pillage should be investigated by the Israeli authorities and those found responsible suitably punished; that deported or transferred persons should be allowed to return home under UN supervision; that confiscated property taken in a manner inconsistent with the Fourth Geneva Convention should be restored to its owners; and that the Israeli authorities should refrain from demolishing houses for reasons not provided for in the Fourth Convention and should provide compensation in all cases of houses demolished in violation of the Convention.[29]

The Special Committee reported that there was 'considerable evidence' of infringements of the right of persons living in the occupied areas to remain there and of the right of those who fled to return to their homes. Israel had been pursuing 'a policy of collective and area punishments ... imposed indiscriminately'. While not contesting the right of the occupying power under the Fourth Convention to restrict the freedom of those who pose a threat to security, the Special Committee considered that this power was 'being abused in that it is exercised too freely'. Individuals were being held in detention 'for indefinite, prolonged periods'. The Committee heard several allegations of destruction of houses and buildings ('in many instances ... unwarranted'), and of confiscation and expropriation of property. Although such destruction is prohibited by the Fourth Convention 'except where such destruction is rendered absolutely necessary by military operations' (Article 53), Israel had had 'unscrupulous recourse' to military necessity in carrying out 'this wanton destruction'. The Special Committee concluded that Israel had been violating human rights in the Occupied Territories. The weight of international public opinion should be brought to bear to persuade Israel to desist from violations. The Special Committee recommended that there should be 'a further and more thorough study of ... the entire question of the protection of human rights in occupied territories', and asked that 'sufficient professional and other staff' should be assigned to the Committee should it be necessary to visit the Middle East again.[30]

The two UN reports were submitted to the parent bodies in 1970. The Human Rights Commission approved its Working Group's report. Israel was condemned for refusing to apply the Fourth Geneva Convention, and called on to take measures to rectify the situation. The Working Group was asked to 'continue to investigate and report' – a strange decision in view of the fact that the General Assembly's Special Committee had an almost identical mandate. In the event, the Working Group did not issue further substantive reports. The report of the Special Committee was placed before the General Assembly, which asked the Special Committee to continue its work 'pending the early termination of Israeli occupation of Arab territories'. Israel was urged to comply with the Fourth Geneva Convention on civilians, and the Special Committee was asked to consult the ICRC to ensure the safeguarding of the human rights of the population of the Occupied Territories.[31]

(5) Although the International Committee of the Red Cross has duties under the Geneva Conventions, its normal practice is to report in confidence only to the government or other authority concerned. In 1970, however, it published a report on territories occupied by Israel in 1967, probably because incomplete and possibly misleading extracts from the ICRC report had already been published.[32]

The ICRC found that, following the 1967 war, problems relating to the treatment of the wounded and prisoners of war were settled 'relatively quickly'. ICRC delegates were usually given freedom of movement to visit POWs. All applications for information with regard to missing prisoners rapidly received official answers from the Israeli military authorities, and requests and suggestions were met in most cases by a positive response. The ICRC was able to arrange for the repatriation of all seriously wounded casualties before the end of 1967. After delay in some cases, 5638 Arab POWs and 19 Israeli POWs were exchanged on a bilateral basis. Detainees and internees were visited, but ICRC delegates encountered difficulties in 1969 and 1970 in visiting Israeli prisoners held in Egypt; in 1970 the same problem was encountered in Syria. There were also difficulties over the repatriation of civilians, but 'some twenty-thousand persons were enabled to return to their homes on one side or other of the cease-fire lines'. Some 3700 family reunions were permitted on compassionate grounds.

Matters were different in the case of the Fourth Convention concerning civilians in the Occupied Territories. The ICRC informed Israel in July 1967 that 'in its opinion the Fourth Convention was applicable'. Israel replied a year later that it wished 'to leave the question ... open for the moment'. This hindered the ICRC in seeking to prevent such prohibited activities as the destruction of houses and the deportation of protected persons.

The Fourth Convention prohibits any destruction of property 'except where such destruction is rendered *absolutely necessary by military operations*' (Article 53, my italics). It also prohibits the punishment of any protected person except for an offence which he or she has *personally* committed (Article 33, my italics); in other words, indiscriminate or collective punishments are banned. The ICRC found that three kinds of destruction were in fact carried out by Israel as measures of punishment: the destruction of villages or town quarters, the destruction of houses, and the so-called 'punishment of neighbours' policy which was directed against 'the houses of persons helping members of al-Fatah'. When the ICRC delegate made representations to the Israeli Ministry of Defence, he was told 'that it was not for the ICRC to interfere in a question that affected directly the security of the State'. The ICRC took the view that, while it deplored all terrorist attacks against civilians, such attacks were in themselves no justification for resorting to reprisals or any other form of collective penalties.

The ICRC had evidence of deportations from the Golan Heights, the West Bank of the Jordan, and the Gaza Strip. The Israeli authorities responded that, in the case of the Golan Heights, there had been no deportations, only 'voluntary departures'. As for the West Bank, those deported were Jordanian citizens engaged in activities detrimental to the interests of the State: deportation, in Israel's view, was more humane than internment. There had been transfers of population within the Occupied Territories, and in most cases the persons transferred had accepted compensation.

The ICRC took the view that 'at least by analogy' the provisions of the Fourth Convention should apply to Jewish communities in Arab countries. The ICRC delegate was able to visit Jews 'assigned to residence in camps' in Libya, and was in 'more or less constant touch' with three communities of Jews with Syrian nationality. Egypt, on the other hand, would not permit ICRC delegates to visit interned Jews.

As the ICRC has not published comparable reports of other situations following armed conflict, it is impossible to judge whether its experience in the Middle East was in any way typical. It would seem that no country complied fully with the obligations it had assumed, yet no country was totally impervious to the appeals of the ICRC.

Following the 1967 war, the Security Council adopted unanimously a resolution which emphasized the inadmissibility of acquiring territory by war, and this resolution was reaffirmed in 1973.[33] In accordance with these decisions, the Council has been concerned at Israeli attempts to change the status of the Occupied Territories and has deplored, censured, and condemned changes in the status of Jerusalem, which changes it has regarded as invalid; it has also regarded as null and void the 1981 decision to impose Israeli laws and administration on the Golan Heights; and it has strongly deplored the construction of Jewish settlements in the Occupied Territories, which it has regarded as a serious obstacle to peace.[34] It has expressed grave concern, deeply regretted, and strongly deplored the deportation of

Palestinians.[35] It also strongly deplored the refusal of Israel to allow the mayor of Al-Khalil to travel to New York to appear before the Security Council, condemned the attempts by Jewish extremists to assassinate the mayors of Nablus, Ramallah, and Al Bireh, and condemned the killing and wounding of defenceless Palestinian civilians.[36]

In 1969, in a debate on the status of Jerusalem, the United States reminded the Security Council that Israel was required by the Fourth Geneva Convention 'to maintain the occupied area as intact and unaltered as possible, without interfering with the customary life of the area'. Israeli actions, said the United States, had led to concern that the eventual disposition of East Jerusalem might be prejudiced. This stance was quoted by another delegate later in the year, following the fire at the Al Aqsa mosque in the Old City of Jerusalem, started by a demented Australian. When the Arab States complained in 1971–72 that Israel was violating the Geneva Conventions, Israel counter-attacked by asking for a meeting of the Council 'to consider the mutual release of all prisoners of war, in accordance with the provision of the Third Convention'. But no meeting was held. In 1976, after another Arab–Israeli war, Islamic States again complained of Israeli violations of the Geneva Conventions, but Israel counter-complained that the Arabs were the main violators of humanitarian norms. At the Camp David meeting in 1978, President Carter reaffirmed the US view that unilateral action by Israel could not change the status of Jerusalem, and that East Jerusalem was occupied territory and hence subject to the international law of belligerent occupation.[37]

After the peace treaty between Egypt and Israel, the Commission on Human Rights adopted a resolution on violations of human rights in territories occupied by Israel. Third World and Communist countries again alleged that Israel was in breach of the Geneva Conventions, and there were calls for mandatory sanctions against Israel under Chapter VII of the UN Charter. Israel denied that it was violating the Geneva Conventions, accused UN organs of using double standards, and alleged that Arabs were the foremost violators of humanitarian principles.[38]

Following Israeli incursions into or invasions of the Lebanon, the Council condemned acts which endanger or take innocent human life and called on all parties to facilitate the work of the ICRC and the UN agency for Arab refugees (UNRWA).[39]

The refusal of Israel to accept *de jure* that the Fourth Geneva Convention applies in occupied territories places the ICRC and the other parties to the Convention in considerable difficulty. Common

Table 3.1 Security Council decisions regarding the implementation of the Geneva Conventions in territories occupied by Israel, 1967–93

1.	14 June 1967	res.237 (S/7968/Rev.3)
2.	24 March 1968	res.248
3.	21 May 1968	res.252 (S/8590/Rev.2)
4.	27 Sept.1968	res.259 (S/8825/Rev.2)
5.	3 July 1969	res.267 (S/9311)
6.	15 Sept.1969	res.271 (S/9445, as amended)
7.	25 Sept.1971	res.298 (S/10337, S/10338/Rev.1)
8.	26 May 1976	1922nd mtg., para.2.
9.	11 Nov.1976	S/12233
10.	22 March 1979	res.446 (S/13171/Rev.2)
11.	20 July 1979	res.452 (S/13461)
12.	14 Nov.1979	S/13629
13.	1 March 1980	res.465 (A/13827)
14.	8 May 1980	res.468 (S/13930)
15.	20 May 1980	res.469 (S/13949)
16.	5 June 1980	res.471 (S/13984)
17.	30 June 1980	res.476 (S/14031)
18.	20 Aug.1980	res.478 (S/14113)
19.	19 Dec.1980	res.484 (S/14306)
20.	17 Dec.1981	res.497 (S/14798)
21.	19 June 1982	res.512 (S/15240)
22.	4 July 1982	res.513 (S/15273)
23.	29 July 1982	res.515 (S/15325)
24.	26 Jan.1984	S/16293
25.	8 Dec.1986	res.592 (S/18506/Rev.1)
26.	22 Dec.1987	res.605 (S/19352/Rev.1)
27.	5 Jan.1988	res.607 (S/19403)
28.	14 Jan.1988	res.608 (S/19352/Rev.1)
29.	26 Aug.1988	S/20156
30.	6 July 1989	res.636 (S/20710)
31.	30 Aug.1989	res.641 (S/20820)
32.	19 June 1990	S/21363
33.	12 Oct.1990	res.672 (S/21859)
34.	24 Oct.1990	res.673 (S/21893)
35.	20 Dec.1990	res.681 (S/22022)
36.	4 Jan.1991	S/22046
37.	24 May 1991	res.694 (S/22633)
38.	6 Jan.1992	res.726 (S/23372)
39.	4 April 1992	S/23783
40.	18 Dec.1992	res.799 (S/24987)

Article 1 of the Fourth Convention obliges the parties to respect the Conventions in all circumstances, and also 'to ensure respect' for them; and the Conventions contains identical articles for dealing with alleged violations (Articles 52/53/132/149). This provides for an inquiry, to be instituted by a party to the conflict; but no party has asked for an inquiry on this matter. The Fourth Convention states that the Convention constitutes no obstacle to humanitarian activities by the ICRC or any other impartial humanitarian organization for the protection and relief of civilians 'subject to the consent of the Parties to the conflict' (Article 10), and that ICRC delegates shall enjoy the same prerogatives as those of a Protecting Power, subject to 'the approval of the Power governing the territories where they will carry out their duties' (Article 143). There is, however, no provision in the Convention for the ICRC to initiate an inquiry into alleged breaches, though Article 6(4) of the statutes of the International Red Cross stipulates that the ICRC shall 'take cognizance of complaints regarding alleged breaches of the humanitarian Conventions',[40] and the ICRC has repeatedly expressed in public the view that the Fourth Convention applies to territories occupied by Israel.

In 1988, Secretary-General Pérez de Cuéllar recommended that the Security Council should appeal to those parties to the Conventions having diplomatic relations with Israel 'to use all the means at their disposal to persuade the Government of Israel to change its position as regards the applicability of the Convention'. The Security Council considered the report of the Secretary-General in five meetings, and a draft resolution was submitted which would have called on Israel to apply the Fourth Convention *de jure* and have recalled the obligation of all parties to the Convention to ensure respect for it. This text received 14 affirmative votes but was vetoed by the United States.[41]

In 1990, following an incident on the Temple Mount in Jerusalem, in which more than 20 Palestinians were killed by police bullets and about 150 people were injured, the Security Council asked the Secretary-General to send a mission to the region. Israel took the view that such a mission was 'unnecessary', but provided the Secretary-General with the report of its own Commission of Investigation. Pérez de Cuéllar reported this response to the Security Council and suggested that the Council might call for a meeting of the parties to the Geneva Convention 'to discuss possible measures that might be taken by them'. After debate over eight meetings, the Council by unanimous vote asked the Secretary-General to cooperate with the ICRC in developing further the idea of a meeting of the parties to the Convention. Consultations with the ICRC proceeded slowly, but the Secretary-General reported to the Council on 9 April 1991 that he had asked the parties to the Convention to submit to him by 1 May 1991 their views about a meeting of parties, and that these replies would be addressed in the Secretary-General's next report.[42] So far as I know, there has been no further report on the matter.

It is difficult to be sure why the idea of a meeting of parties to the Convention was not proceeded with. The ICRC has traditionally tried to avoid involvement in matters with political implications, and it is possible that it feared that a meeting of parties might become enmeshed in acrimonious debates about Palestinian participation. This was certainly possible, as the Palestine Liberation Organization had decided in 1989 to adhere to the Geneva Conventions of 1949 and the Additional Protocols of 1977. The ICRC was not able to determine whether the communication from the PLO could be considered as an instrument of accession, but circulated the communication to the other parties.[43] There has been some consideration in the UN Commission on Human Rights and the Sub-Commission on the Prevention of Discrimination and Protection of Minorities about the possibility of asking the International Court of Justice for an advisory opinion on the legal consequences for States arising from the building by Israel of settlements in the Occupied Territories in breach of Security Council resolutions 446 of 22 March 1979 and resolution 465 of 1 March 1980.

INDIA–PAKISTAN–BANGLADESH, 1971–74

On 13 December 1971, shortly after the Bangladesh war, Pakistan asked the Security Council to accept a number of 'imperatives', of which the fourth was to devise means to ensure scrupulous respect for the Geneva Conventions. Eight days later, the Council called on 'all those concerned' to apply the Geneva Conventions 'in full', and asked the Secretary-General to keep the Council informed on the implementation of the resolution. From time to time, during the following months, Pakistan complained that India was violating the Geneva Conventions and other humanitarian norms, and was ill-treating POWs and detaining them after the cessation of active hostilities. India maintained that those guilty of 'grave crimes such as genocide, war crimes, and crimes against humanity' were not entitled to immunity under the Geneva Conventions and that, in any case, it was India's view that the Convention 'ceases to apply' once hostilities have closed. Subject to the legal position, India said it would respect all humanitarian norms.[44]

Under the terms of the resolution of the Security Council, the UN Secretary-General appointed Vittorio Winspeare Guicciardi as his special representative for humanitarian problems. Winspeare issued two reports on his discussions with the governmental authorities in the area and with Red Cross and other relief organizations. Two crucial issues for the Winspeare mission were the release of Sheikh Mujibur Rahman and the fate of the displaced Biharis. Sheikh Mujibur, who was the elected leader of the people of East Pakistan (which later became Bangladesh) was in prison in West Pakistan, but India took the view that his release was essential if Bangladesh were to become orderly and stable. Secretary-General U Thant had called for Sheikh Mujibur's release some months before the outbreak of war, and Winspeare made a new appeal to President Bhutto and other Pakistani leaders that the Sheikh should be set free. On 8 January 1972, Mujibur was released and proceeded to Bangladesh. When Winspeare visited Dhaka the following month, he was able to have a substantial talk with Mujibur Rahman.[45]

The Biharis (who numbered about 500 000 in 1971–72) are Urdu-speaking Muslims who had opted for East Pakistan at the time of partition but who found themselves unwelcome in Bengali-speaking Bangladesh. Sheikh Mujibur had appealed to his followers in Bangladesh to surrender their arms, but the Biharis had refused. In the ensuing clash with troops and police, many Biharis had been killed. Winspeare visited several camps for Biharis and found evidence of suffering, but he concluded that the authorities in Bangladesh were doing what they could to ameliorate the situation.[46]

The Winspeare mission gave a good deal of attention to providing informal links between the three capitals, as most normal diplomatic contacts had ceased. Winspeare found the Bangladesh authorities 'sympathetic in principle' to the repatriation of West Pakistani officials; as for senior officials of the former East Pakistan government, Bangladesh intended to try them as collaborators. Winspeare found great anxiety in Pakistan about the future of their POWs and about the proposed trials. He was told by the International Committee of the Red Cross that India had agreed to repatriate a number of severely wounded Pakistanis. He believed that outstanding humanitarian problems should be dealt with in direct talks between the parties.[47]

In 1973, Pakistan instituted proceedings against India in the International Court of Justice concerning 195 Pakistani POWs whom India proposed to hand over to Bangladesh to be tried for genocide and crimes against humanity. Pakistan claimed to have exclusive jurisdiction over the POWs in question and that there was no ground in international law for handing them over to Bangladesh. Later in the year, however, Pakistan informed the Court that negotiations were taking place with India, and asked that proceedings in the Court should be discontinued.[48]

CYPRUS SINCE 1964

A resolution of the Security Council in 1974 called on all parties to respect the fundamental human rights of every person.[49] Since 1974, the reports of the Secretary-General to the Security Council on the operations of the UN Force (UNFICYP) have usually included a section on humanitarian assistance.

IRAQ–IRAN, 1980–88

The war between Iraq and Iran was afflicted by an unusually large number of breaches of humanitarian norms: the use of chemical weapons, direct attacks on non-combatants, and ill-treatment of POWs.

The Iranian allegation that Iraq had used chemical weapons was investigated by a group of UN experts. Under the terms of a resolution of the General Assembly in 1982, the UN Secretary-General may seek the assistance of experts in order to investigate alleged uses of chemical or biological (bacteriological) weapons, including the on-site collection and examination of evidence. In the case of the Iraq–Iran war, Pérez de Cuéllar did not cite the resolution of the General Assembly as the authority for his action. Instead he acted on the basis of 'the humanitarian principles embodied in the Charter' and 'the moral responsibilities' vested in the office of the Secretary-General. This action was undertaken with the concurrence of Iraq. The allegation by Iran that chemical weapons had been used was confirmed by the UN experts, and this judgement was endorsed by the Security Council in 1985; and, in the following year, the Council noted that chemical weapons had been used by Iraq 'on many occasions'. The Council repeatedly condemned the use of chemical weapons as contrary to the obligations of the Geneva Protocol of 1925.[50]

Another group of UN experts investigated allegations about attacks on non-combatants and concluded that, while the allegations of Iraq and Iran could not be confirmed, both countries had made attacks which had caused damage to civilian targets. The Council condemned all violations of the Geneva Conventions and other provisions of international humanitarian law, and called for the cessation of attacks against civilians.[51]

When the International Committee of the Red Cross visits POWs or political prisoners, it reports its findings in confidence to the government concerned. Occasionally part of a report has been leaked to the media in such a way as to give an incomplete and misleading picture: in such circumstances, the ICRC has little alternative but to publish its report in full. With that exception, the ICRC does not publicize the difficulties it encounters nor its findings, unless (a) the breaches of international humanitarian law are major and repeated, (b) its delegates have witnessed the violation with their own eyes or the breaches have been established by reliable and verifiable sources, (c) confidential representations to the governments concerned have not succeeded, and (d) such publicity would be in the interests of the victims.[52] The ICRC published three documents on what it learned about the treatment of POWs in Iraq and Iran.

In some respects, the two States met their obligations under the Geneva Conventions. The first public appeal of the ICRC in 1983 drew attention to grave and repeated breaches of international humanitarian law by both sides (summary executions of captured soldiers, abandoning of the wounded on the field of battle, and indiscriminate bombing of towns and villages), as well as to obstacles the ICRC had encountered in exercising its mandate under the Geneva Conventions. In February 1984, the ICRC issued a second memorandum making similar complaints. Later in 1984, in an unusual action, the President of the ICRC made a formal public statement about official allegations in Iran that the ICRC had been spying for Iraq, and reported that Iran had first obstructed and then suspended ICRC activities.[53]

The third public statement had followed an incident in a POW camp in Gorgan in Iran, and this caused Iraq to request a UN inquiry. Another group of experts was appointed by the UN Secretary-General. After a full investigation at POW camps, the UN experts concluded that both Iraq and Iran had failed to uphold the standards and policies which they professed. The Secretary-General visited the two States in 1985 and appealed for the observance of recognized international humanitarian rules.[54]

KUWAIT, 1990–91

Iraq's invasion and intended annexation of Kuwait took place in August 1990. This was by no means the only act of aggression with which the Security Council had been confronted, but it was the first time since the United Nations was founded that a UN Member was simply wiped from the map. Kuwait's human rights record was remarkably dismal. If this Iraqi venture had succeeded, many small and medium-sized countries would have feared being swallowed up by powerful neighbours. According to UN and other impartial sources, Iraq violated many international humanitarian norms during the invasion and occupation of Kuwait.

The first reference to IHL in the decisions of the Security Council came on 13 September 1990, when Iraq was called on to respect IHL, including the Fourth Geneva Convention on civilians. Later that month, the Council reaffirmed the applicability of the Fourth Convention: Iraq was called on to comply fully with all its terms; and Iraq would be held responsible for any grave breaches. In October, the Council demanded that Iraq should cease hostage-taking and other breaches of international law, including the Fourth Geneva Convention. Iraq would be held liable for loss, damage, or injury to nationals of Kuwait or to other non-Iraqi nationals. As part of the ceasefire arrangements in March–April 1991, the Council demanded that Iraq should release all Kuwaiti and third-country nationals and should allow the ICRC to have access to all POWs. Iraq would be held liable under international law for any injury to foreign nationals arising from the invasion and occupation of Kuwait.[55]

Those violations committed in Kuwait during the Iraqi occupation were investigated by a team from the UN Secretariat at the request of Kuwait. In the immediate aftermath of the war, the UN team was not able to provide a definitive or comprehensive report, but an interim report was issued to the Security Council on 29 April 1991. A full report was promised at a later date.[56]

The UN team based its inquiries on two international treaties to which Iraq is a party – the Fourth Geneva Convention and the UN Covenant on Civil and Political Rights. The team received allegations of a wide range of abuses, including cases of arbitrary arrest and/or detention, cruel treatment and torture of detainees, ill-treatment of civilians, deportations, reprisals, collective penalties, and destruction or expropriation of property.

EL SALVADOR SINCE 1991

As part of the settlement of conflicts in Central America, an agreement on human rights was reached on 26 July 1990 between the Government of El Salvador and the armed opposition (the Farabundo Martí Front for National Liberation, usually abbreviated as FMLN). In 1991, the Security Council authorized the Secretary-General 'to monitor' this and other agreements between the parties. In accordance with this mandate, the Secretary-General established an Observer Mission in El Salvador (ONUSAL) the reports of which were published as documents of the Security Council and the General Assembly.

In its first report, ONUSAL distinguished between international human rights law, for which it had a specific mandate in the agreement of 26 July 1990, and international humanitarian law relating to armed conflict. The latter was the responsibility of the ICRC, the reports of which are confidential, whereas ONUSAL's reports were intended for publication. There was, nevertheless, some overlap between the two systems of law, and ONUSAL intended to deal with the latter 'only in cases which can be considered especially significant', giving top priority to cases involving inhumane threats or acts against persons not participating directly in hostilities.[57] Annexed to ONUSAL's second report, covering September and October 1991, was information which dealt in one section with cases relating to Human Rights and Humanitarian Law and, in a separate section, with Situations Affecting Human Rights. The annexes to subsequent reports had separate sections dealing with International Humanitarian Law.[58]

During the first ten months of operation in 1991–92, ONUSAL received 4528 complaints attributable to the Government, or FMLN. It will be seen from Table 3.2, that the proportion of inadmissible cases rose steadily in 1992. The complaints mainly concerned allegations of summary executions, death threats, disappearances, torture and cruel, inhuman, or degrading treatment or punishments, attacks on the life of persons or attacks on civilians, and acts or threats of

Table 3.2 Complaints received by ONUSAL, August 1991–July 1993

	Doubtful or inadmissible cases	*Admissible cases*	*Total*
Aug.–Sept. 1991	56	398	454
Oct. 1991	105	521	626
Nov. 1991	74	489	563
Dec. 1991	119	373	492
Jan. 1992	97	396	493
Feb. 1992	118	288	406
March 1992	148	303	451
April 1992	208	272	480
May 1992	296	267	563
June 1992–Jan. 1993	?	480 (8 months)	?
Feb. 1993	?	160	?
March 1993	?	139	?
April 1993	?	130	?
May 1993	?	121	?
June 1993	?	145	?
July 1993	?	166	?

violence intended to intimidate. ONUSAL also received complaints of war taxes levied by the FMLN.

ONUSAL investigated every complaint and reported on the Security Council 'allegations . . . illustrative of fairly widespread phenomena'. Both parties had committed violations of humanitarian norms. In its second report, ONUSAL expressed concern at 'the magnitude of some actions attributed to FMLN', and ONUSAL's fourth report referred to 'a great many complaints against FMLN regarding violations of the rules protecting the civilian population'.

SOMALIA, 1992

Four days after the Security Council launched the Congo operation in 1960, Secretary-General Hammarskjöld commented to US Ambassador Lodge that this was the first time that the United Nations had had to help a country that had no government.[59]

It was precisely this situation that faced the United Nations regarding Somalia in 1992. Mainly on the basis of reports from the Secretary-General, the Security Council passed a series of resolutions citing Chapters VII and VIII of the Charter, calling for the provision of humanitarian assistance, imposing 'a general and complete' arms embargo, urging the Somali factions to respect international humanitarian law, to observe a ceasefire, to attend a conference for national reconciliation and unity, and establishing a UN Operation in Somalia (UNOSOM) to monitor the ceasefire and provide security for the movement of humanitarian supplies.[60]

These resolutions were noteworthy in two respects. First, internal conditions *within* a State were said to threaten *international* peace and security, thus providing the Security Council with a basis for taking binding decisions under Chapter VII of the Charter. Secondly, the Council expressly cited Chapter VIII of the Charter regarding regional agencies and arrangements, thus providing for cooperation with the Organization of African Unity, the League of Arab States and the Islamic Conference. In the light of the Secretary-General's report on the breakdown of law and order in Somalia, the Council condemned all violations of international humanitarian law and declared that those who ordered or committed such acts would be held individually responsible. It may be noted that an expert appointed by the Human Rights Commission 'received allegations as to human rights violations committed by the United Nations forces in Somalia'.[61]

FORMER YUGOSLAVIA SINCE 1992

Although these things are difficult to measure, it seems likely that there were more serious violations of international humanitarian law during the fighting that followed the break-up of Yugoslavia than in other recent conflicts. This was widely reported by the media and in reports circulated to the Security Council: from the Committee of Experts appointed by the Council in 1992;[62] the Special Rapporteur of the Commission on Human Rights, Tadeusz Mazowiecki;[63] the Co-Chairmen of the International Conference on Former Yugoslavia, Cyrus Vance and Lord Owen;[64] the European Commission;[65] and a number of UN Member States.[66]

The parties to the conflict frequently disregarded the orders of the Security Council. The Council, acting under Chapter VII of the Charter, imposed 'a general and complete embargo on all deliveries of weapons and military equipment to Yugoslavia', later extended to a comprehensive ban in respect of Serbia and Montenegro. The Council also imposed a 'no-fly' zone over Bosnia and Herzegovina.[67]

The parties to the conflict had agreed on 22 May 1992 to respect the main provisions of the four Geneva Conventions (1949), the first Additional Protocol thereto (1977), and the Protocol annexed to the Convention prohibiting mines and booby traps (1980). The Security Council had affirmed that all parties to the conflict were bound to comply with the Geneva Conventions and other obligations under international humanitarian law, 'and that persons who commit or order the commission of breaches of the [Geneva] Conventions are individually responsible in respect of such breaches'. The Council condemned forcible expulsions and attempts to change the ethnic composition of former Yugoslavia, the imprisonment, abduction, and abuse of civilians, the practice of 'ethnic cleansing', and attacks on fleeing civilians. States and international humanitarian organizations were asked to make available to the Council 'substantiated information' regarding grave breaches of the Geneva Conventions and other violations of international humanitarian law.[68]

On 6 October 1992, the Council asked the Secretary-General 'as a matter of urgency' to establish an impartial Commission of Experts to examine and analyse evidence on grave breaches of international humanitarian law. The Commission was to consist of five members serving in their personal capacities. The Commission took as the applicable law:

Hague Convention IV on the laws and customs of war on land, 1907
The Genocide Convention, 1948
The Four Geneva Conventions, 1949
The Hague Convention on the protection of cultural property, 1954
Additional Protocol I to the Geneva Conventions, 1977
The Convention on excessively injurious or indiscriminate weapons, 1980
General Assembly resolutions 2444 (XXIII), 1968 (human rights in armed conflict) and 2675 (XXV), 9 Dec. 1970 (basic principles for the protection of civilian populations in armed conflicts)

The Commission, in an interim report, found evidence 'of uneven value' regarding wilful and mass killings, 'ethnic cleansing', torture, rape, pillage, arbitrary arrests, and destruction of civilian property. The Commission discussed the idea of an *ad hoc* war crimes tribunal, which had been recommended by Lord Owen and Cyrus Vance.[69]

Ideas about the form such a tribunal might take had been submitted in writing by France, Italy, Sweden (on behalf of CSCE), Canada, the Islamic Conference, the Russian Federation, the United States, the Netherlands, and informally by other States and non-governmental organizations. On 22 February 1993, the Council decided to establish an international tribunal 'for the prosecution of persons responsible for serious violations of international humanitarian law' committed in former Yugoslavia since 1991, and asked the Secretary-General to submit specific proposals for implementing the decision.[70]

On 20 March 1993, Bosnia-Herzegovina instituted proceedings in the International Court of Justice against Yugoslavia (Serbia and Montenegro), alleging that the latter had violated the Genocide Convention and other instruments of international humanitarian law. On 8 April, the Court, as a provisional measure, ordered Yugoslavia (Serbia and Montenegro) to take all measures to prevent the crime of genocide.[71]

The Secretary-General's proposals for an international tribunal were issued on 3 May. He suggested that such a tribunal should be established by the Security Council acting under Chapter VII of the UN Charter. Its task should be to apply existing international law, not to develop new law. This existing law would comprise Hague Convention IV on the laws and customs of war on land, 1907; the Charter of the Nürnberg Tribunal, 1945;[72] the Genocide Convention, 1948; and the four Geneva Conventions, 1949. (It is noteworthy that the Secretary-General's list of instruments did not correspond in all respect to those used as a basis by the Commission of Experts.)

The tribunal should have jurisdiction over natural persons and not entities such as associations or organizations. Acting in an official capacity or on the orders of a superior should not relieve a person of criminal responsibility. The tribunal should have primacy over national courts.

The tribunal should consist of 11 independent judges with similar qualifications to the judges of the International Court of Justice. The judges should be elected by the General Assembly from a list submitted by the Security Council. There should be a Prosecutor appointed by the Security Council on the nomination of the Secretary-General, and a Registrar to service the tribunal, appointed by the Secretary-General after consultation with the president of the tribunal. The judges, Prosecutor, and Registrar should serve four-year terms. The seat of the tribunal should be at the Hague.

Accused persons should have a fair and public hearing, and should be presumed innocent until proved guilty. Penalties should be limited to imprisonment and the confiscation of property acquired by criminal conduct, and the tribunal should not be empowered to impose the death penalty. Imprisonment should take place outside former Yugoslavia. 'States should be encouraged to declare their readiness to carry out the enforcement of prison sentences in accordance with their domestic laws and procedures . . .'.[73] The General Assembly held ten ballots in September 1993, as a result of which, the following judges were elected: Georges Michel Abi-Saab (Egypt), Antonio Cassese (Italy), Jules Deschênes (Canada), Adolphus Godwin Karibi-Whyte (Nigeria), Germain Le Foyer De Constil (France), Li Haopei (China), Gabrielle Kirk McDonald (United States), Elizabeth Odio Benito (Costa Rica), Rustam Sidhwa (Pakistan), Sir Ninian Stephen (Australia) and Lal Chand Vohrah (Malaysia).

While an *ad hoc* tribunal may have been the best option in 1993, I regret that a permanent international criminal court had not been created, able to deal with all persons alleged to have committed grave violations of existing international law. I consider this matter in greater detail in Chapter 4.

THE ROLE OF THE SECURITY COUNCIL

The Charter empowers the Security Council to take coercive action against States if this is necessary in order to maintain or restore international peace and security, but there are no provisions in the Charter for acting against individual violators of IHL.

If violations of IHL are so extensive as to threaten the peace, Council is empowered to order non-military or military measures of coercion. If the Council intends to apply enforcement measures, then the ban on intervening in matters which are essentially within the domestic jurisdiction of any State no longer applies.

It is noteworthy that the Council has not used its powers consistently. It invoked Chapter VII of the Charter in the case of Iraq, Somalia, Libya, and Serbia-Montenegro, but not against Israel, which has often been found guilty of violating IHL but has never been threatened by the Security Council with sanctions under Chapter VII.

The Genocide Convention, the four Geneva Conventions, and Additional Protocol I provide for national action if grave breaches are committed against protected persons, namely, wilful killing, torture, or inhuman treatment, or extensive destruction and appropriation of property when this is not justified by military necessity. Additional Protocol I goes further than the Geneva Conventions and prohibits action directed against enemy civilians, attacks against works or installations containing dangerous forces, and attacks against non-defended localities or demilitarized zones, the movement of civilians into occupied territory, unjustifiable delay in repatriating prisoners of war or civilians, and inhuman and degrading practices based on racial discrimination. If there were in existence an international criminal tribunal, it should be authorized to deal with individuals accused of violating IHL.

If a State deliberately infringes IHL, it is possible to take belligerent reprisal action, except against protected persons, until the enemy stops illegalities, but this is of limited value and open to abuse. The International Committee of the Red Cross would like to prohibit completely belligerent reprisals unless

(a) the party alleging violation of IHL has offered the possibility of inquiry and impartial observation of the facts;
(b) the scale of the reprisal is not out of proportion to that of the violation complained of;
(c) the reprisal action is, so far as possible, carried out in the same field as that of the violation;
(d) the reprisal is not contrary to the law of humanity;[74] for example, to torture captured personnel.

In one of the cases reviewed in this chapter, the UN Secretary-General suggested that 'the Security Council might wish to call for a meeting of the high contracting parties [to the Fourth Geneva Convention] to discuss possible measures that might be taken by them under the Convention.'[75] No such meeting has been held.

It is evident that the procedure for dealing with violations of IHL is woefully inadequate. This is known to combatants, who therefore may feel free to violate its provisions when superior officers are looking the other way or, in some cases, when the violation has been ordered by superior officers. If the illegality of one side becomes known to the other side, as will usually be the case, the other side will resort to belligerent reprisals, leading to a general escalation of the means of conducting military operations in a manner contrary to Article 22 of the Regulations attached to the Hague Conventions of 1899 and 1907, namely, 'The right of belligerents to adopt means of injuring is not unlimited.'

4 Terrorism

It is notoriously difficult to define terrorism. The 1973 Convention on terrorism described it as 'criminal acts directed against a State and intended or calculated to create a state of terror in the minds of particular persons, or a group of persons or the general public' (Article 1.2). That definition is satisfactory so far as it goes, but it does not bring out the fact that most terrorist acts that come before the Security Council nowadays are not simply to create a state of terror but are intended to induce governments to act in ways that they had not otherwise intended – to release prisoners, for example.

There has undoubtedly been an increase in that sort of terrorism in recent decades. It is the instrument of those with a grievance but who have inadequate support within their own community or are weak in conventional military terms. Acts of terrorism often, but not invariably, are directed against innocent persons, as a means of exerting pressure on the strong.

It may be noted that the Fourth Geneva Convention on the protection of civilians includes an article prohibiting the taking of hostages (Article 34), which is described as a grave breach (Article 147), preceded by an article prohibiting 'measures ... of terrorism' (Article 33), which are *not* described as grave breaches, and 'measures ... of terrorism' are not defined. The International Committee of the Red Cross might also stress that the Additional Protocols to the Geneva Conventions prohibit acts or threats of violence, the primary purpose of which is to spread terror among the civilian population, in international wars (Additional Protocol I, Article 51.2) and in internal wars (Additional Protocol II, Article 13.2). There are, in addition, a number of international treaties expressly designed to prevent acts of terrorism and to bring the perpetrators to justice:

Convention on Offences and certain Acts committed on board Aircraft, signed at Tokyo on 14 September 1963

Convention for the Suppression of Unlawful Seizure of Aircraft, signed at The Hague on 16 December 1970

Convention for the Suppression of Unlawful Acts against the Safety of Civil Aviation, signed at Montreal on 23 September 1971

Convention on the Prevention and Punishment of Crimes against Internationally Protected Persons, including Diplomatic Agents, adopted by the General Assembly on 14 December 1973

International Convention against the Taking of Hostages, adopted by the General Assembly on 17 December 1979
Convention on the Physical Protection of Nuclear Material, adopted at Vienna on 3 March 1980
Protocol for the Suppression of Unlawful Acts of Violence against the Safety of Civil Aviation, signed at Montreal on 24 February 1988
Convention for the Suppression of Unlawful Acts against the Safety of Maritime Navigation, done at Rome on 10 March 1988
Protocol for the Suppression of Unlawful Acts against the Safety of Fixed Platforms located on the Continental Shelf, done at Rome on 10 March 1988
Convention on the Marking of Plastic Explosives for the Purpose of Detection, done at Montreal on 1 March 1991

It is not easy to decide which cases that came before the Security Council should be included in this chapter. Should one, for example, include the murder in 1948 of the UN mediator for Palestine, Count Folke Bernadotte? This atrocity was perpetrated by an illegal Israeli underground group, one member of which was later to become Prime Minister. Bernadotte had been appointed by the General Assembly, but he had issued 31 reports to the Security Council between May and September, and the preambular paragraph of a resolution of the Security Council after Bernadotte's assassination maintained that the act appeared to have been committed 'by a criminal group of terrorists'.[1] Yet the purpose of killing Bernadotte seems to have been to eliminate a UN appointee in order to damage or destroy his recommendations rather than to pressure governments or the United Nations into acting in ways they had not otherwise intended.

Another possible candidate for inclusion, this time an instance of kidnapping, concerned the capture of Adolf Eichmann in Argentina in 1960 by Israeli secret agents. Israel admitted that its personnel had committed a formal violation of the sovereignty of Argentina, but the purpose had been to bring to justice a man who had participated in the massacre of six million Jews. The resolution adopted by the Security Council on this occasion was notably bland.[2]

Another borderline case arose from a complaint by Guinea in 1969 of aggression by Portugese forces based in Guinea (Bissau). Part of the eventual settlement of the issue involved a mutual exchange of prisoners, and there was a tendency in some quarters to regard these prisoners as hostages until they were repatriated. The

Security Council called on Portugal to release the crew of a captured Guinean aircraft and the passengers from a captured Guinean barge; Portugal said it would do so if Guinea would release 24 of its soldiers detained by Guinea.[3] It may be doubted whether unrepatriated prisoners of war should normally be regarded as hostages.

Some acts which have been loosely labelled as 'terrorist' could equally well be described as grave breaches of international humanitarian law. This would apply, for example, to Iraq's action in using hostages as 'human shields', which was condemned by the Security Council.[4] The same would apply to actions in former Yugoslavia in pursuit of so-called 'ethnic cleansing': indeed, a section of a report of the Secretary-General on the matter is headed 'Acts of terrorism'.[5]

'Terrorism' is sometimes used as a synonym for aggression. Thus, after South Africa had attacked Lesotho in 1982, King Moshoeshoe of Lesotho appealed to the Security Council to restrain South Africa 'from pursuing a strategy of naked terrorism';[6] another case was when Libya, after complaining of US violations of Libyan territorial waters and airspace in 1983, said that the United States was pursuing a policy of terrorism;[7] again, the Soviet Union declared in the Security Council in 1984 that US interference with shipping off the coast of Nicaragua was a policy of State terrorism.[8] But these were not cases of terrorism in its contemporary meaning.

Terrorists often operate in countries with oppressive regimes, so that much of the outside world may sympathize with the *aims* of terrorists, if not with their *methods*. To their supporters and sympathizers, terrorists are often thought of as freedom-fighters. One of the difficulties of dealing with the international implications of terrorism is that the perpetrators of terrorist acts may claim to be the victims of State terrorism, an argument which was often deployed by Palestinian and South African nationalist organizations.[9]

National governments have always found it difficult to deal with terrorism, both its outward manifestations and its underlying causes. Indeed, the more a government respects democratic norms, the more difficult it may be to deal with the outward manifestations of terrorism; yet respect for democratic norms is crucial if the underlying causes of terrorism are to be tackled.

Some terrorist outrages are simply mindless acts of destruction and killing, such as the Sharpeville massacre in South Africa in 1960 or the massacre in the Sabra and Shatila Palestinian refugee camps in 1982. But the hijacking of ships or aircraft or the taking of hostages are usually bargaining ploys: we will release the hostages we hold if you will release named prisoners. During the past quarter of a century, there has been increasing reluctance on the part of Israel and many Western countries to engage in sordid exchanges of this kind.

Many terrorist acts do not have international implications and so are within the domestic jurisdiction of States. Even so, the vast majority of terrorist acts with international implications are not brought to the attention of the Security Council. From time to time, Israel launched attacks on its Arab neighbours, either (in Israel's view) as a preemptive measure to eliminate terrorist bases or in retaliation for Arab terrorist attacks against Israeli targets. Israel had complained to the Security Council that its Arab neighbours were harbouring terrorist gangs or had reported on particular terrorist acts, though without expressly asking the Security Council to act.[10] In 1986, a terrorist incident directed against Israel was narrowly avoided. An Arab, Nezar Hindawi, had persuaded his Irish girlfriend to take on to an Israeli aircraft an item of luggage containing a concealed bomb. This was detected by Israeli security personnel. Hindawi's evidence at the trial implicated Syrian diplomats in London. Britain broke diplomatic relations with Damascus after the trial, though these were restored in 1990. Israel reported the facts of the Hindawi affair to the Security Council and the General Assembly, but no meeting of the Security Council was asked for or held.[11]

Moreover, it is not easy to deal with international terrorism without, at the same time, addressing its underlying causes. Thus, in 1972, Secretary-General Waldheim asked the General Assembly to consider 'Measures to prevent terrorism and other forms of violence which endanger or take innocent human lives or jeopardize fundamental freedoms'. That was a clumsy enough formulation for a UN agenda item, but on the insistence of some strongminded Third World diplomats, the thrust of Waldheim's proposal was altered by the addition of the words 'and study of the underlying causes of those forms of terrorism and acts of violence which lie in misery, frustration, grievance and despair and which cause some people to sacrifice human lives, including their own, in an attempt to effect radical changes'.

Secretary-General U Thant exercised good offices of a sort in several cases of aerial hijacking in 1968 and 1969,[12] but it was not until 1970 that the Security Council formally took up the international repercussions of terrorist acts.

1 HIJACKED AIRCRAFT

A dramatic act of aerial hijacking took place in September 1970, when the Popular Front for the Liberation of Palestine seized four passenger aircraft: an attempt to hijack an Israeli plane failed. One plane was forced to land in Cairo and was blown up on the ground after the passengers were for a time held hostage. The other three aircraft were forced to land at Zerka in Jordan, and some of the passengers were for a time held hostage. Britain and the United States asked for an urgent meeting of the Security Council. In private consultations, the members of the Security Council agreed on the text of a resolution that was adopted by consensus. This called for the release of the passengers and crews of the hijacked aircraft and called on States to take all possible steps to prevent further hijackings. In the event, the hostages were released in stages over the following three weeks, and the aircraft were then blown up. Three days after the final release, seven PFLP prisoners (including Leila Khaled) held in Britain, the Federal Republic of Germany, and Switzerland were flown to Cairo. Although all the records of this incident are not yet in the public domain, it would seem that the International Committee of the Red Cross acted as a neutral intermediary between the governments concerned and the Popular Front for the Liberation of Palestine.[13] Israeli opinion was highly critical of the three European Governments for 'giving in' to terrorists.

2 ATTACK IN LOD AIRPORT

There was a further spate of hijackings of aircraft, culminating in May 1972 in an attack on the airport at Lod (Lydda) in which three Japanese terrorists and 26 passengers were killed. The assault was committed by three members of the United Red Army of Japan, but it was generally believed that they were acting on behalf of a Palestinian faction. The Security Council did not meet immediately: indeed, it did not meet in public at all, but three weeks after the incident, it approved a statement of consensus, expressing concern at and condemning aerial hijacking and other interference with civil aviation, and calling on States to act separately and together to deter such unlawful acts. It is not possible to tell from the published records precisely what transpired in the private consultations. The decision of the Council consisted of four paragraphs, two beginning 'Members of the Security Council . . .', and two paragraphs (expressing similar sentiments) beginning 'The Security Council . . .'. One may speculate that two drafts were considered in the private consultations. Negotiations must have been prolonged, and when it proved impossible to reconcile the two texts, they were simply married and issued by the President as a consensus statement in clumsy form. Indeed, two members of the Council expressed reservations at the procedure followed. India, while valuing informal consultations among Council members, considered that any decision by the Council without a formal meeting, 'could have serious and far-reaching legal and other consequences'. Italy thought that the adoption of a resolution in a formal meeting of the Council would have been preferable to a decision agreed upon through informal consultations: this, maintained Italy, would have avoided certain discrepancies in the statement of consensus.[14]

3 DIVERSION OF ARAB PLANE

On 10 August 1973, Israeli fighters intercepted a Middle East Airways plane *en route* from Beirut to Baghdad and forced it to land at a military base in Israel. This was done in the belief, mistaken as it turned out, that among the passengers was George Habash, leader of the Popular Front for the Liberation of Palestine. The Security Council held five meetings during which the Israeli action was generally condemned, while Israel complained at the failure of the international community to take effective steps to eradicate terrorism. The Security Council resolved to condemn Israel for violating the sovereignty of the Lebanon, as did the International Civil Aviation Organization.[15]

4 ENTEBBE RESCUE

One of the most spectacular acts of counter-terrorism took place at Entebbe in Uganda in 1976. An Air-France passenger aircraft, AF 139, with some 250 passengers and a crew of 12, was hijacked over Corfu by agents of the Popular Front for the Liberation of Palestine. The aircraft stopped at Benghazi in Libya, where one Israeli passenger, a nurse, feigned illness and was allowed to disembark. The passengers had the impression that Libyan cooperation with the hijackers was minimal. The aircraft then proceeded to Entebbe in Uganda, where the hijackers were joined by a number of Arab colleagues. About 150 non-Jewish hostages were released in two stages. The demands of the hijackers were never made entirely precise but related to the release of 53 political prisoners held in Israel, France, the Federal Republic of Germany, Switzerland and Kenya. It was not clear whether President Idi Amin was primarily interested in currying favour with the hijackers or in securing their release, although Yitzhak Rabin, the Israeli Prime Minister, maintained that Amin 'cooperated with the terrorists under a cloak of deception and false pretence'.

The initial reaction of the Government of Israel was to negotiate an exchange of hostages for prisoners, using the good offices of France but, at a later stage, it was decided to attempt a rescue. Four Hercules C-130 aircraft, carrying a Mercedes car, Land Rovers and other vehicles, flew some 2200 miles from Israel to Entebbe. Over 100 hostages and the crew of the French aircraft were rescued. Six hijackers, some 20 Ugandan soldiers, and three hostages were killed, as well as the leader of the rescue force, Jonathan Netanyahu. It had originally been intended that the aircraft would refuel at Entebbe, but this proved impossible for technical reasons, so the planes refuelled in Kenya. One elderly hostage, Dora Bloch, had been taken ill and was in hospital in Kampala. After the rescue operation, she was brutally murdered.

The Organization of African Unity seemed to be more outraged by Israeli aggression against Uganda than by the original terrorist attack and called for an urgent meeting of the Security Council. Five meetings of the Council were held. The African States expressed outrage at the enormity of Israel's offence in violating the sovereignty and territorial integrity of an African State, however moral the pretext.

> the Zionists were caught red-handed in a flagrant violation of the sovereignty and territorial integrity of the Republic of Uganda (Uganda)
>
> Israel wants to introduce the law of the jungle into international relations (Mauritania)
>
> this barbaric act (Cameroon)
>
> the criminal act of aggression committed by the Zionist, racist and terrorist entity (Libya)

> the Israeli authorities have placed themselves beyond the pale of international law and justice (Benin)

> another demonstration of the desperate and cynical attitude which the Zionist regime has for anything that smacks of humanitarianism (Somalia)

> there seems to be a determination to ignore completely, or at least to gloss over, Africa's legitimate complaint. . . . (Tanzania)

Most Western statements were more nuanced in stigmatizing Israel's action at Entebbe as a violation of the UN Charter, while claiming that a legal and moral justification could be made for seeking to protect innocent hostages.

> Whatever the motives, whatever the circumstances, terrorist acts . . . must be categorically and unequivocally condemned. . . . In our view, the Israeli action . . . involved the infringement of the national sovereignty and territorial integrity of Uganda. . . . My Goverment, while unable to reconcile the Israeli action with the strict rules of the Charter, does not find it possible to join in a condemnation. . . . (Sweden)

> Israel's action in rescuing the hostages necessarily involved a temporary breach in the territorial integrity of Uganda. . . . However, there is a well-established right to use limited force for the protection of one's own nationals. . . . (United States)

> At first sight there would not seem to be any doubt that the surprise attack by an armed force on a foreign airport . . . indeed constituted a violation of international law. . . . However, in order to make an objective judgement, we should take into account the circumstances that led up to this action . . . , an unlawful threat to the lives and security of innocent persons (France)[16]

Two draft resolutions were submitted to the Council. One, by the three African members, would have condemned Israel's 'flagrant violation of Uganda's sovereignty and territorial integrity', but the sponsors decided not to insist on this being put to the vote. The other, submitted by Britain and the United States, would have condemned hijacking, deplored the loss of life, and reaffirmed the Charter requirement to respect the sovereignty and territorial integrity of all States. This received the affirmative votes of the five Western members and Japan, none against, but nine members either abstaining or not participating in the vote. The draft resolution was therefore not adopted – an interesting example of the so-called Hidden Veto.[17]

5 US HOSTAGES IN IRAN

The long-drawn-out crisis over US diplomatic and consular hostages in Iran began on 4 November 1979, when a mob of militant students surrounded the US embassy in Tehran. There had been a similar incident the previous February, but this had been contained by the Iranian authorities. In the November incident, two US diplomats (Bruce Laingen and Victor Tomseth) and one security officer (Michael Howland) were at the Foreign Ministry when the incident occurred, and the three of them were detained there. Five consular officers and one attaché managed to escape and take sanctuary in the Canadian embassy, leaving Iran secretly on 29 January 1980. Five female and eight African-American hostages were released on 18 and 19 November 1979, possibly following representations to Iran from the Palestine Liberation Organization; and one hostage who contracted multiple sclerosis was allowed to leave in July 1980. The remaining 52 hostages remained in captivity in frightening conditions for 444 days.

From the start, US Secretary of State Cyrus Vance hoped to solve the problem by resort to international institutions and diplomatic negotiations, if necessary using intermediaries. If these methods did not lead to a prompt resolution of the conflict, non-military coercive measures might be necessary; but he was resolutely opposed to military action of any kind for any purpose. Indeed, there were, from the start, divided counsels in both capitals. It was not clear whether the militant students in Tehran were acting on their own initiative or under the authority of the country's leaders, nor whether the Iranian religious and secular leaders were in full agreement at various stages. President Carter in Washington often received conflicting advice from Vance, who believed that the problem had to be solved without the use of military force, and from Carter's national security advisor, Zbigniew Brzezinski, who favoured tough military action either to rescue the hostages or to punish Iran. Moreover, the United States had great difficulty in persuading its friends and allies to cooperate in imposing coercive non-military measures against Iran. The decision of the United States to use the machinery of the United Nations and the International Court of Justice in the early months helped

Carter to resist internal pressures for imprudent military adventures. As far as Iran was concerned, the United Nations and the Court were simply tools at the disposal of the United States – or 'the Great Satan', as it was often called.

On 9 November, the United States issued to the UN Security Council a brief factual report of the incident and asked the Council to 'urgently consider what might be done to secure the release of the . . . personnel being held'. The President of the Council, following private consultations with Council members, issued a statement:

(i) expressing profound concern at the detention of American personnel;
(ii) emphasizing the inviolability of diplomatic personnel and establishments, in accordance with internationally accepted norms;
(iii) urging 'in the strongest terms' the release of the personnel being held; and
(iv) urging the Secretary-General to use his good offices in attaining this objective.

Iran, in a rather intemperate response, made no reference to the hostages but asked the United States to recognize the guilt of the former Shah and to return to Iran the property and funds of the Shah, members of his family, and the leading members of the former regime.[18]

It was a basic Iranian demand for the next eight months that the Shah should return to Iran and face his accusers. When the crisis erupted, the Shah had just arrived in the United States and was seriously ill in hospital, but on 15 December 1979 he moved to Panama, and on 23 March he left Panama for Egypt. This led to Iranian threats to put the hostages on trial. The Shah died of cancer on 27 July 1980.

On 25 November 1979, the Secretary-General, with the unanimous support of members of the Council, asked that the Security Council should be convened urgently, citing his power under the rarely-used Article 99 of the Charter, which allows him to bring to the attention of the Council 'any matter which in his opinion may threaten the maintenance of international peace and security'. Iran initially welcomed the Secretary-General's initiative, but when the Council met on the date suggested by Iran (1 December), the President of the Council announced that Iran would not be participating in the proceedings. The Secretary-General drew attention to two aspects of the problem: the US demand that the hostages be released, and Iran's grievances about injustices and abuses of human rights during the Shah's regime. The United States, with the general support of Council members and other participants in the debate, said that the hostages must be released *before* Iran's grievances could be dealt with, but Kuwait suggested that the Council might authorize the Secretary-General to establish a consultative body to help in identifying abuses and violations of human rights under the Shah's regime and any other legitimate grievances of the Iranian Government: this was an idea that Cyrus Vance had mentioned to UN Secretary-General Kurt Waldheim the previous week. During the course of the debate, the US Ambassador stated that the United States had initiated proceedings in the International Court of Justice. The Council, by unanimous vote, approved a draft resolution that had been prepared in private consultations. This called on Iran to release the hostages, urged Iran and the United States to exercise restraint and resolve their differences peacefully, and asked the Secretary-General to lend his good offices to secure the immediate implementation of the resolution.[19]

Two important military developments during the crisis affected the policies of the parties. On 27 December 1979, Soviet troops entered Afghanistan to prop up the country's ramshackle Communist regime. US experts found it difficult to assess the overall effect of this act on the strategic situation of the region, but it was a move that worried the West, which was soon arming guerrilla fighters opposed to the new Government in Kabul. Then, on 22 September 1980, Iraq invaded Iran, thus placing strains on the Iranian economy at a time when sanctions were beginning to bite.

The US request to the International Court of Justice received prompt attention. On 15 December, the Court unanimously ordered Iran, as a provisional measure, to release all US hostages immediately and afford them full protection, and to restore diplomatic and consular premises in Tehran to US control. The two Governments were ordered not to aggravate the tension nor render the dispute more difficult of solution.[20]

On 22 December, Secretary-General Waldheim reported to the Security Council in writing that his contacts with the parties had produced no progress but that he would continue his efforts. He subsequently elaborated the written report in an oral statement in the Security Council. On the same day that Waldheim issued his written report, the United States requested an early meeting of the Security Council to consider 'measures which might induce Iran to comply with its international obligations'. The United States assured the Council that, once the hostages were released, it would be 'prepared to discuss Iran's claimed grievances'.[21]

The Council held three meetings at the end of December. Vance said that the Council should now condemn Iran for its failure to comply with the Council's previous decisions and the provisional measures ordered by the International Court of Justice; should ask the Secretary-General to intensify his efforts; and should warn Iran that if the hostages had not been released by an early date, the Council would have to impose non-military sanctions under Article 41 of the Charter. The United States would, in fact, have preferred that the Council should decide on economic sanctions against Iran immediately, but the general view in the Council was to proceed in stages. Several members of the Council, but not Britain, did say that they favoured mandatory sanctions under Article 41. The two Communist members, on the other hand, were opposed to any coercive action. The Soviet Ambassador stressed that the dispute was a bilateral one and did not fall within the ambit of Chapter VII of the UN Charter: sanctions would only exacerbate the situation and create a new threat to peace. A resolution incorporating the US position and deciding to meet again on 7 January 1980 was approved by 11 votes, the two Communist states and two other Council members abstaining.[22]

Waldheim now proceeded to Iran, but it was not a happy visit. He was not able to make progress on the issues between Iran and the United States, and he was attacked by an ill-disciplined crowd while visiting the Cemetery of the Martyrs, from which he made an undignified retreat by helicopter.

The final meeting of the Security Council on the hostage crisis convened on 11 January. The Council had before it a written report of the Secretary-General on his visit to Iran. He had discussed with the Iranian Foreign Minister the idea, mentioned privately by Vance and publicly by Kuwait, of a committee to investigate alleged violations of human rights and other illegal acts under the Shah's regime, but the Secretary-General had stressed in Tehran that the hostages must be released first or, at least, simultaneously. He stated that Iran was continuing to link the release of the hostages to the extradition of the Shah and the return of his assets. Waldheim said that it had been a useful trip in helping him to understand 'the many facets' of the crisis. When the Council convened, the US Ambassador made a brief statement about 'certain suggestions . . . of uncertain authority', whereupon the Council adjourned for two days. These 'suggestions' referred to Waldheim's request that a vote on sanctions be postponed because of indications that Iran was giving serious consideration to the idea of a commission of inquiry to look into Iranian grievances. When the Council resumed on 13 January, no progress on this aspect had been made, so the United States sponsored a draft resolution for comprehensive mandatory non-military sanctions against Iran under Articles 39 and 41 of the Charter. The Soviet Union repeated its view that a bilateral dispute between two States did not fall within Chapter VII of the Charter, and Mexico considered that the imposition of sanctions would be contrary to the Order of the International Court to avoid any action that might aggravate the situation. The US draft received 10 votes in favour but was vetoed by the Soviet Union.[23]

From this point on, the role of the Security Council was simply to be the recipient of documents: from the United States, announcing the severance of diplomatic relations with Iran and the imposition of economic sanctions (8 April 1980), reporting the failure of a rescue attempt (25 April 1980), transmitting the final judgement of the International Court of Justice (9 June 1980) and, at the end of the crisis, informing the Council of the agreements reached for the release of the hostages (20 January 1981); and from Iran, complaining of the US rescue attempt and expressing the suspicion that the United States was supporting Iraq in the Iraq–Iran war.[24]

But if the Security Council was no longer able to take effective action, the responsibilities of the UN Secretary-General had not been exhausted. An elaborate scenario was now worked out for Waldheim to transmit to Tehran. The United States still insisted that the first step should be the release of the hostages, but the United States now withdrew its opposition to a UN commission of inquiry, to be appointed by Waldheim, to hear Iranian grievances. On 20 February, at a press conference in New York, Waldheim announced the names of five members for the Commission, all highly respected, impartial, and strong-minded international figures. Waldheim refused to say whether there was a connection between the release of hostages and the hearing of Iranian grievances: 'All I can say in this delicate situation is that both aspects of the problem have been taken into account.' In fact, it had been agreed that the Commission would issue no report on Iran's grievances unless the Commission, as a minimum, had been able to meet all the hostages.[25]

The UN Commission assembled in Geneva, leaving for Tehran on 23 February. It was a frustrating time for the Commission. Like other UN bodies appointed on a representative basis, the Commission spent much of its time negotiating with itself. The Commission was able to begin the process of collecting information about Iranian grievances, but the expectation that they would be able to see the hostages never materialized. After the Commission had spent more than a fortnight hanging around fruitlessly in Tehran, the Ayatollah Khomeini announced that no hostages could be seen until Iran's grievances had been satisfactorily publicized. The Commission concluded that it could not fulfil its mandate. The next day, it left Tehran, and the expected report on Iran's grievances was never published. Waldheim later made it clear that the Commission was 'ready to resume its work whenever this may appear to be useful and oportune',[26] but the 'useful and opportune' moment never occurred.

On 7 April, the United States at last broke diplomatic relations with Iran and unilaterally imposed economic sanctions, and ten days later, further unilateral US coercive measures were announced. By now, Carter had authorized the rescue mission. Vance was on holiday when the crucial decision was taken on 11 April, but on 21 April he wrote to the President resigning his office – though the letter was not made public until after the rescue attempt. He was succeeded as Secretary of State by Senator Edmund Muskie.

The rescue mission was a daring operation. Eight helicopters were to rendezvous in darkness with six C-130 Hercules transport aircraft at a desert airstrip in Iran. The helicopters were to be refuelled, the C-130s would leave Iran, and the helicopters were to proceed to a remote site near Tehran. The following night, US forces would storm the embassy building and free the hostages, the helicopters would be destroyed, and US forces and the freed hostages would be flown out of Iran in US C-141 aircraft.

Unfortunately for the United States, three of the eight helicopters developed technical malfunctions, and, on the advice of the military and with Carter's agreement, the mission had to be aborted. During the complicated manoeuvring on unfamiliar terrain in darkness, one of the five surviving helicopters collided with one of the C-130s, which then burst into flames. The Iranian authorities now ordered that the 49 hostages should be removed from the US embassy and dispersed throughout the country.

The next event in this long-drawn-out saga was the final judgment of the International Court of Justice, issued on 24 May. The Court commented that, while US frustration was understandable, the rescue attempt was 'of a kind calculated to undermine respect for the judicial process in international relations'. The Court took note of Iran's view that the question of the hostages was of secondary importance and that the Court could not take cognizance of the hostage issue apart from the 'grave, flagrant and continuous violations of all international norms, committed by the United States'. The Court, in response, stated that Iran had not had recourse to the normal remedies open to it. The detention of internationally protected persons was not a marginal or secondary matter. The Court was entitled, under Article 36 of the UN Charter, to make recommendations to the Security Council on a legal dispute. It decided that Iran had violated and was still violating customary international law as well as international conventions in force between the two countries. The Court called on Iran to release the hostages and to make reparations to the United States for the injury caused.[27]

As Iran had ignored the decisions of the Security Council and the International Court of Justice, and as the rescue attempt had failed, the United States now turned to the good offices of intermediaries. Since January, US officials had been discussing the terms of a possible settlement with two Paris-based lawyers (Hector Villalon and Christian Bourquet), who had access to senior Iranian sources. In May, there began a series of meetings in what was then the Federal Republic of Germany. These discussions oscillated between apparent progress and definite retreat. In October, the Iranian Prime Minister, Mohammed Ali Rajai, visited UN headquarters to solicit support over the Iraq–Iran war, and was disconcerted to discover how little backing there was in UN circles for Iran on the hostage issue. On 2 November, the Iranian Majlis (legislature) issued a five-point statement for the settlement of the problem:

(1) The United States to promise not to interfere in the internal affairs of Iran;
(2) The United States to unfreeze all Iranian assets;
(3) The United States to cancel all economic and financial sanctions against Iran;
(4) All the assets of 'the cursed Shah' and his close relatives should be returned to Iran;
(5) In return for these conditions, Iran would release 'all 52 US criminals'.[28]

There was no mention of putting the hostages on trial. Iran suggested that Algeria should exercise good offices. After tortuous negotiations, a settlement was finally reached on 20 January 1981, the day that Ronald Reagan succeeded Jimmy Carter as President, and the hostages were repatriated via Algiers after 444 days in captivity.

The agreement was extremely complicated and consisted of five principal documents. The United States declared that it would not intervene in the internal affairs of Iran. Once the hostages were released, the United States would release Iranian assets and revoke all trade sanctions. The United States would freeze all assets of the Shah within its jurisdiction and would not prevent Iran from engaging in litigation to recover such assets. An international arbitration tribunal would be established to decide claims by nationals of each of the two States against the other, and certain claims of each of the two States against the other.[29]

6 INCIDENT IN THE SEYCHELLES

The attack on the Seychelles in 1981 aroused concern primarily because it was conducted by mercenaries in an attempt to organize a *coup d'état* against President Albert René and in favour of James Mancham (the deposed President), but two incidental issues fall within the scope of this chapter: the taking of hostages and the hijacking of an Air-India aircraft to enable the mercenaries to escape to South Africa. The mercenaries landed at Pointe Larue in the Seychelles, where they took hostage some seventy airport staff and commandeered an Air-India aircraft *en route* for Bombay. The hijacked plane proceeded to Durban. The Security Council adopted two resolutions unanimously, the first condemning the aggression against the Seychelles and appointing a commission to investigate the incident and to evaluate the economic damage suffered by the Seychelles, the second condemning the mercenary aggression against the Seychelles and appealing for economic assistance to the Seychelles to repair the damage, France being designated to coordinate and mobilize the necessary resources.[30]

There was substantial evidence of South African complicity in the affair, but this was consistently denied by the South African Government.

7 THE *ACHILLE LAURO* AFFAIR

The hijacking of the Italian cruise-liner, the *Achille Lauro*, in October 1985 turned out to be an extremely complicated business. The liner was hijacked off Port Said by four members of the Palestine Liberation Front, who demanded the release of 50 Palestinian prisoners being held in Israel. When this demand was resisted, the hijackers killed an elderly American Jewish passenger, Leon Klinghoffer, and had his body and wheelchair thrown into the sea. The Security Council met at the request of Greece, and the President of the Council was authorized to make a statement deploring the death of Klinghoffer and condemning hijacking and other forms of terrorism.[31]

The *Achille Lauro*, with the hijackers in charge, proceeded to Tartus in Syria, but was refused permission to dock: it therefore returned to Port Said, where the hijackers surrendered to the Egyptian authorities: Egypt had no wish to be implicated in the affair, and the four hijackers together with Abu Abbas (who had masterminded the operation) were placed on an Egyptian aircraft for transfer to Tunis. The Egyptian plane was intercepted by US military aircraft and forced to land at a NATO base in Sicily, where the hijackers were arrested by the Italian authorities. The United States demanded that Abbas be arrested and the hijackers extradited to the United States. Italy refused, and Abbas and a Palestinian colleague were allowed to leave for Yugoslavia. This led to dissension within the Italian Government, the resignation of Defence Minister Giovanni Spadolini, and the collapse of Bettino Craxi's coalition government.

8 DIVERSION OF EGYPTIAN PLANE

Six weeks after the *Achille Lauro* affair, Egypt was the victim of a terrorist assault when one of its aircraft was hijacked by four Arabs while *en route* from Athens to Cairo. There was a brief exchange of fire between the hijackers and Egyptian security personnel, the fuselage of the plane was punctured, and the aircraft made an emergency landing at Luga airport in Malta. The hijackers released 13 female passengers and crew, and then asked that the plane be refuelled. When this was refused, the hijackers said they would shoot one of the hostages every hour. While the negotiations and the first shootings were taking place, an Egyptian commando unit stormed the plane, which caught fire. Fifty-seven of the passengers and hijackers died during the rescue attempt.

There has been some uncertainty as to the identity of the organization from which the hijackers came, but it seems likely that they were from a shadowy Arab group backed and financed by the extremist Abu Nidal faction.

The United States called for the Security Council to meet to consider 'acts of hostage-taking and abduction'. The Council, without debate, unanimously adopted a resolution condemning all acts of hostage-taking and abduction, and appealing for effective international action to facilitate the prevention, prosecution and punishment of those responsible for such acts.[32]

9 ATTACKS ON ROME AND VIENNA AIRPORTS

It was almost certainly the Abu Nidal group that was responsible for the simultaneous attacks on the Leonardo da Vinci airport in Rome and the Schwecat airport at Vienna on 27 December 1985. The four Arab terrorists in Rome threw hand-grenades and opened fire on passengers waiting to check in for Israeli and US flights. Fifteen people died and over 70 were injured before Italian police and Israeli security personnel were able to kill or capture the terrorists. The attack in Vienna was directed at passengers waiting to check in for an Israeli flight. Two people were killed and 45 were wounded. One of the terrorists was killed by Austrian police and two surrendered.

At the end of a meeting of the Security Council called to consider a complaint of Lesotho against South Africa, and after a brief suspension of the meeting for consultations, the President of the Council made a statement on behalf of members of the Council, condemning 'the unjustifiable and criminal attacks' which had led to 'the taking of innocent human lives', and urging that those responsible be brought to trial 'in accordance with due process of law'. Governments and other authorities were urged to bring to an end all acts, methods and practices of terrorism.[33]

10 DIVERSION OF ARAB PLANE

Like 3 above, this was an attempt by Israel to capture an alleged terrorist, an attempt which misfired because of faulty intelligence. On 4 February 1986, Israeli fighter aircraft intercepted near Cyprus a Libyan passenger aircraft flying from Tripoli to Damascus and forced it to land at a military airfield in Israel. The passengers included an official Syrian delegation. The Security Council held three meetings at the request of Syria. Israel explained that the plane was believed to be carrying terrorists, but that this had proved to be unfounded, and the plane was allowed to continue its journey. 'Why this matter is a subject for an urgent meeting of the Security Council,' complained Israeli Ambassador Netanyahu, 'I do not know.' Syria responded that Israel was founded on terrorism; 'Israel brought terrorism to the heart of the Arab world.' A draft resolution submitted by five Third World countries would have condemned the Israeli action as a grave violation of international law, but this was vetoed by the United States on the ground that it did not take sufficient account of 'the need to address . . . the overriding issue of terrorism'. Although the United States was in general opposed to the interception of civil aircraft, 'there may arise exceptional circumstances in which an interception may be justified'.[34]

11 US BOMBING OF LIBYA

Tension between the United States and Libya escalated in the spring of 1986, and there were a number of provocative acts by both countries in the Gulf of Sirte, off the Libyan coast.[35] On 5 April, a bomb exploded in a Berlin nightclub (La Belle), killing one US soldier and a young Turkish woman and injuring over 100 other people. The United States, believing that it had 'evidence of direct Libyan involvement', bombed Tripoli, using aircraft based in Britain and aircraft from carriers in the Mediterranean, killing 37 people. The United States claimed to be acting under the self-defence provisions of the UN Charter. This action was widely disapproved of, France and Spain refusing overflying rights to the UK-based aircraft. Britain agreed to the operation so long as it was directed against targets involved in the conduct and support of terrorism, and the British Ambassador told the Security Council that Libya had provided the Provisional IRA with money and weapons. Nine meetings of the Security Council were held at the request of Libya and other Third World countries, one meeting being suspended for a short while because of a security alert. A draft resolution sponsored by five Third World countries would have condemned both the US attack and 'all terrorist activities whether perpetrated by individuals, groups or States', but this was vetoed by Britain, France, and the United States.[36]

12 HOSTAGE-TAKING CONDEMNED

Increasing concern about terrorism led the Security Council to issue a further statement on 28 January 1987. This recalled the Council's previous decision of 18 December 1985 (8 above, pp. 106–7) by which the Council had condemned unequivocally all acts of hostage-taking and abduction, and had called for the immediate safe release of all hostages and abducted persons wherever and by whomever they were being held. 'Conscious of the serious implications of this issue and, in particular, its humanitarian aspects, the members of the Council again condemn all acts of hostage-taking and abduction and demand the immediate and safe release of all hostages and abducted persons.'[37]

13 COLONEL HIGGINS KIDNAPPED

The Security Council's condemnation of kidnappings and abductions did not prevent the Hizbollah group in the Lebanon from kidnapping a UN officer of US nationality, Lt-Col. William R. Higgins, on 17 February 1988. Higgins was serving with the UN Truce Supervision Organization and the UN Interim Force in the Lebanon. His kidnappers alleged that he was a CIA agent. The Security Council, in the course of a meeting on the renewal of the mandate of the UN Force in the Lebanon, unanimously condemned the abduction of Higgins and demanded his immediate release.[38]

In July 1989, Israel kidnapped Sheikh Abdul Karim Obeid in the hope of exchanging him for Israelis held in the Lebanon. The captors of Colonel Higgins then announced that he had been hanged, though it is not certain when this appalling event had actually taken place. The Council held two meetings on 31 July. The President, as agreed in prior consultations, said that it was a tragic irony that the murder of Higgins should have become known when the Council was actively considering the problem of hostage-taking and abduction. The Council then adopted unanimously a resolution sponsored by Canada and Finland, unequivocally condemning all acts of hostage-taking and abduction, and calling on States to use their influence to secure the safe release of all hostages and abducted persons.[39]

14 MARKING OF EXPLOSIVES

On 14 June 1989, probably on the initiative of Britain and arising from the destruction of Pan-American flight 103 over Lockerbie the previous December, the Security Council unanimously adopted a resolution expressing the usual sentiments about terrorism, but in addition calling for research and action directed towards the means of detecting plastic or sheet explosives. In 1991, the Assembly of the International Civil Aviation Organization adopted by consensus a new Convention on the marking of plastic explosives for the purpose of detection.[40]

15 IRAQ TO DISCONTINUE SUPPORT FOR TERRORISTS

One operative paragraph in the ceasefire resolution following the expulsion of Iraqi forces from Kuwait required Iraq to inform the Security Council that it would not commit or support any act of international terrorism or allow any organization directed towards commission of such acts to operate within its territory, and to condemn unequivocally and renounce all acts, methods and practices of terrorism. In response, Iraq stated that it was a party to and was abiding by the obligations of international conventions relating to numerous aspects of terrorism. 'Iraq has not supported any terrorist activities.'[41]

16 LIBYA ASKED TO HAND OVER SUSPECTS

Following the destruction of Pan-American flight 103 over Lockerbie on 21 December 1988 and of the French UTA flight 772 over Niger on 19 September 1989, France asked Libya to cooperate with the French judicial authorities in establishing responsibility for the destruction of UTA flight 772. Britain and the United States claimed to have evidence implicating two Libyan nationals in the destruction of Pan-Am flight 103, Abdelbaset Ali Mohamed Al-Megrahi and Al-Amin Kalifa Fhimah. Warrants for the arrest of the two individuals were duly issued.[42] Libya denied that any of its nationals were involved in the two incidents.[43] In view of Libya's refusal to hand over the two suspects, the Security Council on 21 January 1992 deplored Libya's failure to respond effectively to the requests of the three governments, and asked the UN Secretary-General to seek Libyan cooperation in providing 'a full and effective response'.[44]

The Secretary-General issued two reports to the Security Council, indicating that there had been 'a certain evolution in the position of the Libyan authorities', in that Libya was willing to accede to the French request, but that the Security Council's resolution had not yet been complied with. The Council met on 31 March 1992 and, by 10 votes to 5 (China and four other non-aligned nations) and, acting under Chapter VII of the Charter, imposed specified non-military mandatory sanctions against Libya if Libya had not complied with the Council's previous resolution by 15 April. The sanctions were aimed at prohibiting the supply of arms to Libya, ceasing all cooperation with Libyan Airlines, and reducing the number and level of staff at Libyan diplomatic and consular posts.[45]

Meanwhile, Libya had on 3 March instituted proceedings in the International Court of Justice against Britain and the United States, alleging that the two States had failed to settle their disputes with Libya through the mechanisms of the Montreal Convention for suppressing unlawful acts against civil aviation and asking the Court to indicate provisional measures. The Court's decision, announced on 14 April 1992, was that it was not required to indicate provisional measures. All UN Members were obliged to accept and carry out the decisions of the Security Council, including the decision on sanctions against Libya. According to Article 103 of the Charter, obligations under the UN Charter prevail over obligations under other international agreements. The rights claimed by Libya under the Montreal Convention could not be the basis for provisional measures.[46]

There the matter rested as far as the United Nations was concerned, but the Arab League was engaged in a separate effort to find a solution and, on 5 April 1993, the League urged the Security Council to take no further action for three months which might adversely affect the League's endeavours. This effort did not meet with success, and on 11 November, the Security Council confirmed its sanctions policy and extended them to include a freeze of Libyan assets. This policy was reaffirmed on 10 December 1993.[47]

THE ROLE OF THE SECURITY COUNCIL

According to the US State Department, there were 'more than 600 international terrorist incidents' in 1984.[48] It is a reasonable assumption that 1984 was a typical year, so that since 1970, there have been at least 10 000 international terrorist incidents.

Nine cases of terrorism came before the Security Council. There were also four cases of counter-terrorism, two being the diversion of civil aircraft by Israel in the mistaken belief that terrorists were aboard (3 and 10 above), one being the rescue by Israel of hostages held at

Entebbe (4 above), and one being the air attack on Libya by the United States in retaliation for a terrorist incident in Berlin (11). There was one general condemnation of hostage-taking (12), one request to States to put special markings in plastic or sheet explosives (14), and Iraq was asked to renounce support for terrorist organizations or actions (15). In two of the remaining cases, statements condemning particular acts of terrorism were issued by the President of the Security Council without debate (7 and 9). In four cases, the Security Council denounced particular acts of terrorism, expressed sympathy for the victims, or asked States to cooperate in preventing further terrorist outrages (2, 6, 8 and 13). In the case of the US hostages in Tehran, the Council called for their release and urged the two governments to exercise restraint, but a US proposal to impose non-military sanctions against Iran ran into a Soviet veto (5). The Security Council's action against Libya after the blowing-up of two civilian aircraft was unprecedented in that the Council, acting under Chapter VII of the UN Charter, imposed selective sanctions against Libya after Libya had refused to hand over the suspects (16). In three cases, there were vetoes (5, by the Soviet Union; 10, by the United States; 11, by Britain, France and the United States) and, in one case, the only proposal put to the vote failed to secure sufficient affirmative votes to pass (4).

States take issues to the Security Council from a variety of motives. Sometimes it is because they wish for action, as in cases 5 and 16. Sometimes it is because of a sense of national impotence; public opinion demands that 'something must be done'. To obtain Security Council resolutions, as in cases 1, 6, 8, 15 and 16, or presidential statements, as in cases 7 and 9, enables governments to tell their own public that they did their best by using established international procedures.

Part of the difficulty of dealing with international terrorism is that many of the most outrageous acts are committed by non-State entities, and the perpetrators normally live an underground existence, beyond the reach of law. In some cases, they are given sanctuary and even support by governments. Extradition has not so far proved an effective procedure in the instances that have come before the Security Council, witness case 7 and (at the time of going to press) case 16.

One innovation that might have had a marginal deterrent effect would be the establishment of a permanent international criminal court or tribunal, before which individuals could be brought who were alleged to have committed violations of existing international law. The creation of such a court or tribunal has been on the international agenda since 1947, but some influential governments, while not wishing publicly to oppose the creation of such a court or tribunal, are uneasy about the idea of an institution that might be used against their own nationals. They therefore advocate *ad hoc* arrangements, such as the Nürnberg and Tokyo tribunals established in 1945 and the tribunal relating to former Yugoslavia established in 1993. Although the Nürnberg and Tokyo tribunals did their best to apply existing law, there is something distasteful about the creation of *ad hoc* courts with retroactive jurisdiction and dealing with some but not all grave violations of international law.

A permanent court would have to be composed of independent judges and act without fear or favour. It would deal with alleged violations of international treaty law, such as breaches of international humanitarian law, genocide, international terrorism, crimes against humanity, the illicit traffic in narcotic drugs, the slave trade and the draft Code of Offences against the Peace and Security of Mankind.[49]

The creation of a permanent court or tribunal would, of course, be no panacea. It is rare for the perpetrators of terrorist crimes to fall into the hands of those responsible for the enforcement of law, and extradition has so far proved an inadequate mechanism. Much depends on the outcome of case 16 and, in particular, whether Libya is prepared to hand over the two suspects and, if they are handed over, if independent opinion considers that any subsequent trials were fairly conducted.[50]

5 The Case-by-Case Approach

For the first four decades, the Security Council dealt with most human rights issues on an *ad hoc* basis. The single exception to this practice was the issue of self-determination, which preoccupied many UN organs in addition to the Security Council. There were occasional references to human rights instruments in resolutions[1] or speeches.[2] Occasionally the Council would include in a resolution or statement an appeal in general terms to respect human rights.[3] From time to time, the Council received documents regarding human rights from other UN organs.[4] The Council also received from UN Members documents alleging violations of human rights by other UN Members, but with no expectation that the Council would debate the matter or take a decision. That was probably the situation regarding a Soviet document in 1950 alleging 'unremitting terrorism and mass executions in Greece'. Britain stated in the Council that matters dealt with in the Soviet document 'are clearly within the sphere of Greek domestic jurisdiction, and the United Nations . . . is therefore precluded from discussing them'. The Council rejected the Soviet proposal to include the item in the agenda.[5] Some States that have been criticized for failing to respect the human rights of those for whom they are responsible have turned the tables by criticizing their critics. In 1990, Israel circulated to the Security Council some of the Country Reports on Human Rights prepared by the US State Department, relating to eighteen States that had criticized Israeli policy.[6] A recent, and respectable, use of this procedure was a document from Portugal alleging massive violations of human rights in East Timor.[7]

The Council has, from the earliest years, appealed for death sentences not to be carried out, for the release of political prisoners, or for the release or exchange of POWs: in Kashmir,[8] Indonesia,[9] the Middle East,[10] South Africa,[11] Southern Rhodesia,[12] Namibia,[13] and Portugese Territories.[14] In 1980, the Council condemned the assassination attempts against a number of Palestinian mayors in the territory occupied by Israel.[15]

Beginning in 1980, the Council began appealing for clemency for named persons in South Africa, including on several occasions Nelson Mandela.[16]

THE CONGO (ZAIRE)

There were two exceptions to the reluctance of the Security Council to take up general questions of human rights between 1946 and the 1990s. The first followed the widespread breakdown of law and order in the Congo (Zaire) in the early months of 1961. It was during this period that Patrice Lumumba was murdered.[17] A series of reports from the Special Representative of the Secretary-General in the Congo referred to arbitrary arrests, deportations, and other violations of fundamental rights. The Security Council noted with regret 'the systematic violations of human rights and fundamental freedoms and the general absence of the rule of law in the Congo', and authorized the UN peacekeeping force to use force 'if necessary in the last resort'.[18]

EAST TIMOR

The second case of the Security Council's willingness to take up human rights issues in a particular territory concerned East Timor. The future status of East Timor (then a Portuguese overseas territory) became a matter of controversy after the revolution in Portugal on 23 April 1974. Several Timorese political groupings were formed, but when the Revolutionary Front for the Independence of East Timor (FRETILIN) declared the territory to be independent, Indonesian 'volunteers' entered the territory, and a provisonal government under Indonesian auspices was formed. The Portugese enclave of Oecusse Ambeno was reported to have merged with Indonesia on 13 December 1975, and in July 1976, Indonesia agreed to a 'request' from a Timorese assembly that East Timor should become Indonesia's twenty-seventh province.[19] The matter was considered by the Security Council at the request of Portugal (and also in the General Assembly), and the Council unanimously called on Indonesia to withdraw from East Timor and asked the Secretary-General to send a special representative to the area 'for the purpose of making an on-the-spot assessment of the existing situation' in order to ensure the implementation of the Council's resolution. The Secretary-General appointed Vittorio Winspeare Guicciardi, an experienced UN official, to undertake this assignment. Winspeare, after visiting Lisbon and Djakarta, went to East Timor, but was unable to obtain transport to visit areas that FRETILIN claimed to hold. He concluded that any accurate assessment of the situation as a whole was 'elusive', but he expressed the hope that it might be possible to build on 'the slender common assumption that the people of East Timor should be consulted on the future status of the Territory'. His report was considered by the Security Council, and the Council called on Indonesia to withdraw its forces without delay.[20]

Disturbances in East Timor were reported from time to time, and UN organs continued to call for the withdrawal of Indonesian forces, to no avail. East Timor and the Oecusse Ambeno enclave now formed part of Indonesia, achieved by what the UN committee on decolonization called 'unilateral integration', although there was no evidence that this was what the people of the territories had wanted after the ending of Portuguese colonial rule.[21] A new crisis arose in 1989 when Australia concluded an agreement with Indonesia regarding cooperation in the so-called Timor Gap, an act which many UN Members considered to be a violation of previous UN decisions.[22]

EL SALVADOR

It was not until the 1990s that the Security Council began to concern itself with human rights in a systematic way. The first case concerned El Salvador, deriving from an agreement signed in San José (Costa Rica) on 26 July 1990 between the Government of El Salvador and the Frente Farabundo Martí para la Liberación Nacional (FMLN). This was one of a series of agreements designed to end the civil war through political negotiations, to consolidate democratic institutions, and to reunite and reconcile the antagonistic elements of Salvadorian society. The San José agreement established a set of norms for the protection of human rights, with a UN mission to verify that the agreed norms were being respected and to investigate alleged violations. There already existed a UN Observer Group in the region (ONUCA), and this was replaced in 1991 by a UN Observer Mission (ONUSAL) to monitor all agreements between the Government of El Salvador and the FMLN.[23] This was the first time that a UN peacekeeping operation had been expressly entrusted with responsibilities regarding human rights.

Parallel to the efforts of the Security Council were the fact-finding and related activities since 1981 of two Special Representatives of the UN Commission on Human Rights (José Antonio Pastor Ridruejo and Pedro Nikken).

When ONUSAL began its work, it found the situation characterized by 'serious, systematic and massive violations of human rights'.[24] The Human Rights Division, one of ONUSAL's three functional units, issued eight reports covering the period 26 July 1991 to 31 July 1993.[25] The first phase of the work, spread over three months, was simply to create the necessary *ad hoc* machinery, even though a ceasefire had not yet come into force. This involved the establishment of regional offices, extensive travel by UN staff to all parts of the country as a confidence-building measure, and the beginning of a public information campaign about the tasks and limitations of the operation. During this period, ONUSAL investigated over one thousand complaints of human rights violations attributable to the Government or the FMLN, the largest numbers dealing with illegal or arbitrary detention or forced recruitment for military service. The process of developing systematic criteria for assessing complaints was not easy, partly because what the population wanted did not always fall strictly within ONUSAL's mandate.

During the second phase, a peace agreement was signed in Mexico City and a formal ceasefire began.[26] Various requests were directed to ONUSAL which again fell outside its mandate, including questions relating to the ownership of land, the imposition of war taxes, and labour disputes. The number of complaints averaged four to five hundred a month, but were declining slightly as the fighting stopped.

During the third phase, May to October 1992, ONUSAL was able to institute various processes for the active investigation of complaints. Although the ceasefire had taken hold, the majority of alleged violations (including inadmissible complaints), still averaged some 450 a month and mainly alleged violations of human rights norms rather than of international humanitarian law (IHL). Most of the complaints regarding violations of IHL were attributable to the FMLN rather than the Goverment. ONUSAL was now able to address to the parties detailed comments about the better protection of human rights including, in particular, 'the lack of any institutional response with regard to the protection of the right to life and to integrity and security of person'. ONUSAL undertook an enhanced educational and informational campaign on human rights, mainly by means of training programmes and the dissemination of knowledge.

The fourth phase, beginning in November 1992, was notable for the strict observance of the ceasefire by both parties. Enforced disappearances and allegations of torture had virtually stopped, though there were still some complaints regarding the right to life, integrity and security of person. Of 1480 complaints declared admissible by ONUSAL between June 1992 and January 1993, only 19 related to alleged violation of international humanitarian law. Difficulties for ONUSAL were exacerbated by the inadequacy of Governmental procedures for dealing with ordinary crime. ONUSAL now felt able to offer more advice regarding the judicial system and other institutional mechanisms to uphold human rights. The operation was not directed simply at providing the sponsoring organs with information and verifying that agreements were being implemented: ONUSAL was also able to adopt 'consensus approaches and methods' with the parties to ensure the effective enjoyment of human rights and other goals specified in the agreements between the Government and the FMLN. The attainment of democracy, stated ONUSAL, is a slow and complex process; it does not follow automatically from peace but is 'difficult and fraught with contradictions'.

In October 1993, two leading members of the FMLN were assassinated, causing the Secretary-General to issue a special report on 'some worrying developments' arising from 'the persistence of serious human rights violations'. The Secretary-General was afraid that, unless there was a change in the behaviour of the parties, it would be impossible to hold the general election scheduled for March 1994.

One innovation in 1993 was the establishment of machinery for joint evaluation of human rights issues 'at the highest level'. The initial meetings proved to be 'highly satisfactory'.

One of the agreements between the parties, signed in Mexico City on 27 April 1991, provided for the establishment of a Commission on the Truth, the members to be appointed by the UN Secretary-General after consultation with the parties, the Commission to be 'entrusted with the task of investigating serious acts of violence that have occurred since 1980 and whose impact on society urgently requires that the public should know the truth'. The Commission received no fewer than 22 000 complaints. There was some dissatisfaction on the Government side that the Commission had exceeded its mandate; the FMLN had a number of reservations about the procedure that had been followed but accepted the Commission's recommendations.[27]

A separate agreement related to the so-called 'purification' of the armed forces of the Government and the FMLN, involving an evaluation of past performance by a rigorous and impartial commission. The FMLN was supposed to complete an inventory of weapons that it held, and this was finished on schedule by 30 November 1992. The

Government had agreed to recall all arms distributed to civilians but failed to complete the process on time. The Commission on purification had recommended that the Government should reassign 102 military officers. When it became apparent that 15 of these officers had not been reassigned by the agreed date, the FMLN suspended the destruction of arms and military equipment. By April 1993, the reassignment of the 15 Government military officers had still not taken place. The FMLN resumed the destruction of weapons, however, and had completed the process for those in El Salvador by 11 February 1993, and those outside the country by 1 April.[28]

IRAQ

Iraq committed many violations of international human rights norms following its invasion and purported annexation of Kuwait on 2 August 1990. The International Committee of the Red Cross took the view that the conflict was an inter-State war, bringing into force the four Geneva Conventions and the First Additional Protocol, which *inter alia* prohibit the taking of hostages. Moreover, the Third Geneva Convention prohibits the placing of POWs in areas where they may be exposed to fire in a combat zone or to render areas immune from military operations, that is to say, the use of POWs as 'human shields' (Articles 19 and 23), and such acts took place in January 1991 when POWs were paraded through the streets of Baghdad and thus exposed to public ridicule (Article 13); and the Fourth Convention prohibits the taking of civilians as hostages (Article 34), the placing of protected persons so as to render points or areas immune from military operations (Article 23), and the denial to internees of sufficient food to keep them in a good state of health (Article 89).

Beginning some days after the invasion of Kuwait, Iraq started placing foreign nationals inside or close to military installations and denying food to foreign workers. The Security Council adopted four resolutions, two unanimously and two with Cuba and Yemen abstaining. These resolutions demanded that foreign nationals be allowed to leave Iraq, and that those choosing to remain be given 'immediate access to food, water and basic services'.[29]

During this time, Iraq was committing gross violations of international humanitarian law in Kuwait, particularly by the expulsion of civilians. This led the Security Council to affirm the applicability of the Fourth Geneva Convention (Civilians) and the responsibility of individuals who commit or order grave breaches of the Convention; to condemn attempts by Iraq 'to alter the demographic character of Kuwait'; and (after the ceasefire had entered into force in 1991) to release immediately under the auspices of Red Cross and Red Crescent societies 'all Kuwaiti and third country nationals' and to arrange for immediate access to and release of POWs.[30]

The problems faced by the Iraqi Kurds had been drawn to the attention of the Security Council on two previous occasions: in 1963, by the Soviet Union, and in 1969 by the United States. In neither case had a meeting of the Council been held. In 1991, the question of 'safe havens' for the Kurds was raised in private consultations, in implementation of the Charter requirement of 'respect for, and observance of, human rights and fundamental freedoms' (Article 55.c of the UN Charter). A variety of methods were considered, and in the end, the Security Council adopted a resolution which condemned the repression of Iraqi civilians, especially in the Kurdish areas; called on Iraq to end this repression which threatened international peace and security; and insisted that Iraq allow immediate access to international humanitarian organizations, and make available all necessary facilities to meet the plight of Iraqi civilians. It was presumably in pursuance of this resolution that Iraq agreed to accept the presence of 500 civilian UN guards. This latter agreement provided that UN personnel might include staff co-opted from non-governmental organizations. Their task would be to provide humanitarian assistance. UN guards would be permitted to carry side-arms 'which will be provided by the Iraqi authorities (subject to the approval of the United Nations)'. By October 1991, the full complement of guards had been deployed, representing 35 different nationalities. A 'no-fly' zone was imposed above the 36th parallel, but without the express authority of a UN organ. One UN guard was killed by 'irresponsible Kurdish irregulars', to use the words of official Iraqi sources.[31] As from August 1992, Iraq announced unilaterally that the 120 guards then in Iraq could remain, but no replacements or additional deployments would be permitted.[32]

At the other end of Iraq, known as the Southern Marshes and populated by Sh'ia Muslims, an uprising had broken out in March 1991. This had been suppressed with considerable brutality, especially in regard to religious and cultural matters. The Special Rapporteur of the UN Commission on Human Rights reported that there had been 'mass indiscriminate bombardments' which had violated the rights to life, personal integrity and due process of law. The inflow of basic foodstuffs and pharmaceuticals had been restricted, and the so-called 'Third River Project' for irrigating a central waterway had been terminated. The persons against whom these attacks were directed were said by Iraq to be military deserters or those accused of murder or rape.[33]

There had been informal discussions among the members of the Security Council about action that might be taken to induce the Government of Iraq to cease its threats to the rights of the Shi'a Arabs in the Southern Marshes, but agreement was not forthcoming. In the circumstances, some members of the Council unilaterally imposed a 'no-fly zone' below the 32nd parallel.

FORMER YUGOSLAVIA

It would be necessary to go back to the Holocaust, the Nazi assault against the Jews, to find suitable language to describe the violations of human rights in former Yugoslavia. There had been many acts of brutality in the half-century since the Nazis decided on the Final Solution, but none to which could be applied the term 'ethnic cleansing'. This mainly took place from 1992 onwards in the Serbian-controlled parts of what had formerly been Yugoslavia. To achieve the goal of 'ethnic cleansing' required acts of unprecedented brutality.[34]

The main characteristic of these events was their arbitrary nature: the use of torture, rape, the mutilation of corpses and other forms of instilling terror, the wanton destruction of churches and mosques, of homes, shops, farms, and places of business, attacks on hospitals and other medical institutions, and the mass expulsion of civilians. The Security Council had the will but not the means to prevent such acts, but it could at least collect and publicize the relevant information.[35]

It was the outrageous nature of the policy of 'ethnic cleansing', and the fact that it was apparently ordered or at least tolerated by the Serbian authorities, that led to the demand for a war-crimes tribunal, to which I referred in Chapter 3, pp. 85–8. The United Nations had adopted several resolutions dealing with war crimes and crimes against humanity, but these were limited to acts committed by States: the proposed international criminal tribunal would extend the concept of war crimes so as to deal also with abhorrent acts committed by individuals.[36]

CAMBODIA

When the Security Council first became involved in human rights issues in Cambodia, there were four factions at loggerheads: the National United Front for an Independent, Neutral, Peaceful and Cooperative Cambodia (FUNCINPEC) headed by Prince Norodom Sihanouk; the Khmer People's National Liberation Front (KPNLF) led by Son Sann; the Party of Democractic Kampuchea (PDK) led by Khieu Samphan (Khmer Rouge); and the Kampuchean People's Revolutionary Party, led by Heng Samrin.

The UN reports on human rights in Cambodia differed in style from those relating to El Salvador, Iraq and Yugoslavia. The latter had dealt with abuses and violations of international human rights standards: the published reports from Cambodia were pretty well confined to describing the machinery established by the UN.

One of the main aims of the UN operation was to bring the fighting to an end, and this required the promise of a free and fair election. This, in its turn, had to be based on a general respect for rights and freedoms. In addition to conventional work to bring the judiciary and the police up to civilized standards, the UN Transitional Authority in Cambodia (UNTAC) resorted to a number of innovative techniques for the promotion of human rights: a nationwide drawing contest on Human Rights Day, the use of video units to demonstrate basic human rights concepts, and the presentation of human rights themes on television, on radio, and in comic strips.[37]

An important step was taken when UNTAC persuaded the Supreme National Council of Cambodia to accede to the two UN Covenants on human rights, and subsequently to agree to accede to other human rights instruments. This provided a legal basis for the protection of human rights, though it remains to be seen to what extent the principles of the Covenants will be applied in a concrete manner. UNTAC also undertook a widespread programme of civic education so that international concepts could be given reality for ordinary people. Codes of conduct were developed for the judiciary and for law-enforcement officials. Training programmes were organized for judges and defence lawyers and for other groups of community leaders. A start was made in elaborating procedures for the investigation of human rights abuses.[38]

A much-needed reform of the prison system was instituted, and the International Committee of the Red Cross was given regular and free access to sick prisoners. A Prison Control Commission was established, leading to the release by August 1992 of 258 prisoners who had been detained without trial. UNTAC gave support to indigenous human rights groups, five of which had come into existence by January 1993. These organizations were given small grants for basic office expenses, access to a library and resource centre, and help in making contact with international non-governmental organizations.[39]

Although UNTAC was one of the most elaborate and costly operations ever undertaken by the United Nations, the human rights component was relatively inexpensive. 'The number of human rights officers required may be modest, since all UNTAC staff, operating in all areas of the mandate, would be charged with carrying out human rights functions, as an integral part of their primary duties.'[40]

THE ROLE OF THE SECURITY COUNCIL

The Security Council is the one principal UN organ without express authority to deal with human rights, except when the denial of rights creates a situation in which international peace and security are threatened or breached or aggression occurs, and the Council applies enforcement measures under Chapter VII of the Charter. Until the 1990s, the Council usually kept strictly within that constraint, but it gradually became apparent that the denial of human rights sometimes constitutes a cause of armed conflict. The Charter should not be lightly disregarded, of course, and the ban on intervening in matters which are essentially within the domestic jurisdiction of States is an important provision; but this, like other provisions of the Charter, is bound to evolve in the light of external circumstances. In the early years, the concept was given a strict interpretation, leaving little scope for the Security Council to take up issues of human rights; but over the decades, the Security Council and other UN organs have come to see that matters of domestic jurisdiction must be understood in the light of other principles in the Charter, and in particular the commitment of UN Members to promote respect for human rights and fundamental freedoms (Articles 1.3, 55.c and 56).

Moreover, it is not intervention if the Security Council acts in response to an invitation from governments or *de facto* authorities as, for example, in the cases of Haiti, El Salvador, Cambodia and Angola. There are, to be sure, borderline cases. Technically, the presence of UN guards in the Kurdish areas of Northern Iraq was with the agreement of the Government of Iraq and the local Kurdish organizations, but the Iraqi Government was in such a weakened state in 1991 that it could hardly resist 'proposals' emanating from the UN Coalition. East Timor was a case of decolonization that went wrong, in the sense that a neighbouring State (Indonesia) was able to manipulate the liberation movements so that all except one were asking for or acquiescing in union with Indonesia rather than a precarious independence. Yugoslavia was a special case. A number of powerful States had recognized the independence of some or all of the units of which Yugoslavia had been constituted, and the Security Council had resolved to be acting under Chapter VII of the Charter,[41] so that some of the Council's actions were regarded as 'enforcement measures', as those words are used in Article 2.7 of the Charter.

6 Human Rights and Peace

Whatever the founders of the United Nations may have thought in 1945, it is now widely understood that the perception that human rights are being denied is a frequent cause of armed conflict. The task of 'promoting and encouraging respect for human rights', as the Charter puts it, is primarily the responsibility of the Commission on Human Rights, its subsidiary organs, and the bodies set up by particular human rights treaties. The Security Council comes into the picture when violations of human rights are so gross, extensive and persistent as to endanger world peace. The members of the Security Council recognized this at the special high-level meeting held on 31 January 1992, when they agreed that 'non-military sources of instability . . . have become threats to peace and security'.[1] One scholar has noted that of 53 international instruments or declarations during the period 1945 to 1989, 'a little more than ninety per cent dealt in some fashion with the rights of human beings'.[2] The dividing lines between the various tasks which the UN is asked to perform are often blurred, so that sometimes (as in the cases of Haiti and Iraq, for example) more than one UN organ is involved. Coordination within the UN system is therefore of primary importance.

Moreover, war creates a host of humanitarian problems even if – which regrettably is rare – the belligerents fully respect international humanitarian law (*jus in bello*). Civilians are harmed or displaced as an unintended consequence of attacks on legitimate military targets. Hospitals and places of worship are damaged or destroyed. New waves of refugees and displaced persons leave their homes in search of safe havens. And when the fighting stops, whether from the exhaustion of both sides or the military victory of one side and defeat of the other, the belligerents still have to patch up the quarrel which caused the war in the first place. General Sherman, who knew what he was talking about, said that war was hell for the boys who had to do the fighting. Today we would have to say that war can be an even greater hell for the non-combatants.

The Security Council has increasingly cooperated with the International Committee of the Red Cross regarding the application and strengthening of international humanitarian law. Virtually all States are parties to the four Geneva Conventions of 1949, and the General Assembly regularly appeals to States to become parties to the

Additional Protocols of 1977 as well.[3] A number of further steps are desirable, however. For many years, the International Committee of the Red Cross has urged that the United Nations should itself become a party to the Geneva Conventions and Protocols. One can well understand that the ICRC should believe that this would strengthen the application of international humanitarian law in circumstances in which military units are operating under UN auspices. But one can equally well understand why successive UN Secretaries-General should take the view that 'improved legal protection of human rights in [UN] operations is likely to come from wider acceptance and application of humanitarian conventions by contributing States than it is from having the United Nations undertake obligations whose discharge would involve the exercise of an authority it has not yet been granted'.[4]

Two steps would be open to the Security Council at the present time. First, the Council could urge the Secretary-General not to accept military units for UN operations from States that are not parties to the main treaties comprising international humanitarian law, or at least for the Secretary-General to urge any such States to become parties at the earliest possible date.

The International Committee of the Red Cross has no means of enforcing international humanitarian law or of imposing penal sanctions against confirmed violators. There are, however, two Articles in the first Additional Protocol that have not yet been exploited. One (Article 89) urges the parties to the Protocol to cooperate with the United Nations in situations of serious violations of the Geneva Conventions and the first Additional Protocol. The next Article (90) provides for an international fact-finding commission to inquire into alleged grave breaches of international humanitarian law and to offer its good offices for restoring an attitude of respect for the Conventions and the first Protocol. This procedure was to come into force when 20 of the parties to the first Protocol agreed to accept the competence of the fact-finding commission. The twentieth acceptance of this provision was received on 25 June 1991, and 34 States had accepted the fact-finding procedure by January 1994.

It is already the case that there is duplication within the UN system for dealing with alleged breaches of human rights treaties and the treaties that constitute the basis of international humanitarian law. It would, however, be possible for the Security Council to adopt a resolution or presidential statement urging UN Members, and especially the permanent members of the Security Council, to make formal declarations in favour of the fact-finding procedure set out in Article 90 of the first Additional Protocol, and to invite the Secretary-General to enter into discussions with the International Committee of the Red Cross about cooperation and the avoidance of duplication regarding fact-finding.

It should not be forgotten that the four Geneva Conventions contain provisions for the repression of grave breaches of the Conventions (Articles 49/50/129/146), but these are dependent on actions by the parties, and the Security Council can itself, under Article 34 of the Charter, engage in fact-finding without resorting to the precise procedures laid down in Article 90 of the first Additional Protocol. Personally I greatly regret the failure to implement the Secretary-General's proposal in 1991 for a meeting of the parties to the fourth Geneva Convention to consider what could be done to induce Israel to apply the Convention *de jure*.[5]

It is, I think, evident from the preceding pages that the Security Council dealt with human rights in two phases: from 1946 to 1989, and from 1989 to the present time. In the first phase, the Council acted in a cautious, empirical, and haphazard way. There was uncertainty regarding what was meant by 'matters which are essentially within the domestic jurisdiction of any state', particularly in regard to colonial questions. Some of the colonial powers did their best to maintain the position that events in their dependent territories were matters of domestic jurisdiction and therefore beyond the scope of UN intervention, as the Netherlands did in 1947–49 regarding Indonesia (see pp. 17–18). This contention sometimes delayed Security Council action, but rarely prevented it altogether. In the background was the veto of the Permanent Five. It was not necessary for a permanent member of the Council to cast a negative vote: it was usually sufficient to *threaten* to do so.

It is widely believed that most vetoes in the Security Council have been cast by the Soviet Union; and that certainly was the case up to 1970, by which date there had been over one hundred Soviet vetoes. But the situation began to change after 1970; vetoes cast since then in open meetings of the Council have been as follows:

China	1
France	13
Soviet Union/Russian Federation	10
United Kingdom	24
USA	66

The Soviet veto in 1993 was of some interest. The draft resolution, submitted by Britain, was designed to change the system for financing the UN Force in Cyprus from voluntary contributions to compulsory assessments in accordance with the normal scale. This text was vetoed by the Soviet Union on 11 May, but later in the month, a resolution with virtually the same effect was adopted by the Security Council, the Soviet Union voting in favour.[6]

All but three of the British vetoes were of proposals relating to Southern Africa, joined on 11 occasions by France and on 18 occasions by the United States. Twenty-nine other US vetoes were of proposals to condemn Israel.

The world has been transformed in the past half-dozen years, and so has the United Nations. Until the 1980s, the medium and smaller powers complained that Cold War rivalries rendered the Security Council impotent. They were, however, able to play off one bloc against the other. No sane person wanted all-out war between the two major military blocs, but there were times when weak States found Cold War tensions to be rather convenient so long as the problems were sufficiently distant.

Now there is only one superpower. There are still five states with veto rights, but most decisions of the Security Council are now negotiated in private by two or three or five of the permanent members, and the agreed text is then presented to the full Security Council for approval. There is rarely any public debate nowadays: the Council is presented with a decision, and the non-permanent members are expected to endorse it without being aware of the arguments pro and con the text for which they are expected to cast affirmative votes, or at least to abstain. This procedure avoids polemical rhetoric directed at public opinion at home rather than to influence fellow-diplomats, and it also means that the work of the Council is not delayed by the lengthy speeches of non-members.

It has always been said that the major powers use double standards, and this was often the case during the worst days of the Cold War, and also over Southern Africa and Israel. And of course the big powers were by no means unique in this respect. Now the use of double standards is blatant. In December 1992, Israel deported 415 Islamic militants from the Occupied Territories in retaliation for the murder of a border policeman (Nissim Toledano). This happened at a time when the Security Council was applying Chapter VII sanctions against several Arab States for failing to respect mandatory decisions of the Security Council, but no action was taken against Israel for failing to implement the Security Council's demand that Israel should 'ensure the safe and immediate return to the occupied territories of all those deported'. The resolution also asked the Secretary-General 'to consider dispatching a representative to the area to follow up with the Israeli Government . . . this serious situation'.[7]

The Secretary-General sent three separate missions to the area and spoke several times himself with Prime Minister Rabin and Foreign Minister Peres, but Israel was adamant. The deportees were militant Muslims and supporters of Hamas or Islamic Jihad, they said. The Israeli action was intended to serve as a deterrent and would help to sustain the peace process. The deportees were not only endangering the lives of Jewish Israelis but were intimidating Palestinian supporters of peace. Palestinians who met with one of the UN envoys rashly assured him that the Palestinians would not resume peace talks with Israel unless the deportees were permitted to return.[8]

There the matter rested, but can anyone believe that if the offending State had been Iraq, say, or Libya, the Security Council would have let the matter rest?

It is partly because of dissatisfaction with this state of affairs that there is a growing demand to increase the number of members of the Security Council, so as to reduce the influence of the Permanent Five. Demands for a larger Council are claimed by Germany and Japan. At the present time, the Charter provides that any UN Member can be elected for two years out of three, but permanent membership in the Charter sense carries with it the right to veto substantive proposals.

The Charter states two requirements for the election of non-permanent members: 'due regard being specially paid, in the first instance to the contribution of Members of the United Nations to the maintenance of international peace and security and to the other purposes of the Organization, and also to equitable geographical distribution' (Article 23.1). It is also necessary, as a matter of common sense, for the size of the Council to be such that 'prompt and effective action' is possible in an emergency (Article 24.1).

The Council originally had 11 members when the total UN Membership was in the range 51 to 117. The membership of the Security Council was increased to 15 in 1965, and total UN Membership has now reached 184. With 10 places to be filled by election, it is not now possible to meet the second requirement of 'equitable geographical distribution'; but I doubt whether an enlarged Council would have dealt more effectively with the fifty or so cases with which I have been concerned in this book than did a Council of 11 or 15 members.

It was sometimes said that the United States, or the West in general, had an automatic voting majority in UN organs. That was never true, since diplomats do not decide how to vote until they have seen the precise wording of the proposal. What *was* true for many years was that the United States, or the West in general, could virtually always prevent a hostile coalition from getting their way on substantive matters by the threat or use of the veto or by organizing sufficient abstentions to make action impossible (the so-called Hidden Veto).

The belief that the Council is dominated by one superpower and its friends has led to some unhelpful competition between the General Assembly and the Security Council, as in the case of Nicaragua, and also in a series of reports to, debates in, and decisions taken by the General Assembly on national sovereignty and non-interference in the affairs of States in their electoral processes.[9] It was the intention of the founders that the Security Council and the General Assembly should not deal simultaneously with the same issue (Article 12.1). The practice since 1960 has been to find means of evading that provision.

It is notable how many of the fifty or so cases dealt with in the preceding pages concerned colonial territories or territories only recently emerged from dependent status. In the early years, the colonial powers often said that particular territories for which they were responsible were not yet ready to run their own affairs: I well recall the sense of outrage on the part of colonial powers in 1960 when the General Assembly voted that 'Inadequacy of . . . preparedness should never serve as a pretext for delaying independence.'[10] The people of territories that had been subjected to foreign rule, even if it was altruistic and benevolent, did not find it easy to adjust to the main democratic norms: that opposition is necessary for the healthy working of democratic institutions or that political opponents are as entitled to have their human rights respected as have political allies. One Asian diplomat told me in 1955 that he would rather be governed like hell by his fellow countrymen than governed like heaven by the former metropolitan power. Forty years later, his country is still governed like hell.

One might have thought that the debates and decisions of the Security Council on self-determination in Africa would be replete with references to UN norms regarding human rights, but that was not the case. Only in the case of South Africa does one find references in meetings of the Council to the Universal Declaration of Human Rights and other UN instruments.

The other notable feature of the cases dealt with in Chapter 1 was the resistance of the West to any determination under Chapter VII of the Charter, to make mandatory action possible. None of the decisions regarding Namibia were mandatory, and it was not until after the Unilateral Declaration of Independence by the white minority in Southern Rhodesia that the sanctions regime was progressively brought into force under Chapter VII of the Charter, and only in 1977 that the South African arms ban was made mandatory. Moreover, it was no secret that the decisions of the Security Council on sanctions were widely disregarded, usually with the knowledge of the governments concerned. It is difficult for governments that connived at sanctions-busting over Southern Africa to be taken seriously when they talk of mandatory sanctions against Iraq or Libya.

The Secretary-General suggested in 1992 that, because the United Nations had not been able to act effectively in bringing to an end massive violations of human rights, the Secretary-General himself and expert human rights bodies should be empowered to bring such matters to the attention of the Security Council, together with recommendations for action. When matters of this kind seem to the Secretary-General to threaten international peace and security, he already has the right under Article 99 of the Charter to draw the attention of the Security Council to the threatening situation, as did Waldheim over the hostages in Iran, and Rule 1 of the Council's Provisional Rules of Procedure empowers the President of the Council to call a meeting 'at any time he deems necessary'. I can find nothing in the Charter or the Council's Provisional Rules of Procedure that would prevent the Security Council from acting in the manner suggested by the Secretary-General, but there might be some marginal advantage in institutionalizing the Secretary-General's suggestion.[11]

In reaching a decision on whether the Security Council should become seized of any matter, members of the Council need to weigh up the relative strength of two principles to be found in the Charter: the principle that the UN shall not intervene in matters which are essentially within the domestic jurisdiction of any State unless the Council has decided to apply enforcement measures (Article 2.7), and the principle that UN Members shall cooperate in order to achieve universal respect for and observance of human rights and fundamental freedoms for all without distinction as to race, sex, language or religion (Articles 55.c and 56). It is possible, of course, to amend the Charter *de facto*. Since 1946, an abstention by a permanent member of the Council has been regarded as a concurring vote and not a veto (Article 27.3), and since 24 December 1991 the Russian Federation has been substituted for the Soviet Union as a permanent member of the Security Council (Article 23.1). In neither case was the Charter amended *de jure*.

Whether or not the Charter is amended, the Council has to decide in each case which is the overriding consideration: non-intervention in domestic affairs (Article 2.7) or international cooperation for the promotion of respect for, and observance of, human rights and fundamental freedoms (Articles 55.c and 56). During the first phase, 1946–88, non-intervention in internal affairs tended to be given priority; since 1989, cooperation regarding human rights has increasingly been given pride of place. I would not expect a British ambassador, when faced with a situation of 'unremitting terrorism and mass executions', to say today what one of his predecessors said in 1950, that this was a matter of domestic jurisdiction and therefore beyond the competence of the Security Council.[12] I would expect the Security Council to continue giving increasing pre-eminence to Articles 55 and 56 of the Charter, even if this should erode the strict interpretation of Article 2.7. I would also expect, though I would not necessarily welcome, a proliferation of subsidiary organs, working groups, special rapporteurs, and special representatives of the Secretary-General charged with human rights problems.

The Council is likely to resort increasingly to partial or comprehensive non-military sanctions, as have recently been applied against Iraq, Libya, Serbia, Haiti, UNITA in Angola (not a State but a party or movement within a State), and Liberia. But we have to admit that we do not know much about sanctions: whether they are intended to be symbolic or coercive, which products should be boycotted in any particular case, how the policy should be enforced, how long it would take for coercive sanctions to persuade the guilty party to change its policy, and what exemptions for humanitarian purposes would be appropriate in any particular case. If as much intellectual effort had been directed to how sanctions can be made to work as was directed in universities, research institutes, and foreign offices to nuclear deterrence between 1950 and 1990, we could now more confidently use sanctions as a penultimate means of coercion when human rights are being violated on a massive scale. We should bear in mind, of course, that sanctions tend to be indiscriminate in their effects, thus raising difficult ethical issues regarding the application of *jus in bello* principles.

One could, indeed, envisage a graduated series of coercive measures, beginning with the simple act of placing a matter on the agenda of the Council, passing a resolution of condemnation, engaging in fact-finding or investigation (Article 34 of the Charter), imposing non-military sanctions (Article 41), undertaking military measures of enforcement (Article 42), or suspending or expelling a Member from the Organization (Articles 5 and 6). What happens in fact is that the Security Council decides to apply sanctions under Chapter VII, appoints a subsidiary organ to assemble whatever evidence is available, and this body reports from time to time to the parent body. The Council decided on 6 August 1990 to apply sanctions against Iraq without having much idea how long it would take to have the desired effect (the immediate and unconditional withdrawal of Iraqi forces from Kuwait). At the beginning of November, the most important members of the UN Coalition decided that sanctions were not working, and that military enforcement would be needed before the summer heat would make military operations impossible for mainly white-skinned personnel. What I have not been able to discover is, who decided that sanctions were not working? The military? Diplomats? Politicians? Academic economists? Or was it just a gut feeling that because Iraqi forces were still in Kuwait, that the Iraqi Establishment was still oppressing Kurds in the North and Sh'ia Muslims in the South, and that Saddam Hussein was still in power in Baghdad, then the sanctions policy was not working?

If sanctions are effectively applied, innocent non-combatants will suffer. Indeed, the longer a sanctions regime is in force, the greater the suffering of innocent non-combatants. In my view, we should apply to non-military sanctions the same ethical criteria that we already apply to the conduct of military operations (*jus in bello*), and particularly, to the extent possible, the principles of discrimination and proportion. This is a difficult task, and especially so when the application of sanctions is in support of the human rights of a minority or, as in Southern Rhodesia and South Africa, the rights of an oppressed majority. The predicament over the cases in Southern Africa was lessened for some people since it was the oppressed community that urged the outside world to maintain and step up sanctions.

A most important task regarding the protection and promotion of human rights has been technical assistance in organizing elections and verifying that the process was free and fair. Until the case of Namibia in 1989, the role of the Security Council regarding electoral supervision was haphazard, inconsistent and inadequate. It is clearly of little use for the Council to receive reports from the Secretary-General or one of its own subsidiary organs if these reports are merely derived from the *de facto* authorities or the public media in the area concerned (Madura and Western Java in 1948, the Dominican Republic in 1966). It would no longer be considered adequate for an appointee of the Secretary-General simply to consult community leaders (Bahrain, 1970), though a procedure of this kind might be useful in providing an escape route for a government that has made impossible claims. It would not now be satisfactory for international observers to arrive only twenty-four or forty-eight hours before polling day (Palau, 1986 and 1987).

Until the Namibian operation, the conduct or verification of elections or other means of ascertaining the will of the people had been confined to dependent territories. In these cases, officials of the administering authorities came from countries where periodic free elections were taken for granted. Even junior officials would have a rough idea of the various processes. But after the Namibian operation of 1989, almost all the cases that came to the Security Council were from sovereign States, in many cases with no experience of democratic procedures (e.g. Haiti). As a result, the requesting State often needed advice and help about how to conduct a fair election, as well as the need to confirm that the process had been free and fair.

As the Namibian operation in 1989 had been generally regarded as a success, the Security Council became increasingly willing to authorize the supervision of elections, and the Secretariat has become increasingly competent at doing or supervising the job. For more than a decade, the Council had called for free elections under UN supervision and control as part of a Namibian settlement, and it was a piece of good luck that there was no serious challenge to the decisive result in that case. When requests were received from Haiti in 1990, the Secretary-General stated cautiously that electoral verification by the UN should be an exceptional activity, but he was able to suggest a set of guidelines to be taken into account when requests were received for electoral verification, and these were repeated in a special report to the General Assembly the following year.

It was, in his view, necessary for a request for electoral verification to meet certain criteria. In the case of Haiti, these were that the request should relate to a situation with an international dimension, that the monitoring should cover the entire electoral process, and that the request should have broad public support in the country concerned. These criteria were extended and clarified in the case of Angola: that the Security Council was already seized with the situation as it had established a peacekeeping force to monitor the ceasefire, that the conduct of internationally-supervised elections was a central element in the implementation of an agreed peace accord, and that the introduction of a UN presence in the electoral process had been officially requested by the Government at an important point in the peace process.[13] In some cases, a necessary precondition would also be the release of political prisoners and the return of exiles. The Code of Conduct adopted by political parties in Namibia (pp. 33–4) could serve as a model for other cases of electoral verification.[14]

In all the cases since 1989, the international observers reported that there had been some minor faults in organizing the election, but in no case were these on such a scale as to affect the result. UN officials should exert the greatest possible influence to prevent local registering officers from being paid at a *per capita* rate for every elector placed on the register, as happened in Haiti in 1990. It is too tempting for inexperienced officials in remote areas to succumb to improper pressures to fudge the normal procedures for financial gain or in response to bullying tactics.

The Secretary-General suggests that the criteria for judging whether an election is free and fair should include

> a well-rounded set of rules which provide an adequate legal framework for the electoral process; impartiality of the electoral authorities at all levels; the opportunity for all citizens to compete for elective positions; effective freedom of association, assembly, expression, and movement; a psychological, political, and social climate favourable to free and fair elections; fair and effective provisions for voter registration; effective procedures for polling and counting to prevent fraudulent practices and respect the secrecy of the vote; appropriate methods for processing complaints, petitions, and appeals; adequate access to the media by candidates and parties; a public properly informed of why, where, when, and how to vote; and the necessary access by representatives of opposition parties to all stages of the electoral process.[15]

In all the cases described in Chapter 2, the UN operation was undertaken at the request of the government on whose territory the election was taking place. In such circumstances, it is not reasonable to regard the United Nations as having intervened or interfered in matters which were essentially within the domestic jurisdiction of the State invoking UN assistance, any more than does the provision of other kinds of technical assistance. It is prudent, all the same, to ensure that there is broad public support for the United Nations assuming a supervisory role: that meant, for example, consulting the Democratic Turnhalle Alliance regarding Namibia, UNITA regarding Angola, and the Party of Democratic Kampuchea regarding Cambodia, preferably in a direct and formal manner, but if necessary informally and with the help of trusted intermediaries.

Throughout the election campaign, public officials should realize that they are there to serve the whole people. During the run-up to the plebiscite in Palau in December 1986, government officials were encouraged to campaign for one of the options being submitted to the people. The Soviet Union drew attention to this at a meeting of the Trusteeship Council, which led the British representative to say that the Visiting Mission 'had not been mandated to look into the political campaign preceding the vote; it had not been in Palau for the whole proceedings and therefore it would have been quite wrong to have attempted to pass judgement on that'.

It is, moreover, necessary to observe the registration of voters. In Haiti, for example, in seven out of nine Departments, the number of people registering to vote exceeded the official estimates of the adult population. The Secretary-General ascribed this to two possible causes: the unreliability of the 1982 census figures, and the fact that the inexperienced officials in charge of registration of voters were paid, 'not on the basis of the work done, but on the basis of the number of persons registered'.[16]

It is clear that UN supervisors should be in the country throughout the election campaign, on polling day, and when the votes are counted. They should, moreover, remain until the new government is installed. In Haiti, there was an attempted *coup* between the first round of voting on 16 December 1990 and the inauguration of the new president on 7 February 1991. In Angola, UNITA refused to accept the result of the first round of the election in September 1992 on the ground that there had been massive and systematic fraud. The election, instead of being a gateway to peace, provided a pretext for a renewal of the civil war.[17]

In some cases of electoral verification, it may be desirable for the UN to act in collaboration with other inter-governmental agencies or, occasionally, with non-governmental organizations such as the International Committee of the Red Cross or the Carter Institute or, for specialized tasks, humanitarian agencies such as Amnesty International or the Save the Children Fund. Cooperation by the UN with autonomous bodies with their own distinctive policies and budgets is never easy, especially if the UN or one of the collaborating bodies claims that its distinctive skills entitle it to play a leading role or to have a generous share of international funding, as has sometimes been the case with the International Committee of the Red Cross. It is a disagreeable experience to see humanitarian organizations competing for seats of honour, as it were, and forgetting the tragic conditions all around them.

There can also be competition between different UN agencies, especially when it comes to the organization or verification of elections (as happened over Nicaragua and Haiti). When the Security Council is already seized with issues in the country invoking electoral assistance, it would make sense for the Council to accept the main responsibility for decision-making regarding electoral matters; in other cases, there is no reason why the authorizing resolution should not be taken by the General Assembly. In either event, the operation in the field should be administered by the Secretary-General.

The UN, at the present time, is overloaded and underfunded. Between October 1991 and October 1993, the UN received no fewer than 58 requests for electoral assistance.[18] Some requests had to be turned down because of insufficient lead time or because the request was not sufficiently precise. The authorizing body, whether the Security Council or the General Assembly, must assess the relative importance and urgency of each request before saying 'yes'. It is of no long-term benefit for the UN or the Members of the UN to take on responsibility for electoral verification and then do the job so clumsily as to provide a pretext for one party to challenge the result. Coordination of electoral assistance within the UN Secretariat must be a nightmare. In a recent report, the UN Secretary-General mentioned the following staff units as having some responsibility in the matter:[19]

Centre for Human Rights
UN Development Programme
Department for Development Support and Management Services
Department for Political Affairs
Electoral Assistance Unit
High Commissioner for Refugees

Office for Project Services
Task Force on Electoral Matters
UN Volunteer Programme

It is little wonder that the provision of electoral assistance should place strains on an already overworked Secretariat.

All UN staff and those military units engaged in field operations need to maintain strict impartiality, other than loyalty to the United Nations and its purposes and principles. This is easy to write but difficult to perform in situations of tension. I once asked a senior UN military commander whether he had difficulty with bias of the military units assigned to him. Yes, he said, for the first six months they are strongly biased in favour of party A, and thereafter even more strongly biased in favour of party B. These reactions to local circumstances were not the views of experienced diplomats or scholars, but of ordinary men and women who had to make snap-judgements on the basis of the limited events that they saw with their own eyes.

What is interesting about public attitudes to UN operations is that if you ask people on whose behalf the operation was launched, you tend to get the same sort of reply: for the first six months, they say, we welcomed UN officials or military units with open arms, but then we discovered they were not on our side, so we began to treat them with suspicion. Dissatisfaction with the UN in El Salvador mounted as the people discovered that the tasks they wanted the UN to undertake were not within the mandate agreed by the Security Council.[20] It is for this reason that an essential element in the UN's verification is to engage seriously, promptly and persistently in a variety of confidence-building measures.

In order to do a proper job of supervision, UN staff should report only what they have seen with their own eyes: in the case of second-hand information, which in some instances may properly be reported to UN headquarters, the fact that it is second-hand should be made absolutely clear, and the recipient of the information can then make a judgement as to its reliability.

In cases where cross-border military raids are possible (as in Kashmir and Namibia), or where internal disturbances and tensions might interfere with the rule of law (as in El Salvador and Cambodia), it might be desirable to deploy peacekeeping units along disturbed frontiers or in areas of internal violence. I have used tentative language in the previous sentence, as the United Nations is now overworked, and there is a limit to the number of operations it can take on.

I can understand the uneasiness of some developing countries that UN supervision of elections will inevitably lead to a substantial international presence in fragile countries at a delicate time in their history, and that this might be abused by representatives of powerful States in order to promote their national interests at the expense of those of the host country. It is natural that former colonies should be on their guard against such abuses. The UN Secretary-General nearly always reports that, in any particular election, there were minor cases where proper procedures were not fully followed by local officials, but not to such an extent as to affect the result. It would not be surprising if there were also minor cases of improper action by some of the international supervisors, but also not to such an extent as to affect the result.

There are, in any case, certain safeguards. During and since the Namibia case in 1989, there has not been a single veto in the Security Council of a proposal for electoral assistance. The main hesitation in the Council came in 1990 regarding Haiti. After lengthy private consultations with the Secretary-General, the members of the Council, 'without prejudice to their positions on the competence of the organs of the United Nations on electoral assistance if requested', expressed the hope that another UN body (the General Assembly) would take 'urgent action' at Haiti's request.[21]

A substantial safeguard lies in the presence of regional observers in cases where the UN invites or accepts collaboration with a regional agency. In the forthcoming election in Mozambique, for example, the United Nations will almost certainly agree to collaborate with the Organization of African Unity (OAU). UN officials might hesitate to report any malpractices by UN colleagues to the head of the operation or even to headquarters, but does anyone believe that African observers from the OAU would fail to report any but the most trivial infractions of proper procedures?

We can, however, expect further resolutions of the General Assembly on respect for national sovereignty in cases where the UN is supervising elections, especially if the country concerned is politically unstable or has little or no experience of democratic procedures.[22]

In reviewing the cases in the preceding pages, there are only four matters over which the author is seriously disappointed. First, the absence of sophisticated procedures for making sanctions effective, for identifying violations, and for applying penal measures against confirmed violators, whether they be states, liberation movements, business enterprises, or individual persons. The few cases in which the Security Council has authorized military enforcement had the effect, as wars tend to have, of solving some problems at the expense of creating new ones. Every effort should be made to use successfully coercive measures short of armed conflict, as is envisaged in Article 41 of the Charter.

My second disappointment is the failure of the Security Council to deal more effectively with cases of international terrorism. One cannot be precise about how many cases of international terrorism there have been in any particular period but, using the figures of the US State Department, it would seem that there have been over 10 000 cases of terrorism with international implications since 1970, of which nine were considered by the Security Council. Of the nine cases of straightforward terrorism, one ended in a Soviet veto (no. 5 in Chapter 4, p. 102).

One is driven to the conclusion that UN Members have had little faith in the capacity of the Security Council to act effectively. Even in the case of the Hindawi affair, Israel reported the facts to the Security Council,[23] but there was no request for the Security Council to meet.

Part of the difficulty is to separate acts of terrorism from the conditions of injustice which cause grievance and despair to such an extent that a sustained campaign of terrorism might seem a plausible means of obtaining a remedy. This is illustrated by the fate of Kurt Waldheim's initiative in 1972 when his proposal for a study of terrorism was emasculated (if that is the right word) by the addition of a study of the underlying causes of terrorism.

Another difficulty has been that most of the terrorist acts that came before the Security Council were committed by Muslims, who risked their own lives as well as those of innocent victims. It is hazardous to describe the beliefs of religious faiths other than one's own, but my understanding is that Muslims think it praiseworthy for a Muslim to risk martyrdom in a cause that Islam considers righteous.

A further problem is that most acts of international terrorism are committed by non-State entities who are given sanctuary by sympathetic governments or powerful elements in such governments. It used to be said that foreign aid should not have political strings attached, but might there not be circumstances when international aid should be dependent on the recipient State renouncing all support for terrorism? The ceasefire resolution after the UN-authorized campaign to liberate Kuwait included the following operative paragraph:

> Requires Iraq to inform the [Security] Council that it will not commit or support any act of international terrorism or allow any organization directed towards commission of such acts to operate within its territory and to condemn unequivocally and renounce all acts, methods and practices of terrorism.[24]

Admittedly, to withhold international aid will harm the innocent, but so do acts of terrorism.

Finally regarding my second disappointment, I believe that the creation of an international criminal court would have a marginal deterrent effect.

That leads to my third regret, which is the ludicrous way UN organs have dealt with the need for an international criminal court. It is now 47 years since the International Law Commission was asked to study the matter.[25] The timetable thereafter was as follows (somewhat simplified):

1950	General Assembly establishes committee of 17 members to prepare one or more preliminary draft conventions or proposals relating to an international criminal court.[26]
1952	General Assembly appoints new committee to explore the implications and consequences of establishing an international criminal court.[27]
1953	Committee submits report as requested, but General Assembly postpones a decision of substance.
1954	General Assembly again postpones consideration of report pending progress on related issues.[28]
1956	Consideration of matter again deferred.
1957	Matter deferred yet again.[29]
1968	Matter resuscitated by Saudi Arabia; General Assembly decides to take the matter up 'at such time as it [the General Assembly] resumes consideration of the question . . . or at such other time as it deems appropriate'.[30]
1990 and 1991	General Assembly asks International Law Commission to consider further and analyse the question of international criminal jurisdiction.[31]
1992	General Assembly asks International Law Comission to elaborate a draft statute as a matter of

priority. International Law Commission establishes working group.[32]

1993 Working group submits draft statute.[33]

The issues raised in this connection are undoubtedly complex, but they were solved on a narrower basis after the Second World War for Nürnberg and Tokyo, and more recently for former Yugoslavia. In these three cases, the defendants were charged with war crimes, but a permanent tribunal would have to deal with all breaches of international law such as international terrorism and the traffic in narcotic drugs. I suspect, though I have no evidence, that some governments (including my own) do not relish the idea of a court that would have to act impartially, even against their own nationals.

My final regret concerns the failure of the Security Council to operate according to consistent standards. I happened to be in the Middle East in August 1990, just after Iraq had invaded and annexed Kuwait. With a single exception, everyone I spoke to, whether taxi-drivers or senior government officials, condemned Saddam Hussein's use of military force in Kuwait, but then went on to complain of the West's double standards in failing to act equally robustly regarding Palestinian grievances.

If circumstances were suitable, I agreed with the Arab complaint, and then gave a series of explanations. I soon found that my interlocutor had stopped listening.

My own expectation is that the Security Council will increasingly be asked to take up issues of human rights. The fact that many of such cases barely satisfy the Charter requirements for Security Council action will undoubtedly trouble some of the most talented international lawyers for whom the wording of the Charter is on a par with holy writ. The problem in the future will not only concern legal aspects, but how the UN system can cope effectively with all the demands made on it.

Notes

INTRODUCTION

1. Sydney D. Bailey, *How Wars End* (Oxford: Clarendon Press, 1982), Vol. 1, p. 10.
2. 'International Definitions and Principal International Humanitarian Law Treaties', *International Review of the Red Cross*, no. 296 (Sept.–Oct. 1993), p. 427.
3. A/48/640, 11 Oct. 1993.

1 SELF-DETERMINATION IN AFRICA

1. GA res. 1514 (XV), 14 Dec. 1960; GA res. 2200A (XXI), 16 Dec. 1966.
2. *Juridical Yearbook, 1964*, pp. 228–37.
3. SCOR, Supplement for Jan. to March 1961, p. 145, S/4738; 945th mtg. (14 March 1961), para. 107, S/4769; 946th mtg. (15 March 1961), para. 165.
4. SCOR, Supplement for April to June 1961, pp. 57–9, S/4816 and Adds. 1 and 2; 950th mtg. (6 June 1961), para. 38, S/4828; 955th mtg. (9 June 1961), paras 65–8, S/4833/Rev. 1; SC res. 163 (S/4835), 9 June 1961.
5. SCOR, Supplement for July to Sept. 1963, pp. 6–10, S/5347; 1044th mtg. (26 July 1963), para. 4, S/5372; 1048th mtg. (30 July 1963), para. 21, S/5379; SC res. 180 (S/5380), 31 July 1963.
6. SCOR, Supplement for Oct. to Dec. 1970, p. 51, S/9987; 1558th mtg. (22/23 Nov. 1970), para. 7, S/9988; 25th year, Special Supplement no. 2, S/10009; SC res. 289 (S/9990/Rev. 2), 23 Nov. 1970; SC res. 290 (S/10030), 8 Dec. 1970.
7. SCOR, 943rd mtg. (10 March 1961), para. 53; 945th mtg. (14 March 1961), para. 81.
8. SC res. 163 (S/4835), 9 June 1961; SC res. 180 (S/5380), 31 July 1963; SC res. 183 (S/5481), 11 Dec. 1963; SC res. 218 (S/6953/Rev. 1, as amended), 23 Nov. 1965; SC res. 290 (S/10030), 8 Dec. 1970; 1603rd mtg. (30 Nov. 1971), para. 5; SC res. 312 (S/10607/Rev. 1), 4 Feb. 1972; SC res. 322 (S/10838/Rev. 1), 22 Nov. 1972.
9. SC res. 180 (S/5380), 31 July 1963; SC res. 218 (S/6953/Rev. 1, as amended), 23 Nov. 1965; SC res. 312 (S/10607/Rev. 1), 4 Feb. 1972.
10. GA res. 3205 (XXIX), 17 Sept. 1974; GA res. 3365 (XXX), 16 Sept. 1975; GA res. 31/44, 1 Dec. 1976.
11. SCOR, 1064th mtg. (9 Sept. 1963), para. 6; 1068th mtg. (12 Sept. 1963), paras 101–3.
12. SCOR, 1257th mtg. (12 Nov. 1965), paras 13, 15–16, 18–19, 21–4, 33; 1263rd mtg. (17 Nov. 1965), paras 10, 23; 24th year, 1479th mtg. (19 June 1969), paras 30–3.

13. SCOR, 1278th mtg. (17 May 1965), paras 36–7; 1532nd mtg. (12 March 1970), para. 41.
14. SC res. 216 (S/6921/Rev. 1), 12 Nov. 1965.
15. SC res. 217 (S/6955, as amended), 20 Nov. 1965.
16. SC res. 221 (S/7236/Rev. 1), 9 April 1966; SC res. 232 (S/7621/Rev. 1, as amended), 16 Dec. 1966.
17. SC res. 217 (S/6955, as amended), 20 Nov. 1965; SC res. 232 (S/7621/Rev. 1, as amended), 16 Dec. 1966; SC res. 318 (S/10747), 28 July 1972; SC res. 415 (S/12404/Rev. 1), 29 Sept. 1977; SC res. 423 (S/12597), 14 March 1978; SC res. 460 (S/113699), 21 Dec. 1979; SC res. 463 (S/13777/Rev. 1), 2 Feb. 1980.
18. SCOR, Supplement for Oct. to Dec. 1965, p. 354, S/6896.
19. SCOR, 1276th mtg. (9 April 1966), para. 10; Supplement for April to June 1966, pp. 29–32, 46–8, 62–3, S/7237, S/7238, S/7240, S/7241, S/7261*, S/7272.
20. SCOR, 1428th mtg. (29 May 1968), paras 2–4.
21. SCOR, 1531st mtg. (11 March 1970), paras 5–6; 34th year, 2142nd mtg. (27 April 1979), paras 3–5, 7–8, 15, 37–8, 82, 84.
22. SCOR, 1663rd mtg. (27 Sept. 1972), para. 26.
23. SCOR, Supplement for Jan. to March 1968, pp. 214–15, S/8443; SC res. 253 (S/8601), 29 May 1968.
24. SC res. 202 (S/6329/Rev. 1), 6 May 1965; SC res. 217 (S/6955, as amended), 20 Nov. 1965; SC res. 253 (S/8601), 29 May 1968; SC res. 277 (S/9709, as amended), 18 March 1970; SC res. 445 (S/13140), 8 March 1979; SC res. 460 (S/13699), 21 Dec. 1979.
25. SC res. 463 (S/13777/Rev. 1), 2 Feb. 1980.
26. SC res. 217 (S/6955, as amended), 20 Nov. 1965; SC res. 232 (S/7621/Rev. 1, as amended); SC res. 253 (S/8601), 29 May 1968; SC res. 277 (S/9709, as amended), 18 March 1970; SC res. 288 (S/9980), 17 Nov. 1970; SC res. 314 (S/10541/Rev. 1), 28 Feb. 1972; SC res. 318 (S/10747), 28 July 1972; SC res. 320 (S/10804/Rev. 1), 29 Sept. 1972; SC res. 333 (S/10927), 22 May 1973; SC res. 409 (S/12339), 27 May 1977.
27. SC res. 386 (S/12013), 17 March 1976.
28. SC res. 460 (S/13699), 21 Dec. 1979; SC res. 463 (S/13777/Rev. 1), 2 Feb. 1980; GA res. S-11/1, 25 Aug. 1980.
29. GA res. 2145 (XXI), 27 Oct. 1966; GA res. 2248 (S–V), 19 May 1967; SC res. 264 (S/9100), 20 March 1969; SC res. 276 (S/9620/Rev. 1), 30 Jan. 1970; ICJ Reports, 1971, paras 131, 133; SC res. 301 (S/10372/Rev. 1), 20 Oct. 1971; GA res. 2871 (XXVI), 20 Dec. 1971; SC res. 385 (S/11950), 30 Jan. 1976; SC res. 431 (S/12792), 27 July 1978.
30. SCOR, Supplement for April to June 1978, pp. 17–19, S/12636; 2082nd mtg. (27 July 1978), paras 91–3, 263–5; SC res. 431 (S/12792), 27 July 1978; SC res. 532 (S/15803), 31 May 1983; SC res. 539 (S/16085/Rev. 2), 28 Oct. 1983; SC res. 632 (S/20466), 16 Feb. 1989; SC res. 640 (S/20808/Rev. 1), 29 Aug. 1989; SC res. 643 (S/20923/Rev. 1), 31 Oct. 1989.
31. SCOR, Supplement for July to Sept. 1978, pp. 33–6, S/12827; 2087th mtg. (29 Sept. 1978), paras 11–22; SC res. 435 (S/12865), 29 Sept. 1978.
32. SCOR, Supplement for July to Sept. 1982, pp. 12–13, S/15287.
33. S/20109-A/43/521, 11 Aug. 1988; S/20129, 17 Aug. 1988, Annex; S/20325–

A/43/964, 14 Dec. 1988, Annex; S/20345, 22 Dec. 1988, Annex; S/20346–A/43/989, 22 Dec. 1988, Annex; S/20566, 4 April 1989, Annex; See also SC res. 628 and 629 (S/20399 and S/20400), 16 Jan. 1989.
34. GA res. S-18/1, 23 April 1990.
35. SC res. 269 (S/9384), 12 Aug. 1969; SC res. 439 (S/12922), 13 Nov. 1978; SC res. 566 (S/17284/Rev. 2), 19 June 1985.
36. SC res. 319 (S/10750, as amended), 1 Aug. 1972; SC res. 323 (S/10846, as amended), 6 Dec. 1972; SC res. 385 (S/11950), 30 Jan. 1976.
37. SC res. 246, 14 March 1968; SC res. 264 (S/9100), 20 March 1969; SC res. 269 (S/9384), 12 Aug. 1969; SC res. 276 (S/9620/Rev. 1), 30 Jan. 1970; SC res. 301 (S/10372/Rev. 1), 20 Oct. 1971; SC res. 310 (S/10608/Rev. 1), 4 Feb. 1972; SC res. 385 (S/11950), 30 Jan. 1976; SC res. 439 (S/12922), 13 Nov. 1978; SC res. 532 (S/15803), 31 May 1983; SC res. 539 (S/16085/Rev. 2); SC res. 566 (S/17284/Rev. 2), 19 June 1985; SC res. 601 (S/19242), 30 Oct. 1987.
38. SC res. 245, 25 Jan. 1968; SC res. 246, 14 March 1968; SC res. 269 (S/9384), 12 Aug. 1969; SC res. 276 (S/9620/Rev. 1), 30 Jan. 1970; SC res. 283 (S/9891), 29 July 1970; SC res. 301 (S/10372/Rev. 1), 20 Oct. 1971; SC res. 310 (S/10376/Rev. 2), 4 Feb. 1972; SC res. 323 (S/10846, as amended), 6 Dec. 1972; SC res. 566 (S/17284/Rev. 2), 19 June 1985; SC res. 601 (S/19242), 30 Oct. 1987.
39. SC res. 310 (S/10608/Rev. 1), 4 Feb. 1972; SC res. 366 (S/11579), 17 Dec. 1974; SC res. 385 (S/11950), 30 Jan. 1976.
40. SC res. 245, 25 Jan. 1968; SC res. 246, 14 March 1968; SC res. 366 (S/11579), 17 Dec. 1974; SC res. 385 (S/11950), 30 Jan. 1976.
41. SCOR, Supplement for Jan. to March 1960, pp. 58–9, S/4279 and Add. 1; 851st meeting (30 March 1960), paras 10–12, 17, 26–9, 46–58, 116; 852nd meeting (30 March 1960), paras 6–17; 854th meeting (31 March 1960), paras 8–9, 86–8; 855th meeting (1 April 1960), paras 10, 18–22, 58–64; SC res. 134 (S/4300), 1 April 1960.
42. SCOR, Supplement for April to June 1960, pp. 2–3, S/4305; Supplement for Jan. to March 1961, pp. 51–3, S/4635; Brian Urquhart, *Hammarskjold* (London: The Bodley Head, 1972), pp. 494–9.
43. GA res. 1761 (XVII), 6 Nov. 1962.
44. SCOR, 1129th mtg. (10 June 1964), paras 12–13, 106; 1132nd mtg. (15 June 1964), paras 17–19; 1135th mtg. (18 June 1964), para. 53.
45. SC res. 134 (S/4300), 1 April 1960.
46. GAOR, 18th session, Annexes, Addendum to agenda item 30, pp. 49–70 (S/5418-S/5310, A/5453-S/5353); SCOR, Supplement for July to Sept. 1963, pp. 11–14, S/5348; 1050th mtg. (31 July 1963), para. 42; 1054th mtg. (6 Aug. 1963), para. 19; 1076th mtg. (3 Dec. 1963), para. 5; SC res. 181 (S/5386), 7 Aug. 1963; SC res. 182 (S/5471), 4 Dec. 1963; SC res. 191 (S/5773), 18 June 1964; SC res. 282 (S/9882/Rev. 2), 23 July 1970; SC res. 311 (S/10609/Rev. 1), 4 Feb. 1972.
47. SC res. 300 (S/10365/Rev. 1), 12 Oct. 1971; SC res. 326 (S/1087 Rev. 1), 2 Feb. 1973; SC res. 328 (S/10898/Rev. 1), 10 March 1973; SC res. 387 (S/12030), 31 March 1976; SC res. 393 (S/12158), 30 July 1976.
48. SC res. 418 (S/12436), 4 Nov. 1977; SC res. 421 (S/12477), 9 Dec. 1977; SC res. 466 (S/13887), 11 April 1980; SC res. 473 (S/13995), 13 June

1980; SCOR, Supplement for July to Sept. 1980, pp. 95–108, S/14179; SC res. 558 (S/16860), 13 Dec. 1984; SC res. 569 (S/17354/Rev. 1), 26 July 1985; SC res. 591 (S/18474), 28 Nov. 1986; S/18961 and Adds., 30 June 1987–2 Feb. 1958; S/21015, 11 Dec. 1989.

49. S/18705, 19 Feb. 1987; S/PV.2738, 20 Feb. 1987, p. 67.

50. SC res. 428 (S/12692), 6 May 1978; SC res. 447 (S/13197), 28 March 1979; SC res. 454 (S/13601), 2 Nov. 1979; SC res. 475 (S/14024), 27 June 1980; SC res. 527 (S/15524), 15 Dec. 1982; SC res. 545 (S/16226), 20 Dec. 1983; SC res. 546 (S/16247/Rev. 1), 6 Jan. 1984; SC res. 567 (S/17286), 20 June 1985; SC res. 568 (S/17291), 21 June 1985; SC res. 571 (S/17481, as amended), 20 Sept. 1985; SC res. 574 (S/17531), 7 Oct. 1985; SC res. 577 (S/17667), 6 Dec. 1985; SC res. 580 (S/17701), 30 Dec. 1985; SC res. 581 (S/17817/Rev. 1), 13 Feb. 1986; S/18195, 30 June 1986; SC res. 602 (S/18291), 25 Nov. 1987; SC res. 606 (S/18379, as amended), 23 Dec. 1987; S/19959, 24 June 1988.

51. SC res. 181 (S/5386), 7 Aug. 1963; SC res. 182 (S/5471), 4 Dec. 1963; SCOR, Supplement for April to June 1964, pp. 31, 41, paras 50 and 116 of Annex to S/5658; SC res. 282 (S/9882/Rev. 2), 23 July 1970; 1555th mtg. (21 Oct. 1970), para. 4; SC res. 311(S/10609/Rev. 2), 4 Feb. 1972; SCOR, 1806th mtg. (29 Oct. 1974), paras 25, 51, 77, 80; SC res. 392 (S/12103), 19 June 1976; SC res. 473 (S/13995), 13 June 1980; SC res. 556 (S/16791), 23 Oct. 1984; SC res. 591 (S/18474), 28 Nov. 1986; S/18808, 16 April 1987.

52. SC res. 556 (S/16791), 23 Oct. 1984; SC res. 581 (S/17817/Rev. 1), 13 Feb. 1986.

53. SC res. 181 (S/5386), 7 Aug. 1963; SC res. 182 (S/5471), 4 Dec. 1963; SC res. 190 (S/5761), 9 June 1964; SC res. 191 (S/5773), 18 June 1964; SC res. 311 (S/10609/Rev. 1), 4 Feb. 1972; SC res. 417 (S/12309/Rev. 1), 31 Oct. 1977; S/13842, 13 March 1980; SC res. 473 (S/13995), 13 June 1980; SC res. 556 (S/16791), 23 Oct. 1984; SC res. 560 (S/17013/Rev. 1), 12 March 1985; SC res. 569 (S/17354/Rev. 1), 26 July 1985; S/17413, 21 Aug. 1985; S/18808, 16 April 1987.

54. SC res. 392 (S/12103), 19 June 1976; SC res. 417 (S/12309/Rev. 1), 31 Oct. 1977; SC res. 556 (S/16791), 23 Oct. 1984; SC res. 569 (S/17354/Rev. 1), 26 July 1985; S/18157, 13 June 1986.

55. SC res. 190 (S/5761), 9 June 1964; SC res. 191 (S/5773), 18 June 1964; S/13226, 5 April 1979; S/14361, 5 Feb. 1981; SC res. 503 (S/14960), 9 April 1982, S/15444, 4 Oct. 1982; SC res. 525 (S/14511), 7 Dec. 1982; SC res. 533 (S/15815), 7 June 1983; SC res. 547 (S/16271), 13 Jan. 1984; S/17408, 20 Aug. 1985; S/17575, 17 Oct. 1985; SC res. 610 (S/19627), 16 March 1988; SC res. 615 (S/19940), 17 June 1988; SC res. 623 (S/20290), 23 Nov. 1988.

56. SC res. 417 (S/12309/Rev. 1), 31 Oct. 1977; S/13549, 21 Sept. 1979; S/14794, 15 Dec. 1981; SC res. 554 (S/16700), 17 Aug. 1984; SC res. 556 (S/16791), 23 Oct. 1984.

57. S/PV. 3095–6, 15 and 16 July 1992; SC res. 765 (S/24288), 16 July 1992.

58. S/24389, 7 Aug. 1992; SC res. 772 (S/24422), 17 Aug. 1992; see also A/46/401, 16 Sept. 1991.

59. S/24314 and S/24315, 20 July 1992; S/24389, 7 Aug. 1992, paras 62, 79;

S/24541, 10 Sept. 1992; S/24544, 9 Sept. 1992; S/25004, 22 Dec. 1992; S/25315, 12 April 1993; S/26347, 24 Aug. 1993; GA res. 48/1, 8 Oct. 1993; S/26714-A/48/22, 17. Nov. 1993, paras 3–70; S/26785, 23 Nov. 1993; S/26883, 16 Dec. 1985.

2 ASCERTAINING THE WILL OF THE PEOPLE

1. A/C.4/351, 20 Feb. 1957.
2. SCOR, 3rd year, Special Supplement no. 1, S/649/Rev. 1, pp. 67–8, Appendix VIII; 256th mtg. (26 Feb. 1948), pp. 304–10; Supplement for June 1948, pp. 25–41, S/786; SC res. 40 (S/689), 28 Feb. 1948; Alastair M. Taylor, *Indonesian Independence and the United Nations*, pp. 111–13, 115–16.
3. SCOR, Supplement for June 1948, pp. 11–24, S/729; Taylor, pp. 113–16.
4. SC res. 63 (S/1150), 24 Dec. 1948; SC res. 64 (S/1164), 28 Dec. 1948; Philip C. Jessup, *The Birth of Nations* (New York; Columbia University Press, 1974), pp. 71–8.
5. SCOR, 400th mtg. (14 Jan. 1949), p. 8; SC res. 67 (S/1234), 28 Jan. 1949; *Foreign Relations of the United States*, 1949, Vol. VII pt. 1, pp. 144–6, 163–6, 180–1; Dirk V. Stikker, *Men of Responsibility* (New York, Harper and Row, 1966), p. 145; Taylor, pp. 186–92.
6. SCOR, 421st mtg. (23 Mar. 1949), pp. 5, 25–6.
7. SCOR, 4th year, Special Supplement no. 6, S/1417, para. 52; Taylor, pp. 232–5.
8. P. L. Lakhanpal (ed.), *Essential Documents and Notes on Kashmir Dispute* (Delhi, International Books, 2nd edn, 1965), pp. 42, 55–7, 72–3, 75; K. Sarwar Hasan, with the cooperation of Subeida Hasan (eds), *The Kashmir Question* (Karachi, Pakistan Institute of International Affairs, 1966), pp. 13, 55–7; Alastair Lamb, *Kashmir: A disputed legacy* (Hertingfordbury, Roxford, 1991), pp. 148–246.
9. SCOR, Supplement for Nov. 1948, S/1100, pp. 67–87, 139–44 (Annexes 6 and 28).
10. SC res. 47 (S/726), 21 April 1948; SCOR, Supplement for Nov. 1948, p. 33, S/1100, para. 75; SC res. 51 (S/819), 3 June 1948; SCOR, 4th year, Special Supplement no. 7, S/1430, pp. 63–4; *FRUS*, 1949, Vol. VI, pp. 1691–3, 1700 n. 3, 1706, 1709–10, 1715, 1722–3, 1740–2, 1744–5, 1748.
11. SCOR, 231st mtg. (22 Jan. 1948), p. 165; 236th mtg. (28 Jan. 1948), pp. 268, 272, 274–6; 239th mtg. (3 Feb. 1948), pp. 314, 318, 327–31; 240th mtg. (4 Feb. 1948), pp. 361–2; 241st mtg. (5 Feb. 1948), pp. 23–4; 242nd mtg. (6 Feb. 1948), pp. 37–41, 51–3; 244th mtg. (11 Feb. 1948), pp. 94–7; 266th mtg. (10 March 1948), pp. 68–77; 269th mtg. (18 March 1948), pp. 117–31; 285th mtg. (19 April 1948), pp. 4–5, 28–31; Supplement for May 1948, pp. 92–3, S/756; Supplement for Nov. 1948, p. 66, Annex 3 to S/1100.
12. SCOR, Supplement for Nov. 1948, S/1100, pp. 31–3, 43, 55–7, paras 75–6, 97, 146–53.

13. SCOR, Supplement for Jan. 1949, S/1196, pp. 22–5, 33–45, paras 10–16 and Annexes 3–6.
14. SCOR, 4th year, Special Supplement no. 7, S/1430, pp. 137–40, 143–7, 173–5, 183–5, Annexes 32, 36, 48–51.
15. Ibid., pp. 52, 61–2, paras 249–50, 283.
16. SC res. 80 (S/1469), 14 March 1950; SCOR, 5th year, 471st mtg. (12 April 1950), p. 5.
17. SCOR, Supplement for Sept. to Dec. 1950, pp. 24–52, S/1791.
18. GA res. 91 (S/2017/Rev. 1), 30 March 1951; SCOR, 543rd mtg. (30 April 1951), paras 12–22.
19. SCOR, 548th mtg. (29 May 1951), para. 8a (S/2181); SC res. 96 (S/2392), 10 Nov. 1951; SC res. 98 (S/2883), 23 Dec. 1952; SC res. 122 (S/3779), 24 Jan. 1957; SC res. 126 (S/3922), 2 Dec. 1957.
20. SCOR, 236th mtg. (28 Jan. 1948), p. 281; 237th mtg. (29 Jan. 1948), p. 290; 241st mtg. (5 Feb. 1948), p. 8; 532nd mtg. (21 Feb. 1951), paras 15, 22; 537th mtg. (21 March 1951), paras 20–1; 606th mtg. (6 Nov. 1952), para. 17; 797th mtg. (25 Oct. 1957), para. 11; 1090th mtg. (10 Feb. 1946), para. 99.
21. SC res. 161 (S/4741), 21 Feb. 1961; GA res. 1600 (XV), 15 April 1961.
22. SCOR, Supplement for April to June 1961, pp. 69–76, S/4841-A/4786 and Adds. For a clear and fair account of this episode, see Catherine Hoskyns, *The Congo since Independence* (Oxford: Oxford University Press, 1965, under the auspices of the Royal Institute of International Affairs), pp. 374–80.
23. SCOR, Supplement for July to Sept. 1961, pp. 14–15, 54–7, 61, 66–9, 74–6, S/4865, S/4911 and Adds., S/4913-A/4830, S/4917, S/4923; Brian Urquhart, *Hammarskjold* (London, The Bodley Head, 1972), pp. 547, 549.
24. SCOR, Supplement for July to Sept. 1961, pp. 9–10, 52–3, S/4863, S/4908.
25. SCOR, 1202nd mtg. (6 May 1965), para. 36; SC res. 203 (S/6355), 14 May 1965; SCOR, 1212th mtg. (19 May 1965), paras 156–9, 208; SC res. 205 (S/6376), 22 May 1965; SCOR, Supplement for April to June 1965, pp. 160, 223–4, 295–6, S/6370, S/6408, and S/6432; SCOR, Supplement for July to Sept. 1965, pp. 92–3, S/6530*, paras 14, 28–33; SCOR, 1233rd mtg. (26 July 1965), para. 2.
26. SCOR, Supplement for Oct. to Dec. 1965, pp. 423–4, S/6991 and Add. 1; Supplement for April to June 1966, pp. 93, 111–15, 124–5, 132–42, 145–8, S/7303, S/7324, S/7332, S/7338 and Adds. 1–4, S/7342.
27. SCOR, 1477th mtg. (17 June 1969), para. 4.
28. SC res. 445 (S/13140), 8 March 1979; SC res. 448 (S/13282), 30 April 1979.
29. On Iran's plicy towards Bahrain, see Rouhallah K. Ramazani, *The Persian Gulf* (University Press of Virginia, 1972), pp. 45–56.
30. SCOR, 25th year, Supplement for Jan. to March 1970, pp. 175–6, S/9726; U Thant, *View from the UN* (London, David and Charles, 1978), pp. 50–1.
31. SCOR, Supplement for April to June 1970, pp. 143–4, S/9737, S/9738.
32. Ibid., pp. 166–70, S/9772.

33. Ibid., pp. 175, 178, S/9779, S/9783; 1536th mtg. (11 May 1970); SC res. 278 (S/9792), 11 May 1970; GA res. 2752 (XXVI), 21 Sept. 1971.
34. SCOR, 2nd year, Supplement no. 8, S/281; SC res. 21 (S/318), 2 April 1947; SCOR, 4th year, Supplement for March 1949, pp. 1–2, S/916; SC res. 70 (S/1280), 7 March 1949; SCOR, 415th mtg. (7 March 1949), pp. 1–11.
35. See my article 'The Future composition of the Trusteeship Council', *International Organization*, Vol. XIII, no. 3 (1959), pp. 412–21.
36. The reports of the missions of observation were issued as Supplements to the Official Records of the Trusteeship Council as follows:
Mariana Islands, 17 June 1975: 43rd session, no. 2, T/1771
Pacific Islands other than Mariana Islands, 12 July 1978: 46th session, no. 2, T/1795
Marshall Islands, 1 March 1979: 46th session, no. 3, T/1805
Palau, 9 July 1979: 47th session, no. 1, T/1813
Palau, 10 Feb. 1983: 50th session, no. 3, T/1851
Federated States of Micronesia, 21 June 1983: 51st session, no. 1, T/1860
Marshall Islands, 7 Sept. 1983: 51st session, no. 2, T/1865
Palau, 21 Feb. 1986: 53rd session, no. 2, T/1885
Palau, 2 Dec. 1986: 54th session, no. 1, T/1906
Palau, 30 June 1987: 54th session, no. 2, T/1919
Palau, 21 Aug. 1987: 54th session, no. 3, T/1920
Palau, 6 Feb. 1990: 57th session, no. 1, T/1942
37. T/1865, para. 49; T/1942, p. 42.
38. T/1771, paras 83 and 110; SCOR, 41st year, Special Supplement no. 1, S/18238, para. 211; S/PV. 2972, 22 Dec. 1990, pp. 6–7; SC res. 683 (S/22001), 22 Dec. 1990.
39. T/1860, para. 70; SCOR, 41st year, Special Supplement no. 1, S/18238, para. 211; SC res. 683 (S/22001), 22 Dec. 1990; SC res. 703, 9 Aug. 1991.
40. T/1805, paras 22–31; T/1865, para. 49; SCOR, 41st year, Special Supplement no. 1, S/18238, para. 211; SC res. 683 (S/22001), 22 Dec. 1990; SC res. 704, 9 Aug. 1991.
41. In addition to the reports of missions to observe referenda (see note 36), see also the following Special Supplements no. 1 to SCOR: 40th year, S/17334, para. 262; 41st year, S/18238, para. 211; 42nd year, S/19596, para. 202; 43rd year, S/20168, para. 120; 44th year, S/20843, para. 172; 45th year, S/22212, para. 152; 46th year, S/23554, para. 111; also S/21662, 28 Aug. 1990; S/22008*, 18 Dec. 1990; SC res. 683 (S/22001), 22 Dec. 1990.
42. SC res. 385 (S/11950), 30 Jan. 1976; SC res. 431 (S/12792), 27 July 1978; SC res. 435 (S/12865), 29 Sept. 1978; SC res. 439 (S/12922), 13 Nov. 1978; SC res. 532 (S/15803), 31 May 1983; SC res. 539 (S/16085/Rev. 2), 28 Oct. 1983; SC res. 632 (S/20466), 16 Feb. 1989; SC res. 640 (S/20808/Rev. 1), 29 Aug. 1989; SC res. 643 (S/20923/Rev. 1), 31 Oct. 1989.
43. GA res. 3111 (XXVIII), 12 Dec. 1973; GA res. 31/146, 20 Dec. 1976; SCOR, Supplement for July to Sept. 1983, p. 66, S/15943, para. 17; S/20412, 23 Jan. 1989, paras 26–7; S/20635-A/44/280, 16 May 1989.

44. SCOR, Supplement for April to June 1978, p. 19, S/12636, para. 9; S/20412, 23 Jan. 1989, paras 24–5; S/20635/A/44/280, 16 May 1989.
45. SCOR, Supplement for Oct. to Dec. 1985, pp. 141–2, S/17658; S/20412, 23 Jan. 1989; S/20457, 9 Feb. 1989.
46. South African complaints about SWAPO incursions can be found in UN documents S/20557, 3 April 1989; S/20565, 4 April 1989; S/20567, 5 April 1989; S/20576, 7 April 1980. Extracts from Pérez de Cuéllar's oral report to the Security Council may be found in *Blue Helmets* (United Nations, 2nd edn, 1990), pp. 361–7. See also S/20883, para. 13, and Robert S. Jaster, *The 1988 Peace Accords and the Future of South Western Africa* (London: International Institute for Strategic Studies, 1990), Adelphi Paper 253, pp. 36–7.
47. S/20412, 23 Jan. 1989, para. 42; S/20883, 6 Oct. 1989, paras 13–15; S/20943, 3 Nov. 1989, para. 8.
48. S/20883, 6 Oct. 1989, paras 5–12.
49. S/20883, 6 Oct. 1989, paras 47–50; S/20683, 12 June 1989, pp. 5–6; S/20883/Add. 1, 16 Oct, 1989; S/20943, 3 Nov. 1989, para. 12.
50. S/20883, 6 Oct. 1989, paras 28–38, 51–3, and pp. 26–8; S/20683, 12 June 1989, pp. 7–19; S/20967, 14 Nov. 1989, para. 1.
51. S/20883, 6 Oct. 1989, paras 40–2; S/20943, 3 Nov. 1989, para. 14.
52. S/20479, 21 Feb. 1989; S/20847, 13 Sept. 1989; S/20871, 26 Sept. 1989; S/20883, 6 Oct. 1989, para. 22; S/20967, 14 Nov. 1989, para. 2.
53. S/20967, 14 Nov. 1989, paras 2, 5–7, 9, and p. 10; S/20967/Add. 2, 16 March 1990.
54. S/19085-A/42/521, 31 Aug. 1987; S/20491-A/44/140, 14 Feb. 1989.
55. A/44/210, 5 April 1989; A/44/304, 6 June 1989; A/44/375*, 7 July 1989.
56. A/132/424, 16 Dec. 1977.
57. GA res. 43/24, 15 Nov. 1988; S/20491-A/44/140, 27 Feb. 1989; SC res. 637 (S/20752), 27 July 1989; GA res. 44/10, 23 Oct. 1989, paras 7–8; S/20856, 28 Aug. 1989; S/20857, 20 Sept. 1989; SC res. 644 (S/20951), 7 Nov. 1989.
58. A/44/642 and Corr. 1, 17 Oct. 1989; A/44/834, 7 Dec. 1989; A/44/917, 31 Jan. 1990; A/44/921, 22 Feb. 1990; A/44/927, 30 March 1990; GA res. 45/15, 20 Nov. 1990; *Observing Nicaragua's Elections, 1989–1990* (Atlanta, Georgia, n.d).
59. GA res. 45/15, 20 Nov. 1990.
60. A/45/1, 16 Sept. 1990, p. 12; A/46/609 and Corr. 1, 19 Nov. 1991, paras 55–67, 75–82.
61. A/46/609, 19 Nov. 1991, para. 37; A/44/965 and Corr. 1 and Add. 1, 973, and 979, 17 July, 21 Aug. and 17 Sept. 1990; A/45/234, 25 Sept. 1990; S/21845–7, 5 Oct. 1990; GA res. 45/2, 10 Oct. 1990.
62. A/45/PV. 29, 10 Oct. 1990, pp. 57–68.
63. A/44/973, 21 Aug. 1990, Annex II; A/44/979, 17 Sept. 1990, Annex; A/45/870, 14 Dec. 1990, paras 2, 11, 100–2; A/46/609, 19 Nov. 1991, para. 39; S/21847, 5 Oct. 1990.
64. For this and subsequent paras, see A/45/870 and Add. 1, 14 Dec. 1990 and 22 Feb. 1991; *The 1990 General Elections in Haiti* (Atlanta, Georgia, Council of Freely-Elected Heads of Government, and Washington, DC, National Democratic Institute for International Affairs, 1991);

Report on the Elections of December 16, 1990 (Washington, DC, Washington Office on Haiti, 1991).

65. E/CN.4/1992/50, 31 Jan. 1992, paras 51–80.
66. A/46/695-S/23230, 20 Nov. 1991.
67. S/PV. 3011, 3 Oct. 1991.
68. GA res. 46/7, 11 Oct. 1991; GA res. 46/138, 17 Dec. 1991; S/23691-A/46/891, 11 March 1992; SC res. 841 (S/25957), 16 June 1993; S/25958, 16 June 1993. See also Commission on Human Rights res. 1992/77, 5 March 1992.
69. A/47/908, 24 March 1993, paras 5, 6, 13, 58–81, and pp. 8–32; A/47/960, 3 June 1993, paras 5, 39; SC res. 841 (S/25957), 16 June 1993; S/26063-A/47/975, 12 July 1993; S/26085, 15 July 1993; S/26297-A/47/1000, 13 Aug. 1993; S/26352, 25 Aug. 1993; S/26361, 26 Aug. 1993; SC res. 862 (S/26384), 31 Aug. 1993; S/26480 and Add. 1, 21 and 22 Sept. 1993; SC res. 867 (S/26484 as amended), 23 Sept. 1993; S/26567, 11 Oct. 1993; S/26668, 30 Oct. 1993.
70. S/26297-A/47/1000, 13 Aug. 1993, paras 5, 10; S/26352, 25 Aug. 1993; S/26361, 26 Aug. 1993; SC res. 861 (S/26364), 27 Aug. 1993; S/26361, 26 Aug. 1993; SC res. 861 (S/26364), 27 Aug. 1993; SC res. 862 (S/26384), 31 Aug. 1993; S/26460, 17 Sept. 1993; S/26480, 21 Sept. 1993; SC res. 867 (S/26484 as amended), 23 Sept. 1993; S/26471*-A/47/1023*, 23 Sept. 1993; S/26567, 11 Oct. 1993; S/26573, 13 Oct. 1993; SC res. 873 (S/26578), 13 Oct. 1993; SC res. 875 (S/26586), 16 Oct. 1993; S/26633, 25 Oct. 1993; S/26668, 30 Oct. 1993; S/26683-A/48/659, 2 Nov. 1993; S/26724*, 12 Nov. 1993; S/26725, 12 Nov. 1993; S/26747, 15 Nov. 1993; 26802, 26 Nov. 1993.
71. S/20338, 17 Dec. 1988; SC res. 626 (S/20339), 20 Dec. 1988; S/22609, 17 May 1991, pp. 2, 42, 45–7; SC res. 696 (S/22652), 30 May 1991; S/22678, 6 June 1991; S/23191, 31 Oct. 1991, para. 29.
72. S/23556, 7 Feb. 1992; S/23671, 3 March 1992, paras 1–8, 18–33; SC res. 747 (S/23743, as amended), 24 March 1992.
73. S/24145 and Corr. 1, 24 June and 1 July 1992; S/PV. 3092 and S/24249, 7 July 1992.
74. S/24556, 9 Sept. 1992; S/24623, 6 Oct. 1992; S/24573, 18 Sept. 1992.
75. S/24623, 6 Oct. 1992; S/24720*, 28 Oct. 1992; SC res. 785 (S/24738), 30 Oct. 1992; S/24858, 25 Nov. 1992.
76. SC res. 793 (S/24863), 30 Nov. 1992; S/24996, 21 Dec. 1992; S/25076, 8 Jan. 1993; S/25140, 21 Jan. 1993; SC res. 804 (S/25187), 29 Jan. 1993; SC res. 811 (S/25399), 12 March 1993; SC res. 823 (S/25694), 30 April 1993.
77. S/24996, 21 Dec. 1992; S/25002, 22 Dec. 1992; S/25076, 8 Jan. 1993; S/25140, 21 Jan. 1993; S/25840, 25 May 1993; SC res. 834 (S/25857), 1 June 1993; S/25899, 8 June 1993; S/26060, 12 July 1993; SC res. 862 (S/26384), 31 Aug. 1993; S/26434, 13 Sept. 1993; SC res. 844 (S/26445), 15 Sept. 1993; S/26644, 27 Oct. 1993; S/26677, 1 Nov. 1993; S/26872*, 14 Dec. 1993.
78. Brian Urquhart, *Hammarskjold* (London: The Bodley Head, 1972), p. 310; SCOR, Supplement for July to Sept. 1966, pp. 108–9, S/7478.
79. SCOR, Supplement for April to June 1964, pp. 74, 130–2, S/5666,

S/5697; SC res. 189 (S/5741), 4 June 1964; SCOR, Supplement for July to Sept. 1964, pp. 101–12, 347–9, S/5832*, S/5952.

80. SCOR, Supplement for Jan. to March 1979, pp. 3–4, 17, 27, S/13003, S/13022, S/13027.
81. Ibid., pp. 83, 97, 89, 144, S/13111, S/13117, S/13119, S/13162.
82. S/21404-A/45/353, 23 July 1990; S/21689-A/45/472, 31 Aug. 1990; S/21732-A/45/490, 17 Sept. 1990; S/21788-A/45/519, 18 Sept. 1990; SC res. 668 (S/21800), 20 Sept. 1990.
83. S/21866-A/45/620, 10 Oct. 1990; S/21908-A/45/671, 25 Oct. 1990; S/22059-A/46/61, 11 Jan. 1991; S/22733-A/46/267, 24 June 1991; S/22740-A/46/271, 26 June 1991; S/22808-A/46/310, 18 July 1991; S/23097 and Add. 1, 30 Sept. 1991; SC res. 717 (S/23145), 16 Oct. 1991; S/23177-A/46/608, 30 Oct. 1991; SC res. 718 (S/23180), 31 Oct. 1991.
84. A/45/605, 10 Oct. 1990, paras 15–16.
85. S/23177-A/46/608, 30 Oct. 1991, part II (pp. 13–14), Annex 1.D (pp. 25–7), Annex 3 (pp. 40–1); S/23613, 19 Feb. 1992, paras 23–48; A/47/668, 18 Nov. 1992, para. 30.
86. S/23331, 30 Dec. 1991; SC res. 728 (S/23383), 8 Jan. 1992; S/23613, 19 Feb. 1992, paras 23–51, 80; SC res. 745 (S/23561), 28 Feb. 1992.
87. S/24090, 12 June 1992; S/24091, 12 June 1992; SC res. 766 (S/24320), 21 July 1992.
88. S/24578, 21 Sept. 1992; SC res. 783 (S/24652), 13 Oct. 1992; S/24800, 15 Nov. 1992; SC res. 792 (S/24856), 30 Nov. 1992.
89. S/25124, 25 Jan. 1993; S/25289, 13 Feb. 1993; SC res. 810 (S/25376), 8 March 1993; S/25658*, 26 April 1993; S/25669, 27 April 1993; S/25784, 15 May 1993.
90. SC res. 826 (S/25803 as amended), 20 May 1993. See also S/25003, 22 Dec. 1992; S/25530, 5 April 1993; S/25822, 22 May 1993; SC res. 810 (S/25376), 8 March 1993; SC res. 835 (S/25876), 2 June 1993; S/25879, 2 June 1993; S/25896, 8 June 1993; S/25913, 10 June 1993; SC res. 840 (S/25931), 15 June 1993; S/26090, 16 July 1993, para. 23; S/26529, 26 Aug. 1993; SC res. 860 (S/26362), 27 Aug. 1993; S/26529, 5 Oct. 1993; S/26531, 5 Oct. 1993; S/26546, 7 Oct. 1993; S/26649, 27 Oct. 1993; SC res. 880 (S/26687), 4 Nov. 1993.
91. GA res. 3292 (XXIX), 13 Dec. 1974; ICJ Reports, 1975, para. 162.
92. SCOR, 1849th and 1850th mtgs. and 1852nd to 1854th mtgs. (20 Oct. to 6 Nov. 1975); SC res. 377 (S/11858), 22 Oct. 1975; 379 (S/11865), 2 Nov. 1975; 380 (S/11870), 6 Nov. 1975.
93. SCOR, Supplement for Oct. to Dec. 1975, pp. 27–8, 33–6, 40–1, S/11863, S/11874, S/11876, S/11880.
94. GA res. 40/50, 7 Dec. 1985; A/41/673, 3 Oct. 1986; GA res. 41/16, 31 Oct. 1986; A/42/601, 1 Oct. 1987; GA res. 42/78, 4 Dec. 1987.
95. S/21360, 18 June 1990, pp. 5–12; S/PV. 2826, 20 Sept. 1988; SC res. 621 (S/20193), 20 Sept. 1988; A/43/680*, 7 Oct. 1988.
96. S/21360, 18 June 1990, pp. 13–24; S/PV. 2929, 27 June 1990; SC res. 658 (S/21376), 27 June 1990; A/44/634 and Corr. 1, 12 Oct. 1989; A/45/644 and Corr. 1, 18 Oct. 1990.
97. S/22464, 19 April 1991; S/22532, 24 April 1991; S/PV. 2984, 29 April

1991; SC res. 690 (S/22525), 29 April 1991; S/22779; S/23008, 4 Sept. 1991; S/23043 and S/23044, 17 Sept. 1991; A/46/589, 23 Oct. 1991.

98. S/23299, 19 Dec. 1991; S/PV. 3025, 31 Dec. 1991; SC res. 725 (S/23330), 31 Dec. 1991.
99. *The Western Sahara: The referendum process in danger*, Report by George A. Pickart to the Committee on Foreign Relations of the US Senate, Jan. 1992.
100. S/23662, 28 Feb. 1992, S/23754–5, 25 March 1992.
101. S/24464, 20 Aug. 1992; S/24484, 24 Aug. 1992; S/24504, 31 Aug. 1992; S/24644, 2 Oct. 1992; S/24645, 9 Oct. 1992; 25008*, 24 Dec. 1992; S/25170, 26 Jan. 1993; SC res. 809 S/(S/25340*), 2 March 1993; S/25861, 28 May 1993.
102. S/25818, 21 May 1993; S/26185, 28 July 1993, Annex II; S/26239, 4 Aug. 1993; S/26797, 24 Nov. 1993; S/26848, 6 Dec. 1993.
103. S/24406, 10 Aug. 1992; S/24635, 8 Oct. 1992, pp. 12–18; S/24642, 9 Oct. 1992; SC res. 782 (S/24650 as amended), 13 Oct. 1992; S/24719, 27 Oct. 1992; S/24892 and Corr. 1 and Add. 1, 3 Dec. 1992; SC res. 797 (S/24941), 16 Dec. 1992.
104. S/25518, 2 April 1993, paras 38–44; SC res. 818 (S/25591), 14 April 1993; S/26034, 30 June 1993, paras 16–17; S/26385, 30 Aug. 1993, paras 23–4; A/48/590, 18 Nov. 1993, pp. 31–2; SC res. 863 (S/26426), 13 Sept. 1993; S/26666, 1 Nov. 1963, paras 9–12; SC res. 882 (S/26694), 5 Nov. 1993.
105. S/22133, 22 Jan. 1991; S/23886, 7 May 1992; SC res. 788 (S/24827), 19 Nov. 1992; S/25402, 12 March 1993; SC res. 813 (S/25469, as amended), 26 March 1993; S/25918, 9 June 1993.
106. S/26200*, 4 Aug. 1993, para. 12; S/26272, 9 Aug. 1993, p. 11; SC res. 856 (S/26259), 10 Aug. 1993; S/26422, 9 Sept. 1993, paras 32–6, 39; SC res. 866 (S/26477, as amended), 22 Sept. 1993; S/26868, 13 Dec. 1993, paras 26, 30; S/26886, 17 Dec. 1993.
107. 'The emerging right to democratic governance', *American Journal of International Law*, Vol. 86, no. 1 (Jan. 1992), pp. 46, 47, 52.
108. A/47/668, 18 Nov. 1992, paras 24–7 and pp. 22–31 (Annex II).
109. A/46/609, 19 Nov. 1991, para. 58.
110. A/45/1, 16 Sept. 1990, p. 12; A/46/609, 19 Nov. 1991, paras 55, 59, 79; A/47/668, 18 Nov. 1992, paras 53, 57–9, 65–6; A/47/668/Add. 1, 24 Nov. 1992, paras 8, 13.

3 INTERNATIONAL HUMANITARIAN LAW

1. See *International Humanitarian Law and Human Rights* (Geneva, United Nations fact sheet no. 13, 1991); *Bulletin of Human Rights*, New York, United Nations, 91/1, pp. 1–61.
2. Hague Conventions of 1899 and 1907, preamble; the four Geneva Conventions of 1949, articles 63/62/142/158; the two Additional Protocols of 1977, Article 1 and preamble respectively; 1981 Convention on excessively harmful or indiscriminate weapons, preamble.

3. *Trial of the Major War Criminals before the International Military Tribunal*, Nürnberg, 1947, pp. 253–4; ICJ Reports, 1986, para. 218; see also Rosemary Abi Saab, 'The "General Principles" of humanitarian law according to the International Court of Justice', *International Review of the Red Cross*, July–Aug. 1987, pp. 367–75.
4. A/7720, 20 Nov. 1969; A/8052, 18 Sept. 1970; A/8370 and Add. 1, 2 Sept. and 5 Oct. 1971; A/8781 and Corr. 1, 20 Sept. and 11 Oct. 1972; A/9215, 7 Nov. 1973; A/9669 and Add. 1, 12 Sept. and 19 Nov. 1974; A/10195 and Add. 1, 5 Sept. 1975; A/31/163, 18 Aug. 1976; A/32/144, 15 Aug. 1977.
5. Annual Report of the International Committee of the Red Cross for 1963, pp. 49–50; A/7720, 20 Nov. 1969, para. 114 and Appendix D, p. 102; letter from the International Committee of the Red Cross, 2 Oct. 1992.
6. *The International Committee of the Red Cross in Palestine* ICRC, 1948, pp. 5–7; *Hospital Localities and Safety Zones*, ICRC, 1952, pp. 23–30; Folke Bernadotte, *To Jerusalem* (London: Hodder and Stoughton, 1951), pp. 85, 140; Pablo de Azcárate, *Mission in Palestine, 1948–52* (Washington, DC: Middle East Institute, 1966), pp. 47–8, 53, 124–5; Jacques de Reynier, *A Jérusalem un drapeau flottait sur la ligne de feu* (Neuchâtel, Histoire et Société d'Aujourd'hui, 1950), pp. 86–9, 93–4; SCOR, Supplement for July to Sept. 1957, pp. 38–9, para. 3 of S/3892; Supplement for July to Sept. 1967, pp. 27–30, S/7930/Add. 20.
7. SC res. 84 (S/1558), 7 July 1950; SC res. 90 (S/1995), 31 Jan. 1951; *FRUS*, 1951, Vol. VII, pt. 1, p. 152.
8. *FRUS*, 1950, Vol. VII, pp. 678, 712 n. 1, 793 n. 2; SCOR, Supplement for Jan. to March 1953, pp. 48–9, S/2970.
9. Public Record Office, F0371 99565/FK1071/52, 99569/FK1071/151, and 99631/FK1551/33.
10. Conflit de Corée: recueil de documents, ICRC, 1952, Vol. I, pp. 42–3.
11. US National Archives, C 66228, Ridgway to Joint Chiefs of Staff, 1 April 1952; *FRUS*, 1952–4, Vol. XV, pt. 1, pp. 144, 162, 183, 204, 373 n. 2.
12. US National Archives, c 51870, Clark to Joint Chiefs of Staff, 13 July 1952; *FRUS*, 1952–4, Vol. XV, pt. 1, pp. 341, 373 n. 2, 380 n. 1, 447; Walter G. Hermes, *United States Army in Korea, Vol. 2, Truce Tent and Fighting Front* (Washington, DC: US Government Printing Office, 1966), p. 514.
13. GA res. 610 (VII), 3 Dec. 1952; SCOR, Supplement for July to Sept. 1953, pp. 30–4 (paras 51–9), 35–41, S/3079.
14. GAOR, 7th session, Annexes, Agenda item 16, p. 7, para. 2 (A/2228); SCOR, Supplement for Oct. to Dec. 1952, pp. 38 (S/2836) and 47 (S/2837); Mark W. Clark, *From the Danube to the Yalu* (New York: Harper, 1954), pp. 279–82; US National Archives, CX 63652, Clark to Joint Chiefs of Staff, 13 July 1952; *FRUS*, 1952–4, Vol. XV, pt. 1, pp. 412–13 and pt. 2, pp. 1199, 1378 n. 3.
15. Hermes (note 11), pp. 514–15; GAOR, 8th session, Supplement no. 18, A/2641, p. 3, para. 2 and p. 108.

16. GAOR, 8th session, Supplement no. 18, A/2641, pp. 115–23, 126–41, 149–51; Supplement no. 19, A/2642, paras 44–58, 69, 72 and pp. 28–34; S. N. Prasad, *History of the Custodian Force (India) in Korea, 1953–4* (Delhi: Ministry of Defence, 1976), pp. 88–93.
17. Organization of American States doc. 47, 8 May 1965, pp. 14–15.
18. SCOR, Supplement for April to June 1965, pp. 171–4, S/6371/Add. 1 and Annex, S/6371/Add. 2, para. 11.
19. SC res. 237 (S/7987/Rev. 3), 14 June 1967; SC res. 512 (S/15240), 19 June 1982; SC res. 513 (S/15273), 4 July 1982; SC res. 515 (S/15325), 29 July 1982.
20. SCOR, 1358th mtg. (13 June 1967), para. 225; 1360th mtg. (14 June 1967), paras 125–32; SC res. 237 (S/7968/Rev. 3), 14 June 1967.
21. See, for example, the remarks of ambassadors Blum and Netanyahu in SCOR, 2131st mtg. (19 March 1979), paras 120–6 and S/N. 2774, 16 Dec. 1987, p. 74; also S/19443, 21 Jan. 1988, para. 23. See also Meir Shamgar, 'The Observance of International Law in the Administered Territories', *Israel Yearbook on Human Rights*, Vol. 1 (1971), pp. 262–77; Dov Shefi, 'The Protection of Human Rights in Areas Administered by Israel: United Nations findings and reality', *Israel Yearbook on Human Rights*, Vol. 3 (1973), pp. 337–61; Yoram Dinstein, 'The International Law of Belligerent Occupation and Human Rights', *Israel Yearbook on Human Rights*, Vol. 8 (1978), pp. 104–43; Nissun Bar-Yaacov, 'The Applicability of the Laws of War to Judea and Samaria (the West Bank) and to the Gaza Strip', *Israel Law Review*, Vol. 24 (1990), pp. 485–506; Adam Roberts, 'Prolonged Military Occupation: the Israeli-Occupied Territories since 1967', *American Journal of International Law*, Vol. 84 (1990), pp. 44–103.
22. Annual Report of the International Committee of the Red Cross for 1968, pp. 33–4; *International Review of the Red Cross*, Aug. 1970, p. 427; *Annual Reference Report of* the International Committee of the Red Cross for 1990, p. 79.
23. SC res. 237 (S/7968/Rev. 3), 14 June 1967; GA res. 2252 (ES-V), 4 July 1967; SCOR, Supplement for July to Sept. 1967, pp. 199–209, S/8124-A/6787; Supplement for Oct. to Dec. 1967, pp. 80–154, S/8158-A/6797.
24. GA res. 2254 (ES-V), 14 July 1967; SCOR, Supplement for July to Sept. 1967, pp. 232–86, S/8146-A/6793.
25. Human Rights Commission, res. 6 (XXIV), 27 Feb. 1968 and res. 6 (XXV), 4 March 1969.
26. SC res. 259 (S/8825/Rev. 2), 27 Sept. 1968; SCOR, Supplement for Oct. to Dec. 1968, pp. 74–6, S/8851.
27. GA res. 2443 (XXIII), 19 Dec. 1968; A/7495 and Adds. 1 and 2, 28 May, 19 and 24 June 1969.
28. SCOR, Supplement for April to June 1968, pp. 126–33, S/8553-A/7085; Supplement for July to Sept. 1968, pp. 73–95, S/8699-A/7149; A/8164, 13 Nov. 1970.
29. E/CN. 4/1016 and Adds. 1–5, 20 Jan.–20 Feb. 1970.
30. A/8089, 26 Oct. 1970.
31. Human Rights Commission res. 10 (XXVI), 23 March 1970; GA res. 2727 (XXV), 15 Dec. 1970.

32. *International Review of the Red Cross,* Aug. 1970, pp. 424–58 and Sept. 1970, pp. 485–511; A/8089, 26 Oct. 1970, paras 52, 149.
33. SC res. 242 (S/8247), 22 Nov. 1967; SC res. 338 (S/11036), 22 Oct. 1973.
34. See Table 3.1, nos 3, 5–11, 13, 17, 18, 20. The reports arising from SC res. 446 (Table, p. 136, 22 March 1979) are in SCOR, Supplement for July to Sept. 1979, pp. 16–59, S/13450 and Add. 1 and Supplement for Oct. to Dec. 1979, pp. 106–12, S/13679.
35. See Table 3.1, nos 12, 14, 15, 19, 27, 28, 30, 31, 35, 37, 38.
36. See Table 3.1, nos 13, 16, 26, 33, 34, 39, 40. The report arising from SC res. 605 (Table, p. 136, 22 December 1987) is in S/19443, 21 Jan. 1988, and that from SC res. 672 (Table, p. 136, 12 October 1990) is in S/21919 and Corr. 1, 1 Nov. 1990.
37. SCOR, 1483rd mtg. (1 July 1969), para. 97; 1512th mtg. (15 Sept. 1969), para. 111; 1579th mtg. (16 Sept. 1971), paras 28, 82; 1651st mtg. (18 July 1972), para. 192; Supplement for July to Sept. 1972, p. 72, S/10739; 1916th mtg. (4 May 1976), paras 30–2; 1917th mtg. (5 May 1976), paras 58, 81, 139; 1918th mtg. (19 May 1976), para. 30; 1919th mtg. (12 May 1976), para. 101; 1920th mtg. (14 May 1976), para 32; 1921st mtg. (20 May 1976), para. 29; 1922nd mtg. (26 May 1976), paras 112, 121; *Search for Peace in the Middle East: Documents and Statements, 1967–79*, report prepared by the Congressional Research Service for the US House of Representatives (1979), 27.
38. S/13419-A/34/338, 11 July 1979; SCOR, 2123rd mtg. (9 March 1979), paras 70, 148; 2124th mtg. (12 March 1979), paras 12, 33, 100, 130; S/PV. 2125, 13 March 1979, p. 66; SCOR, 2127th mtg. (15 March 1979), paras 7, 23, 43, 72, 122–6, 151; 2128th mtg. (16 March 1979), paras 49, 63–4, 74; 213lst mtg. (19 March 1979), paras 120–6, 150–1; 2134th mtg. (22 March 1979), para. 8; S/PV. 2125, 13 March 1979, pp. 21, 31, 47–8, 66, 71.
39. SC res. 332 (S/10916/Rev. 1), 21 April 1973; SC res. 347 (S/11275), 24 April 1974; SC res. 436 (S/12883), 6 Oct. 1978; SC res. 450 (S/13392), 14 June 1979; SC res. 512 (S/15240), 19 June 1982; SC res. 513 (S/15273), 4 July 1982; SC res. 521 (S/15402), 19 Sept. 1982; SC res. 542 (S/16179), 23 Nov. 1983; S/17215, 24 May 1985; SC res. 564 (S/17232), 31 May 1985.
40. 'Action by the ICRC in the event of breaches of international humanitarian law', *International Review of the Red Cross*, March–April 1981, pp. 76–83.
41. S/19443, 21 Jan. 1988, para. 27; S/PV. 2785–7, 2789–90, 27 Jan.–1 Feb. 1988; S/19466, 29 Jan. 1988.
42. SC res. 672 (S/21859), 12 Oct. 1990; S/21919 and Add. 3, 31 Oct. and 1 Nov. 1990; SC res. 681 (S/22022), 20 Dec. 1990; S/22472, 9 April 1991.
43. *International Review of the Red Cross*, Jan.–Feb. 1990, pp. 64–5.
44. SCOR, 1613th mtg. (13 Dec. 1971), para. 291; SC res. 307 (S/10465), 21 Dec. 1971; SCOR, Supplement for Oct. to Dec. 1971, p. 121, S/10468-A/8641; Supplement for Jan. to March 1972, pp. 2–3, 14–20, 60, 69–70, 73–4, S/10490, S/10512, S/10560, S/10571, S/10579; Supplement for April to June 1972, pp. 24–5, S/10589.
45. SCOR, Supplement for Oct. to Dec. 1971, p. 81, S/10410, para. 4;

Supplement for Jan. to March 1972, pp. 14–20, S/10512 and Add. 1. I am indebted to Erik Jensen, who was a member of the Winspeare mission, for some background information. There is a useful study of the mission in B. G. Ramcharan, *Humanitarian Good Office in International Law* (The Hague: Nijhoff, 1983), pp. 100–8.

46. SCOR, Supplement for Jan. to March 1972, pp. 15–19, S/10512, paras 14–15 and S/10512/Add. 1, paras 2–3, 6–9.
47. Ibid., pp. 16–17 and 19–20, S/10512, paras 16, 20, 24, and S/10512/Add. 1, paras 14, 17, 19.
48. GAOR, 28th session, Supplement no. 5, A/9005, paras 44–8; 29th session, Supplement no. 5, A/9605, paras 24–5.
49. SC res. 361 (S/11479), 30 Aug. 1974.
50. GA res. 37/98D (XXXVIII), 13 Dec. 1982; SCOR, Supplement for April to June 1984, pp. 108–14, S/16433-A/39/210; Supplement for April to June 1985, pp. 48–9, S/17127 and Add. 1; S/PV. 2576, 25 April 1985, pp. 2–3, S/17130; S/PV. 2667, 21 March 1986, S/17932; S/PV. 2524, 30 March 1984, pp. 2–7, S/16454; SC res. 582 (S/17859), 24 Feb. 1986; SC res. 612 (S/19869), 9 May 1988; SC res. 620 (S/20151), 26 Aug. 1988.
51. SCOR, Supplement for April to June 1983, pp. 112–22, S/15834; S/16627, 15 June 1984; SCOR, Supplement for July to Sept. 1984, pp. 67–8, S/16750; Supplement for Jan. to March 1985, pp. 14–16, 28–9, S/16897, S/16920; SC res. 540 (S/16092), 31 Oct. 1983; S/17004 and S/17036, 6 and 15 March 1985; SC res. 582 (S/17859), 24 Feb. 1986; SC res. 588 (S/18383), 8 Oct. 1986; S/18538, 22 Dec. 1986; S/18610, 16 Jan. 1987; S/19626, 16 March 1988.
52. *International Review of the Red Cross*, March–April 1981, p. 81.
53. Annual Report of the ICRC for 1983, pp. 56–7; Annual Report for 1984, pp. 60–1; Annual Report for 1987, pp. 76–7; Memoranda issued by the ICRC, 10 Feb. 1984 and 23 Nov.
54. SCOR, Supplement for Jan. to March 1985, pp. 48–72, S/16962; Supplement for April to June 1985, pp. 21–2, S/17097.
55. SC res. 666 (S/21747), 13 Sept. 1990; SC res. 670 (S/21816), 25 Sept. 1990; SC res. 674 (S/21911), 29 Oct. 1990; SC res. 686 (S/22298), 2 March 1991; SC res. 687 (S/22430), 3 April 1991.
56. S/22333–4, 6 March 1991; S/22536, 29 April 1991.
57. S/21541-A/44/971, 16 Aug. 1990; SC res. 693 (S/22616), 20 May 1991; S/23037-A/45/1055, 16 Sept. 1991, paras 17–25, 50–2.
58. S/23222 and Corr. 1, 15 and 29 Nov. 1991, Annex, paras 11–90 and 91–145, and pp. 48–9, Appendix II; S/23580-A/46/876, 19 Feb. 1992, Annex, paras 109–49 and 170–2; S/24066-A/46/935, 5 June 1992, Annex, paras 40–3, 56; S/24375-A/46/955, 12 Aug. 1992, Annex, paras 69–77 and 103–6; S/25521-A/47/912, pp. 64–75 S/26033-A/47/968, 2 July 1993; S/26416-A/47/1012, 15 Sept. 1993, p. 28.
59. *FRUS*, 1958–60, Vol. XIV, p. 320.
60. SC res. 733 (S/23461), 23 Jan. 1992; SC res. 746 (S/23722 as amended), 17 March 1992; SC res. 751 (S/23834), 24 April 1992; SC res. 767 (S/24347 as amended), 24 July 1992; SC res. 775 (S/24997 as amended), 28 Aug. 1992; SC res. 794 (S/24863), 3 Dec. 1992; SC res. 814 (S/25472 as amended), 26 March 1993; SC res. 837 (S/25889), 6 June 1993.

61. SC res. 733 (S/23461), 23 Jan. 1992, para. 5; S/24859, 27 Nov. 1992; SC res. 794 (S/24863), 3 Dec. 1992; SC res. 814 (S/25472, as amended), 26 March 1993; A/48/510, 26 Oct. 1993.
62. S/25274, 10 Feb. 1993.
63. S/24516-A/47/418, 3 Sept. 1992; S/24766-A/47/635, 6 Nov. 1992; S/25341-A/48/92, 26 Feb. 1993; S/25792, 10 May 1993; S/26383, 30 Aug. 1993; S/26469, 28 Sept. 1993; 5/26765, 20 Nov. 1993.
64. S/25221, 2 Feb. 1993, Annex 1, paras 5–8.
65. S/25240, 3 Feb. 1993.
66. S/24583, 23 Sept. 1992; S/24705, 23 Oct. 1992; S/24768, 5 Nov. 1992; S/24791, 10 Nov. 1992; S/24918, 8 Dec. 1992; S/25171, 27 Jan. 1993; S/25377, 6 March 1993; S/25392, 10 March 1993; S/25393, 10 March 1993; S/25586, 13 April 1993; S/25613, 19 April 1993; S/26016, 30 June 1993.
67. SC res. 713 (S/23067), 25 Sept. 1991; SC res. 757 (S/24037), 3 May 1992; SC res. 781 (S/24736), 9 Oct. 1992; SC res. 787 (S/24808/Rev. 1 as amended), 16 Nov. 1992; SC res. 816 (S/25440), 31 March 1993.
68. SC res. 752 (S/23927 as amended), 15 May 1992; SC res. 764 (S/24267), 13 July 1992; S/24378, 4 Aug. 1992; SC res. 771 (S/24422), 13 Aug. 1992; SC res. 780 (S/24618), 6 Oct. 1992; S/24744, 30 Oct. 1992; SC res. 808 (S/25314), 22 Feb. 1993; S/25520, 3 April 1993; S/26717, 9 Nov. 1993; S/26726, 12 Nov. 1993.
69. SC res. 780 (S/24618), 6 Oct. 1992; S/24657*, 14 Oct. 1992; S/25274, 10 Feb. 1993; S/25221, 2 Feb. 1993, para. 9; S/25704, 3 May 1993, paras 13–14.
70. S/25266, 10 Feb. 1993; S/25300, 17 Feb. 1993; S/25307, 18 Feb. 1993; S/25504, 1 April 1993; S/25512*-A/47/920*, 5 April 1993; S/25537, 6 April 1993; S/25575, 12 April 1993; S/25594, 14 April 1993; S/25716, 4 May 1993; SC res. 808 (S/25314), 22 Feb. 1993.
71. The Order of the Court was circulated to the Security Council as S/25686, 29 April 1983.
72. The Nürnberg Principles were affirmed in General Assembly res. 95 (I), 11 Dec. 1946.
73. S/25704, 3 May 1993.
74. *Reaffirmation and Development of the Laws and Customs Applicable in Armed Conflicts* (Geneva, ICRC, 1969), pp. 83–7.
75. S/21919, 31 Oct. 1990, para. 24.

4 TERRORISM

1. SC res. 57, 18 Sept. 1948.
2. SC res. 138 (S/4349), 23 June 1960.
3. SCOR, 1522nd mtg. (15 Dec. 1969), paras 62–6; SC res. 275 (S/9574), 22 Dec. 1969.
4. S/23685/Add. 1, 9 March 1992, paras 128–32; SC res. 674 (S/21911), 29 Oct. 1990.

5. S/24600, 28 Sept. 1992, paras 10–18.
6. SCOR, 2406th mtg. (14 Dec. 1982), para. 37.
7. SCOR, 2415th mtg. (22 Feb. 1983), para. 46.
8. SCOR, 2528th mtg. (3 April 1984), paras 40–1, 49.
9. See, for example, SCOR, 2296th mtg. (28 Aug. 1981), paras 8–24.
10. See, for example, SCOR, Supplement for July to Sept. 1976, pp. 53–4, S/12186-A/31/182S; 2375th mtg. (6 June 1982), paras 23–66; 2376th mtg. (8 June 1982), paras 26–33.
11. SCOR, Supplement for April to June 1986, pp. 37–8, S/18020-A/41/302.
12. U Thant, *View from the UN* (London and Newton Abbot: David and Charles, 1978), pp. 302–8, 317–18; GAOR, 24th session, Supplement no. 2 (A/7602), paras 466–71.
13. SCOR, 25th year, Supplement for July to Sept. 1970, pp. 142, 145–6, S/9931, S/9932, S/9948-A/8075; 1552nd mtg. (9 Sept. 1970); SC res. 286 (S/9933/Rev. 1 and Corr. 1), 9 Sept. 1970; Thant (see note 12), pp. 341–4.
14. SCOR, 27th year, Supplement for April to June 1972, pp. 51–2, 85, 100–2, 107, 128, 132–4, S/10639, S/10668, S/10683, S/10692, S/10705, S/10709, S/10711.
15. SCOR, Supplement for July to Sept. 1973, pp. 5, 25, 27–8, 37–8, S/7930/Add. 2082, S/10983, S/10984, S/10990, S/11002; mtgs. 1736–40 (13–15 Aug. 1973); SC res. 337 (S/10987), 15 Aug. 1973.
16. SCOR, Supplement for July to Sept. 1976, pp. 3–8, S/12123-A/31/122, S/12124, S/12126, S/12128; 1939th to 1943rd mtgs. (9–14 July 1976).
17. SCOR, Supplement for July to Sept. 1976, pp. 15–16, S/12138, S/12139; 1943rd mtg. (14 July 1976), paras 147, 162.
18. SCOR, Supplement for Oct. to Dec. 1979, pp. 61, 68–9, S/13615, S/13616, S/13626.
19. SCOR, Supplement for Oct. to Dec. 1979, pp. 83–5, S/13646, S/13650; 2172nd and 2175th to 2178th mtgs. (27 Nov. and 1–4 Dec. 1979); SC res. 457 (S/13677), 4 Dec. 1979.
20. The full text of the Court's Order was issued as a document of the Security Council, S/13697, 19 Dec. 1979.
21. SCOR, Supplement for Oct. to Dec. 1979, pp. 139–40, S/13704, S/13705; 2182nd mtg. (29 Dec. 1979), paras 5–9.
22. SCOR, 2182nd to 2184th mtgs. (29–31 Dec. 1979); SC res. 461 (S/13711/Rev. 1), 31 Dec. 1979.
23. SCOR, Supplement for Jan. to March 1980, pp. 4–5, 10–11, S/13730, S/13735; 2191st mtg. (11 and 13 Jan. 1980).
24. SCOR, Supplement for April to June 1980, pp. 8–9, 28–9, 34, S/13879, S/13908, S/13915, S/13989, 9 June 1980; SCOR, Supplement for Jan. to March 1981, p. 12, S/14338.
25. UN Press Release BN/80/1, 21 Feb. 1980.
26. GAOR, 35th session, Supplement no. 1 (A/35/1), p. 3.
27. ICJ Reports, 24 May 1980; see also S/13989, 9 June 1980.
28. A translation of the text was issued by the State Department on 6 Nov. 1980.

29. US State Department, *Selected Documents no. 19*, 12 March 1981.
30. SCOR, Supplement for Oct. to Dec. 1981, p. 47, S/14783; 37th year, Special Supplement no. 2 (S/14905/Rev. 1), esp. paras 103–20; Special Supplement no. 3 (S/15492/Rev. 1); mtgs. 2314 (15 Dec. 1981), esp. paras 9–10; 2359 (20 May 1982); 2361 (21 May 1982); 2365 (24 May 1982); 2367 (25 May 1982); 2370 (28 May 1982); SC res. 496 (S/14793), 15 Dec. 1981; SC res. 507 (S/15127) 28 May 1982.
31. SCOR, Supplement for Oct. to Dec. 1985, pp. 19–20, 42, 55, S/17548, S/17555, S/17556, S/17574; S/PV. 2618 (9 Oct. 1985) (S/17554).
32. SCOR, Supplement for Oct. to Dec. 1985, p. 183, S/17685; S/PV. 2637 (18 Dec. 1985); SC res. 579 (S/17686), 18 Dec. 1985.
33. S/PV. 2639 (30 Dec. 1985), pp. 55–6 (S/17702).
34. SCOR, Supplement for Jan. to March 1986, pp. 46–50, S/17785-A/41/132, S/17787, S/17792-A/41/135, S/17796 and Rev. 1; S/PV. 2651 (4 Feb. 1986), esp. pp. 14–16, 32; S/PV. 2653 (5 Feb. 1986); S/PV. 2655 (6 Feb. 1986), esp. p. 112.
35. SCOR, Supplement for Jan. to March 1986, pp. 149–51, S/17938, S/17940, S/17941, S/17943-A/41/234; Supplement for April to June 1986, pp. 18–19, S/17982, S/17983; S/PV. 2668–2671 (26–31 March 1986) and 2672–3 (12 and 14 April 1986).
36. SCOR, Supplement for April to June 1986, pp. 22–6, 36–7, S/17990, S/17991, S/17999, S/18016/Rev. 1; mtgs. 2674–80 and 2682–3 (15–24 April 1986).
37. S/18641, 28 Jan. 1987.
38. S/19617, 14 March 1988; S/20053, 25 July 1988, para. 2; S/PV. 2822 (29 July 1988); SC res. 618 (S/20070), 29 July 1988.
39. S/PV. 2872 and S/PV. 2873, 31 July 1989; SC res. 638 (S/20757), 31 July 1989.
40. S/PV. 2869, 14 June 1989; SC res. 635 (S/20690), 14 June 1989; S/20691, 14 June 1989; S/22393 and Corr. 1, 22 March and 4 April 1991.
41. SC res. 687* (S/22430), 3 April 1991, para. 32; S/22689, 11 June 1991, para. 7.
42. S/23306/-A/46/825*, 31 Dec. 1991; S/23307*-A/46/826*, 31 Dec. 1991; S/23308*-A/46/827*, 31 Dec. 1991; S/23309*-A/46/828*, 31 Dec. 1991; S/23317-A/46/831.
43. S/23221, 16 Nov. 1991; S/23226-A/46/660, 20 Nov. 1991; S/23416-A/46/844, 13 Jan. 1992; S/23417-A/46/845, 13 Jan. 1992.
44. S/PV. 3033, 21 Jan. 1992; SC res. 731 (S/23422), 21 Jan. 1992.
45. S/23574, 11 Feb. 1992; S/23672, 3 March 1992; S/PV. 3063, 31 March 1992; SC res. 748 (S/23762), 31 March 1992.
46. ICJ Communiqués nos 92/8 and 9, 14 April 1992.
47. S/25531, 5 April 1993; S/26629, 26 Oct. 1993; SC res. 883 (S/26701), 11 Nov. 1993; S/26861, 10 Dec. 1993.
48. *Current Policy no. 744*, Bureau of Public Affairs, US State Department, 1985, p. 2.
49. See GA res. 47/33, 25 Nov. 1992, para. 4.
50. For the report of a Working Group of the International Law Commission, see GAOR, 48th session, Supplement no. 10 (A/48/10), pp. 255–335.

5 THE CASE-BY-CASE APPROACH

1. SC res. 191 (S/5773), 18 June 1964, South Africa; SC res. 246 (S/8429), 14 March 1968, Namibia; SC res. 366 (S/11579), 17 Dec. 1974, Namibia; SC res. 385 (S/11950), 30 Jan. 1976, Namibia; SC res. 556 (S/16791), 23 Oct. 1984, South Africa.
2. SCOR, 1127th mtg. (8 June 1964), para. 116, South Africa; 2552nd mtg. (29 Aug. 1984), para. 13, Middle East.
3. SC res. 361 (S/11479), 30 Aug. 1974, Cyprus; SC res. 512 (S/15240), 19 June 1982, Middle East; SC res. 513 (S/15273), 4 July 1982, Middle East.
4. See, for example, S/1291, 16 March 1949.
5. SCOR, Supplement for June to Aug. 1950, pp. 150–4, S/1735 and Corr. 1; 493rd mtg. (31 Aug. 1950), pp. 22–3, 30.
6. S/21230-A/45/202 to S/21293-A/45/272, 4 April to 9 May 1990. The countries in question were Afghanistan, Bahrain, Bangladesh, Burkina Faso, Cuba, Iraq, Laos, Libya, Malaysia, Mali, Mauritania, Pakistan, Saudi Arabia, Senegal, Somalia, Sudan, Syria, Yemen.
7. S/23258-A/46/716.
8. SC res. 47 (S/726), 21 April 1948.
9. SC res. 63 (S/1150), 24 Dec. 1948; SC res. 64 (S/1164), 28 Dec. 1948; SC res. 67 (S/1234), 28 Jan. 1949.
10. SC res. 111 (S/3538), 19 Jan. 1956; SC res. 316 (S/10722) 26 June 1972; SC res. 317 (S/10742), 21 July 1972; SC res. 347 (S/11275), 24 April 1974.
11. SC res. 181 (S/5386), 7 Aug. 1963; SC res. 182 (S/5471), 4 Dec. 1963; SC res. 190 (S/5761), 9 June 1964; SC res. 191 (S/5773), 18 June 1964; SC res. 311 (S/10609/Rev. 1), 4 Feb. 1972; SC res. 417 (S/12309/Rev. 1), 31 Oct. 1977; S/13226, 5 April 1979; SC res. 556 (S/16791), 23 Oct. 1984.
12. SC res. 202 (S/6329/Rev. 1), 6 May 1965; SC res. 253 (S/8601), 29 May 1968; SC res. 328 (S/10898/Rev. 1), 10 March 1973; SC res. 463 (S/13777/Rev. 1), 2 Feb. 1980.
13. SC res. 245, 25 Jan. 1968; SC res. 246 (S/8429), 14 March 1968; SC res. 366 (S/11579), 17 Dec. 1974; SC res. 385 (S/11950), 30 Jan. 1976.
14. SC res. 312 (S/10607/Rev. 1), 4 Feb. 1972.
15. SC res. 471 (S/13984) 5 June 1980.
16. SC res. 473 (S/13995), 13 June 1980; S/14361, 5 Feb. 1981; SC res. 503 (S/14960), 9 April 1982; S/15444, 4 Oct. 1982; SC res. 525 (S/14511), 7 Dec. 1982; SC res. 533 (S/15815), 7 June 1983; SC res. 547 (S/16271), 13 Jan. 1984; SC res. 569 (S/17354/Rev. 1), 26 July 1985; SC res. 610 (S/19627), 10 March 1988; SC res. 615 (S/19940), 17 June 1988; SC res. 623 (S/20290), 23 Nov. 1988.
17. The inconclusive UN report on Lumumba's murder was issued in SCOR, Supplement for Jan. to March 1961, pp. 95–101, S/4688 and Adds. 1 and 2; Supplement for Oct. to Dec. 1961, pp. 67–129, S/4976-A/4964.
18. SCOR, Supplement for Jan. to March 1961, pp. 131–7, 154–61, 177, 189–90, 203–9, S/4727 and Adds. 1 to 3, S/4745 and Add. 1, S/4752

(para. 10 and Annex VIII), S/4753*, S/4757 and Add. 1; 940th mtg. (20 Feb. 1961), paras 2–6; SC res. 161 (S/4741), 21 Feb. 1961.

19. SCOR, Supplement for Oct. to Dec. 1975, p. 74, S/11923; Supplement for Jan. to March 1976, pp. 120, 122, S/12011, Annex, paras 15–18, 39; Supplement for April to June 1976, pp. 60–6, S/12097-A/31/109, S/12104.
20. SC res. 384 (S/11915), 22 Dec. 1975; SCOR, Supplement for Jan. to March 1976, pp. 121–3, S/12011, Annex, paras 21–44; SC res. 389 (S/12056), 22 April 1976.
21. SCOR, Supplement for April to June 1977, pp. 37–40, 44–7, S/12327, S/12336; Supplement for July to Sept. 1977, pp. 86–8, S/12408; S/14640-A/36/448, 26 Aug. 1981; SCOR, Supplement for Oct. to Dec. 1983, pp. 16–17, 140–5, S/16034, S/16215, Supplement for July to Sept. 1984, pp. 13–15, 73–5, S/16668-A/39/345, S/16759; Supplement for Oct. to Dec. 1985, pp. 69–70, S/17592; S/18930-A/42/352, 17 June 1987, S/18944-A/42/362, 24 June 1987; S/18963-A/42/379, 2 July 1987; S/23235-A/46/694, 22 Nov. 1991; S/23242-A/46/699, 22 Nov. 1991; S/23258-A/46/716, 12 Nov. 1991.
22. S/21028-A/46/60, 15 Dec. 1989; S/22249-A/46/93, 20 Feb. 1991; S/22285-A/46/97, 28 Feb. 1991; S/23339-A/47/65, 18 Dec. 1991.
23. S/21541-A/44/971; 16 Aug. 1990; SC res. 644 (S/20951), 7 May 1989; SC res. 693 (S/22616), 20 May 1991; SC res. 729 (S/23411), 14 Jan. 1992.
24. A/CONF. 157/PC/61/Add. 12, 2 March 1993, para. 16.
25. S/23037-A/45/1055, 16 Sept. 1991; S/23222-A/46/658, 15 Nov. 1991; S/23580-A/46/876, 19 Feb. 1992; S/24066-A/46/935, 5 June 1992; S/24375-A/46/955, 12 Aug. 1992; S/25521-A/47/912, 5 April 1993; S/26033-A/47/968, 2 July 1993; S/26371, 30 Aug. 1993; S/26416-A/47/1012, 15 Sept. 1993.
26. S/23402, p. 7, Annex, 10 Jan. 1992; S/23501-A/46/864, 30 Jan. 1992.
27. S/23130-A/46/553, 9 Oct. 1991, Annex, section IV; S/25812, 21 May 1993, paras 49–55; S/25812/Add. 3, 25 May 1993.
28. S/23501-A/46/864, 30 Jan. 1992, Annex, section 3; S/25006, 23 Dec. 1992; S/25078, 9 Jan. 1993; S/25200, 29 Jan. 1993; S/25516, 2 April 1993; S/25812, 21 May 1993, paras 4–7, 15; S/26689, 3 Nov. 1993; S/26695, 5 Nov. 1993; S/26685–6, 11 Dec. 1993
29. SC res. 664 (S/21562), 18 Aug. 1993; SC res. 666 (S/21747), 13 Sept. 1993; SC res. 667 (S/21774), 16 Sept. 1993; SC res. 674 (S/21911), 29 Oct. 1993.
30. SC res. 670 (S/21816), 25 Sept. 1993; SC res. 677 (S/21966), 28 Nov. 1993; SC res. 686 (S/22298), 2 March 1991; S/23012, 12 Sept. 1991; S/25441, 19 March 1993.
31. SCOR, Supplement for July to Sept. 1963, pp. 4–5, S/5345; Supplement for Jan. to March 1969, p. 65, S/8987.
32. SC res. 688 (S/22448), 5 April 1991; S/22513, 22 April 1991, and S/22663, 31 May 1991; S/23803, 10 April 1992; A/46/612, 4 Nov. 1991, para. 28; S/24311, 17 July 1992; S/24509, 2 Sept. 1992; S/24511, 2 Sept. 1992.
33. S/23685/Add. 1, 9 March 1992, paras 118–27; S/24386, 5 Aug. 1992, paras 7–16; A/48/600 and Add. 1, 18 and 19 Nov. 1993.

34. S/24516-A/47/418, 3 Sept. 1992, paras 6–32; S/24809-A/47/666, 17 Nov. 1992, paras 8–27; S/25792, 10 May 1993, paras 5–42.
35. SC res. 771 (S/24422), 13 Aug. 1992; SC res. 780 (S/24618) 6 Oct. 1992.
36. S/25704, 3 May 1993, paras 50–9.
37. S/25124, 25 Jan. 1993, paras 19, 25.
38. S/23613, 19 Feb. 1992, paras 10–18; S/23870, 1 May 1992, paras 12, 14; S/24578, 21 Sept. 1992, paras 6, 8; S/25124, 25 Jan. 1993, paras 16–19; S/25719, 3 May 1993, paras 18–19.
39. S/24578, 21 Sept. 1992, paras 9–11; S/25124, 25 Jan. 1993, paras 20–2.
40. S/23613, 19 Feb. 1992, paras 21–2; S/24578, 21 Sept. 1992, para. 7.
41. SC res. 724 (S/23285), 15 Dec. 1991.

6 HUMAN RIGHTS AND PEACE

1. S/23500, 31 Jan. 1992.
2. Dorothy V. Jones, *Code of Peace* (Chicago: University of Chicago Press, 1991), p. 155.
3. GA res. 47/30, 25 Nov. 1992.
4. A/7720, 20 Nov. 1969, p. 102 and para. 114; Umesh Palwankar, 'Applicability of international humanitarian law to United Nations peacekeeping forces', *International Review of the Red Cross*, no. 294 (May–June 1993), pp. 227–40.
5. SC res. 681 (S/22022), 20 Dec. 1990; S/22472, 9 April 1991, para. 6.
6. S/25693, 29 April 1993; SC res. 831 (S/25831), 27 May 1993.
7. SC res. 799 (S/24987), 18 Dec. 1992.
8. S/25149, 25 Jan. 1993.
9. GA res. 157, 8 Dec. 1988; 146, 147, 15 Dec. 1989; 150, 151, 18 Dec. 1990; 130, 137, 17 Dec. 1991; 130, 138, 18 Dec. 1992.
10. GA res. 1514 (XV), 14 Dec. 1960.
11. GAOR, 47th session, Supplement no. 1 (A/47/1), para. 101.
12. SCOR, 493rd mtg. (31 Aug. 1950), pp. 22–3.
13. A/45/870/Add. 1, 22 Feb. 1991, paras 69–75; A/46/609, 19 Nov. 1991, paras 55–82; A/47/668, 18 Nov. 1992, paras 63, 65; A/48/590, 18 Nov. 1993, paras 59–60.
14. S/20883, 12 Sept. 1989.
15. A/48/590, 18 Nov. 1993, para. 62.
16. A/45/870, 14 Dec. 1990, para. 58.
17. SCOR, 42nd year, p. 33, para. 65 and p. 34, para. 76.
18. A/47/668, 18 Nov. 1992, para. 3; A/48/590, 18 Nov. 1993, para. 3.
19. A/48/590, 18 Nov. 1993, paras 5–11.
20. S/23037-A/45/1055, 16 Sept. 1991, para. 16 of Annex; S/23222-A/46/658, 15 Nov. 1991, paras 3–4; S/23580-A/46/876, 19 Feb. 1992, para. 5 of Annex; A/47/668, 18 Nov. 1992, para. 58.
21. S/21847, 5 Oct. 1990.
22. See GA res. 47/130, 18 Dec. 1992. The voting was 99 in favour, 45 against (including the UK), and 16 abstaining or absent.
23. SCOR, Supplement for April to June 1986, pp. 37–8, S/18020-A/41/302.

24. SC res. 687, 3 April 1991, para. 32.
25. GA res. 260B (III), 9 Dec. 1948.
26. GA res. 489 (V), 12 Dec. 1950.
27. GA res. 687 (VII), 5 Dec. 1952.
28. GA res. 898 (IX), 14 Dec. 1954.
29. GA res. 1187 (XII), 11 Dec. 1957.
30. GAOR, 23rd session, Annexes, Agenda item 55, A/7342, para. 104; GA res. 2392 (XXIII), 26 Nov. 1968.
31. GA res. 45/41, 28 Nov. 1990; GA res. 46/54, 9 Dec. 1991.
32. GA res. 47/33, 25 Nov. 1992.
33. GAOR, 48th session, Supplement no. 10 (A/48/10), pp. 255–335.

Index